44 00/90E

career planning,
development, and
management

public affairs and administration
(editor: James S. Bowman
(vol. 1)

Garland reference library
of social science
(vol. 145)

the public affairs and administration series

James S. Bowman, editor
Florida State University

1. career planning, development, and management
    an annotated bibliography
       Jonathan P. West
       University of Miami

2. professional ethics
    an annotated bibliography
    and resource guide
       James S. Bowman
       Florida State University
       Frederick A. Elliston
       Illinois Institute of Technology
       Paul Lockhart
       State University of New York

career planning, development, and management
an annotated bibliography

Jonathan P. West

Garland Publishing, Inc. · New York & London
1983

© 1983 Jonathan P. West
All rights reserved

Library of Congress Cataloging in Publication Data

West, Jonathan P. (Jonathan Page), 1941–
  Career planning/development/management.

  (The Public affairs and administration series ; v. 1)
(Garland reference library of social science ; v. 145)
  Includes indexes.
  1. Vocational guidance—Bibliography. 2. Personnel management—Bibliography. I. Title. II. Series.
III. Series: Garland reference library of social science ; v. 145.
Z7164.V6W45 1983   016.3317′02   82-25150
[HF5381]
ISBN 0-8240-9183-3

Design by Laurence Walczak

Printed on acid-free, 250-year-life paper
Manufactured in the United States of America

contents

Series Foreword   vii

Preface by Douglas T. Hall   ix

Introduction   xi

Section I: Individual Career Planning
1. Career Planning—General   1
2. Career Information/Vocational Interests   15
3. Vocational Guidance and Counseling   23
4. Career Choice   35
5. Job Search: Resumes and Interviews   47
6. Planning to Advance   57
7. Continuing Education   65
8. Career Changes in the Adult Years   69

Section II: Individual Career Development
9. Career Development—General   83
10. Prediction of Career Advancement   93
11. Motivation and Needs   101
12. Work Outcomes   109
13. Burn out/Stress/Obsolescence   121
14. Career Switches   127
15. Career Mobility   133
16. Specific Occupations/Professions/Careers   139
17. Career Development of Women   147

Section III: Organizational Career Management
18. Career Management—General   171
19. Organizational Career Planning   185
20. Organizational Career Development   191
21. Organizational Entry   201
22. Counseling/Coaching/Mentoring   209
23. Management Assessment/Training/Development   215

24. Managing Mobility	227
25. Managing Mid-Life Transitions	239
26. Managing the Older Worker	249
27. Public Sector	257
Author Index	267
Title Index	279

series foreword

The twentieth century has seen public administration come of age as a field of study and practice. This decade, in fact, marks the one hundredth anniversary of the profession. As a result of the dramatic growth in government, and the accompanying information explosion, many individuals—managers, academicians and their students, researchers—in organizations feel that they do not have ready access to important information. In an increasingly complex world, more and more people need published material to help solve problems.

The scope of the field and the lack of a comprehensive information system has frustrated users, disseminators, and generators of knowledge in public administration. While there have been some initiatives in recent years, the documentation and control of the literature have been generally neglected. Indeed, major gaps in the development of the literature, the bibliographic structure of the discipline, have evolved.

Garland Publishing, Inc., has inaugurated the present series as an authoritative guide to information sources in public administration. It seeks to consolidate the gains made in the growth and maturation of the profession.

The Series consists of three tiers:
1. core volumes keyed to the major subfields in public administration such as personnel management, public budgeting, and intergovernmental relations;
2. bibliographies focusing on substantive areas of administration such as community health;
3. titles on topical issues in the profession.

Each book will be compiled by one or more specialists in the area. The authors—practitioners and scholars—are selected in open competition from across the country. They design their work to include an introductory state-of-the-art essay, a wide variety of bibliographic materials, and, where appropriate an information resource section. Thus each contribution in the collection provides a systematic basis for managers and researchers to make informed judgments in the course of their work.

Since no single volume can adequately encompass such a broad, interdisciplinary subject, the Series is intended as a continuous project that will incorporate new bodies of literature as appropriate. The titles in preparation represent the initial building blocks in an operating information system for public affairs and administration. As an open-ended endeavor, it is hoped that not only will the Series serve to summarize knowledge in the field but also will contribute to its advancement.

This collection of book-length bibliographies is the product of considerable collaboration on the part of many people. Special appreciation is extended to the editors and staff of Garland Publishing, Inc., to the individual contributors in the Public Affairs and Administration Series, and to the anonymous reviewers of each of the volumes. Inquiries should be made to the Series Editor.

James S. Bowman
Tallahassee

preface

Writing about careers has mushroomed in the last 10 years. Probably the best-known example of this phenomenon has been the paperback self-help book aimed at corporate climbers, job seekers, career changers, women, minorities, management developers, succession planners, two-career couples, or life planners. Various influences have stimulated this wave of career material. The continuing trend toward self-fulfillment, going back to the 1960's, has generated sustained interest in ways individuals can achieve personal growth within the realities of institutional constraints. Affirmative action activities in organizations have led to greater management interest in career development for *all* employees. Third, a changing success ethic emerged giving rise to what I call the "protean career," a sense of the career as something to be self-directed rather than controlled externally. This, in turn, has led to more interest in personal career planning. Increased concerns for quality of life (both personal and occupational) have produced attempts to plan lives for better balance between work life and personal life. And more recently (but very importantly) an economic environment fluctuating between recession and stagnation has produced more involuntary job changes, career plateaus, and early retirements, all of which call for careful planning. Thus, there have been many needs for material on career planning, development, and management.

Unfortunately, this work has been widely scattered. It has been in academic journals, but these have also been diverse—psychology, education, counseling, management, and personnel. More has been in the popular literature—mass market paperbacks, magazines, and newspapers. Some has been geared to the user (the individual careerist) and part to the practitioner (counselor, personnel specialist, consultant, or manager).

Professor West's bibliography is an admirable integration of this diverse literature. It is organized in such a way that different groups can easily find what they need without getting bogged down. The amount of information in each summary is adequate to give the reader an idea of what could be found in that reading, without presenting excessive detail. I look forward to having this bibliography available to recommend to various groups: people in my career planning seminar, graduate students doing research on careers, individuals interested in better organizational career management, and management consulting clients looking for help in developing career programs. No other single publication currently available has a comparable range of career information.

On behalf of all of his readers, my gratitude goes to Professor West for his efforts to organize and synthesize this exploding literature.

Douglas T. Hall
Boston University

introduction

Substantial literature has emerged in recent years on the subject of career planning, development, and management. Academic research by economists, educators, political scientists, psychologists, and sociologists has made the study of careers in organizations an important interdisciplinary focus in the social sciences. The trade press has also produced a number of published works on career-related concerns. This proliferation of materials has resulted from a growing concern with such career issues as quality of life, job opportunities for minorities and women, economic downturns, career mobility, and the changing success ethic. This annotated bibliography seeks to bring together in a single volume significant academic research from various disciplines and the popular literature dealing with careers in organizations.

the literature

Before discussing the terminology and organizing concepts used in this book, a brief commentary on the state of the literature is in order. While the literature on careers is diverse and expanding, it is not a well-defined field with established consensus about its subject matter and parameters. Nevertheless, there are some recurring themes which can be identified. Much of the published research on career planning, development, and management can be related to one of the following themes.

   1. Career theories and instruments (i.e., occupational classification systems, personality typologies, methodological issues)
   2. Vocational aspirations and career choices of young

people prior to initial employment (i.e., information processing, vocational decision making)
3. Assessment and measurement (i.e., vocational interest inventories; instrument development; validity, reliability; measures of skills, abilities and aptitudes)
4. Process of matching individuals with specific jobs (i.e., job search, recruitment, selection)
5. Worker motivation and work outcomes (i.e., job satisfaction/involvement, performance, turnover, job stress, quality of work life)
6. Biases that affect careers (i.e., sex, race, socioeconomic status and culture)
7. Issues relating to women and work (i.e., changing women's sex roles; the implications of sex membership on career development)
8. Life span aspects of careers (i.e., how careers unfold; worker adjustments to career demands across a life span)
9. Career interventions (i.e., techniques, treatments, and materials to provide career assistance)
10. Organizational efforts to assist employees in planning, developing, and managing their careers (i.e., programs for career education, stress reduction, quality of work life)

In recent years there has been a broadening of perceptions regarding what is relevant to the field. While attention continues to be focused on such traditional variables as career theories, interests, job satisfaction, and assessment, recent emphasis has also been placed on developmental experiences of adults, on women's careers, on the relationship of work and nonwork, and on worker adjustment problems. In addition to these traditional and emerging areas of career-related research (both of which are included in the previously mentioned research themes), there is a need for further studies on the effects of organizational factors on career decisions, attitudes, and behaviors; on the ways individual and personality variables affect career treatment success; on the impact of work experiences on career identities; and on the effects of organizational interventions on career outcome measures.

introduction *xiii*

There is a need for both experimental and comparative studies which evaluate career interventions and assess the costs and benefits of different interventions. Also more interdisciplinary, theory-based research is necessary incorporating longitudinal designs.

terminology

In order to highlight some important conceptual and practical distinctions in the literature, I will focus on the terms "career," "career planning," "career development," and "career management" as ways to organize the materials. These four terms are sometimes used interchangeably and often are subject to multiple interpretations when they appear in the ten themes listed above.

This book defines career as "the combination and sequence of roles played by a person during the course of a lifetime." (item 309) For the other three terms the operational definitions used by Leibowitz and Schlossberg (803) are accepted for this work:

1. career planning: "A deliberate sequence and process of determining one's own career-related interests, values, and skills, assessing career options, deciding on a course of action and designing a meaningful, realistic career plan."
2. career development: "The sum outcome or total of what happens to each employee in his or her career. Each employee's career develops irrespective of their effort to plan or not."
3. career management: "Includes those activities, processes, and systems which result in the organization's ability to describe the career characteristics of its employees and to plan and predict the career capabilities required for its future."

Accordingly, career planning and career development, as these terms are used here, will focus on the individual, while career management will have an organizational focus. Career planning activities are voluntary in the sense that employees can choose to participate in them (e.g., workshops, counseling or planning sessions with organizational superiors), while career management activities are non-voluntary for the individual (e.g., performance evaluation reviews, contributing to a skills system). It is often assumed that successful career outcomes (i.e., career development) are more likely to occur for employees who engage in career planning and who are deliberate about their career choices.

organization

With these distinctions in mind, the annotated entries were organized into three sections and 27 chapters. Sections I and II on Career Planning and Career Development have an individual focus; Section III on Career Management has an organizational emphasis. An item is listed in the section or chapter where it appears to have the most important implications.

Each entry includes a short annotation summarizing its contents. Annotations are descriptive rather than critical. Each reference is assigned a number (1 to 973) and these numbers are cumulative throughout all 27 chapters. Cross references, which appear as parenthetical item numbers in some annotations, direct the reader to other related items in the reference list. A more detailed elaboration of the Table of Contents and a discussion of representative works follows as a guide to users of this bibliography.

The first section starts by examining conceptual approaches to the literature on career life planning. Chapter 1 includes theories, models, and methods of career planning including general articles on vocational decision making and practical self-assessment workbooks.

Chapters 2 through 5 look chronologically at such pre-employment planning concerns as: finding and using occupational information, measuring and predicting vocational interests and choices (Chapter 2); vocational guidance and career counseling (Chapter 3); influences affecting career preferences, aspirations, and choices (Chapter 4); and job-finding methods such as resumes, letters of recommendation, interviews, and executive search firms (Chapter 5).

introduction

The next three chapters concentrate on post-employment planning strategies for employees seeking to move up in their organizations (Chapter 6), contemplating enrollment in continuing education programs (Chapter 7), and confronting career crossroads (Chapter 8).

The second section begins by considering some of the major writings on vocational behavior and career development and on forces affecting career outcomes (Chapter 9). The next four chapters look at: predictors of career development such as technical qualifications, personality characteristics, marital status, scholastic/managerial attitudes, and patronage (Chapter 10); mobility motivations, the need for achievement, career anchors, and the fear-of-success concept (Chapter 11); various work outcomes such as job involvement/organizational commitment, job satisfaction/dissatisfaction, role conflicts, personal and social alienation, and career adaptivity (Chapter 12); and the causes and consequences of burnout, job stress, and professional obsolescence as well as personal strategies for dealing with these (Chapter 13).

Articles and books on career switches, mid-life career changes, and second careers are found in Chapter 14; references on career mobility (organizational, occupational, and geographic) are treated in Chapter 15.

Chapter 16 contains references on selected occupations, professions, and careers such as personnel managers, human resource development/training professionals, elected public officials, and corporate leaders. The burgeoning literature on women's careers is covered in Chapter 17. This chapter looks at issues such as women's career patterns, obstacles and opportunities for women in the workplace, and home-career conflict.

In the third section of the book the focus shifts from the individual to the enterprise's efforts to manage careers. It begins with a general chapter of references on matching personal career goals with organizational requirements and on corporate and government programs/activities in career management (Chapter 18).

Chapters 19 and 20 are linked to Chapters 1 and 9 by their common concern with planning and developing employees' careers. While the earlier two chapters look at personal strategies to plan or enhance one's career; the later two provide administrative guides to career planning and development.

The next seven chapters deal sequentially with the organization's career management activities for employees from the time of initial hire through the employee's career to his or her eventual retirement or departure from the enterprise. Chapter 21 examines organizational entry by exploring works on recruitment, selection, socialization, and organizational climate. Chapter 21 is linked to Chapter 12 with the former considering administrative strategies for cultivating organizational identification, commitment, and involvement. Chapter 22 provides citations on coaching, counseling, and mentoring. Chapter 23 covers management assessment, training, and development. Chapter 24 is the organizationally focused counterpart to Chapter 15 on individual career mobility. It examines issues such as managing promotions, successions, and relocations. The next two chapters on managing mid-life transitions (Chapter 25) and managing older workers (Chapter 26) offer prescriptions for administrators. The content of these two chapters can be related to earlier chapters on adult career changes (Chapter 8); burnout, stress, and obsolescence (Chapter 13); and career switches (Chapter 14). Chapter 27, the last in the volume, deals exclusively with career management in the public sector.

The assignment of references into chapters and sections was most difficult for Chapters 16 (Specific Occupations/Professions/Careers), 17 (Career Development of Women), and 27 (Public Sector). While each of these chapters is singled out for special treatment in only one of the three sections of the book, there are several references to women's career issues, specific occupations, and careers of public employees that have been assigned to other sections and chapters because the principal contribution of the publication coincides more closely with the theme of this other section and chapter. For example, articles on personal pre-retirement plans of bankers, on organizational programs providing mentors for female workers, or on individual career mobility of government employees may be assigned to Chapters 8, 22, and 15, respectively, rather than to 16, 17, and 27.

Some examples of representative works from each section of the book might be useful. Typical of the practical publications

introduction

on career/life planning are those of Bolles (6, 84, 85, 177); Bachhuber and Bolyard (2); Klingner and Davis (186); Kotter, Faux, and McArthur (23); Montana and Higginson (30), Moore (32); and Zenger (51). Representative of more scholarly work on career planning and career choice are the works of Blau and associates (130), Ginzberg (101), Holland (143, 144), Kroll (24), Osipow (36), Roe (159), and Super (46, 124, 309). An excellent overview of career development for readers who have a theoretical orientation is provided by Hall (326, 341). Related works of interest include Dalton, Thompson, and Price (320); Korman (362, 412, 413); Pietrofesa and Splete (334); Tarnowieski (342); Tiedeman and O'Hara (344); and Van Maanen and Katz (431). Readers with practitioner-oriented interests in career development might gain useful insights from Buskirk (318), Haldane (220), Jones (464), Kaufman (448), Robbins (472), and/or Schein (336, 395, 474). Hall and Hall (622) effectively introduce key problems and solutions in career management, some of which are also treated in Epstein (614), Haire (696), Kellog (628), Leider (669), Schein (649, 650, 651), Scott (652), and Walker (658, 680, 681). A quick scan of the alphabetized title index will be helpful in identifying other references which may more specifically speak to the interests of different readers. An author index further facilitates access to citations.

sources

In identifying items for this bibliography, both manual and computer searches were conducted. The bulk of the literature search was done manually. To find relevant items I examined the holdings of four major college and university research libraries (at the University of Arizona, the University of Miami, Florida International University, and Miami-Dade Community College), the Miami Dade Public Library System (which has numerous books and periodicals relating to careers that are not available in the academic libraries), and some smaller public and academic libraries. The University of Miami's inter-library loan office obtained many items from various libraries throughout the country.

The initial list of journals to review was selected after a preliminary search of several indexes and abstracts, *The Work Related Abstracts, Personnel Literature, Personnel Management Abstracts, Psychological Abstracts, Women Studies Abstracts, Sociological Abstracts,* and *Business Periodicals Index.* While annotated entries are included from over 100 academic journals, 12 journals contributed 20 or more studies. These included the following:

Journals	Number of Articles
Business Horizons	25
Harvard Business Review	26
Journal of Applied Psychology	30
Journal of Counseling Psychology	48
Journal of Vocational Behavior	62
Personnel	27
Personnel Administrator	59
Personnel Journal	34
Public Administration Review	23
Public Personnel Management	23
Training and Development Journal	67
Vocational Guidance Quarterly	25

Articles from these 12 journals comprise 46 percent of the total entries annotated. Additional academic journals, popular magazines, and professional or trade publications were identified by reviewing the most frequently cited references on careers. The tables of contents of relevant publications were reviewed for the period 1960–1982. While the 1960 date is somewhat arbitrary, it roughly denotes the beginning of serious scholarship on careers; however, a handful of "classic" articles or books published before 1960 are included. To identify relevant books, the author scanned *Books in Print 1981–82,* the *Cumulative Book Index for 1981,* and previously published bibliographic literature reviews (see below) on career planning, development, and management.

To supplement the manual search, three computer searches were pursued in September 1981. They included the *Social Science Index* back to 1972, *ABI/INFORM* to 1974, and *Dissertation Abstracts* to 1861. In each case career-related descriptors were crossed with such entry terms as executive, professional, manager, administrator, and supervisor. The com-

introduction

puter search had some utility in guiding the manual search by identifying entries which could then be obtained and annotated by the author. However, the manual search was a much more fruitful approach with only 200 of the 973 entries coming initially from computerized data files.

related works

Career Planning, Development, and Management is the first comprehensive book-length annotated bibliography on this subject although there have been other attempts to organize, synthesize, and interpret the literature. The 128-item annotated bibliography on career development published in 1979 by Columbia University's Center for Research in Career Development is the latest and most useful example (89 items overlap with this work). The 291-item annotated bibliography on career planning and career management by Pinto and associates (37), while containing many of the items annotated herein (115 items overlap), remains a valuable resource. However, its scope is more limited than the present volume including only those items published over a 5-year time frame from 1969 to 1974. Campbell and associates (89) have published over 643 abstracts on career guidance methods with more than 130 references under the heading of career development programs, career guidance, and career planning. Authors of the latter volume searched the ERIC system and published sources from 1960 to 1972; but, the heavy emphasis on career guidance methods in educational settings and the more restricted time frame distinguish Campbell's volume from this bibliography.

Readers might also consult published literature reviews. Each year since 1976 the lead article in the October issue of the *Journal of Vocational Behavior* has summarized literature on vocational behavior and career development published in the previous year (315, 317, 322, 332, 345, 349). The *Review of Educational Research* also contains literature reviews on career development (346, 343, 333, 329). And the *Annual Review of Psychology* summarizes career-related literature and suggests needed future research (341, 25, 107). The October 1980 and January 1982 issue of the *Personnel Administrator* and the July 1981 and February 1982 issues of the *Training and Development Journal* were devoted to career planning, career development, and career management.

While the previously published bibliographies and literature reviews continue to be valuable, the current book collects and supersedes them with its larger range of entries (973), its more expansive coverage (career planning, development, and management), its interdisciplinary scope, its broader time frame (1960 to 1982), and its combination of academic and popular sources.

envoi

My aim in compiling this bibliography is to bring together under one cover a comprehensive list of previously scattered materials on careers in organizations. In so doing, I hope that scholars, students, practitioners, and other readers interested in career planning, development, and management will use this book as a benchmark to guide future research, stimulate critical insights, prompt administrative initiatives, and assist them in plotting their careers. Despite the increase in scholarly and popular publications on careers, further research and experimentation are needed if we are to more effectively plan, develop, and manage careers.

acknowledgments

I am grateful to the following people for their assistance: four graduate students at the University of Miami—George Gutierrez, Janice McBeath, Larry Milov, and Adam Wilson—provided research and proofreading assistance in the preparation of this volume; Lyn MacCorkle and Wanda Williams of the University of Miami's Richter Library assisted with the computerized searches and made special efforts to obtain materials for me; Professor James S. Bowman of Florida State University and Julia Johnson of Garland provided helpful editorial advice and encouragement; and my wife, Colleen West, graciously put up with my typing camera-ready copy on the kitchen table for two months.

section I
individual career planning

CAREER PLANNING--GENERAL

1. Anderson, Stephen D. "Planning for Career Growth." *Personnel Journal*, 52, No. 5 (1973), 357-362.

   If the individual is going to assume primary responsibility for personal career development, he must review his needs and interests and determine the extent to which his goals are compatible with those of the organization. Six steps for effective career planning are presented.

2. Bachhuber, Thomas D., and Richard K. Harwood. *Directions: A Guide to Career Planning*. Boston: Houghton Mifflin, 1978.

   A "self-help" text and resourcebook organized around a three-phase career development model: (1) awareness and exploration, (2) decision making, and (3) implementation. Academic planning (choice of courses, major, and type of higher educational institution) is considered within the context of overall career planning. Exercises, references, activities, and general information for post-high school students are provided.

3. Barkhaus, Robert S., and Charles W. Bolyard. *Threads: A Tapestry of Self and Career Exploration*. Dubuque, Iowa: Kendall/Hunt, 1977.

   This career planning workbook outlines a learner-centered model for career decision making. The authors encourage learners to make a self assessment of their interests, values, and skills in relation to educational alternatives and occupational choices. Individual activities, group exercises, and data from testing instruments are outlined to help learners to identify their personal goals, interests, and skills.

4. Begosh, Donald G. "Career Planning: Not Leaving the Future to Chance." *SAM Advanced Management Journal*, 40, No. 2 (1975), 43-49.

   Managers can either be classified as career "planners"

or "wingers", but successful managers are usually planners. Planning principles should be applied to careers just as they are to getting the work done.

5. Best, Fred. "Breaking Out of the Lockstep." *The Wharton Magazine*, 5, No. 2 (1980), 13-21.

    The inflexibility of today's life schedules create problems as people become trapped in the "lockstep flow from school to work to retirement." (p. 13) We need more flexibility in scheduling the days, weeks, and years of our lives. The author suggests ways to reschedule existing work time and to reduce work time.

6. Bolles, Richard N. *The Three Boxes of Life*. Berkeley: Ten Speed Press, 1978.

    Suggests that the three stages in our lives (education, work, retirement) have become boxes for learning, achievement, and leisure. Bolles describes some useful tools which can integrate learning, achieving, and playing into all the stages of our lives. One of these tools is the "Quick Job-Hunting Map" (84).

7. Brenner, Marshall H. "Use of High School Data to Predict Work Performance." *Journal of Applied Psychology*, 52, No. 1 (1968), 29-30.

    Data were obtained from a sample of high school graduates (e.g., teacher's work habits and cooperation ratings, absenteeism, grade point average) employed in an aircraft plant and related to worker performance criteria (e.g., supervisory ratings, absenteeism, and tardiness records). Results show significant relationships between the high school predictors and work performance indicators.

8. Cleveland, Harlan, et al. "Is Career Planning A Useless Exercise?" *SAM Advanced Management Journal*, 40, No. 3 (1975), 52-62.

    Reports the replies of eight businessmen who were asked whether they thought career planning was worthwhile, what role planning played in their careers, and what advice concerning career planning they had for would-be managers.

9. Cosgrave, Gerald P. *Career Planning: Search for a Future*. Toronto: University of Toronto, 1973.

    A guide to aid students in making choices about their schooling and initial employment. Students are instructed to take stock of their thoughts about work and career planning. Self assessment of occupational interests and values is encouraged and guidelines for making educational and career decisions are presented. Special attention is devoted to women and careers, careers for the disenchanted, coping with change, post-high-school educational opportunities, and occupations for which educational programs provide preparation.

10. Djeddah, Eli. *Moving Up*. Berkeley: Ten Speed Press, 1977.

    Presents a program for job relocation and advancement. The author explains how to obtain a job which provides the highest possible pay as well as opportunities for personal effectiveness. The advice provided is as appropriate for job-seekers in mid-life as it is for those just starting out.

11. Ferrari, Erma P. *Careers for You*. New York: Abingdon-Cokesbury, 1963.

    An individual's choice of his/her life work causes questions which are addressed in this book: Will you suit the job? Will the job suit you? Where to find out about occupations? Where are the jobs? How can I make a success of my career?

12. Fletcher, Frank M. "Concepts, Curiosity, and Careers." *Journal of Counseling Psychology*, 13, No. 2 (1966), 131-138.

    As a basis for career planning, a theoretical framework is presented for explaining the development and modification of interests, values, and attitudes. The author discusses principles and propositions regarding this developmental process.

13. Ford, George A., and Gordon L. Lippett. *Planning Your Future: A Workbook for Personal Goal Setting*. La Jolla, Cal.: University Associates, 1972.

    Provides a step-by-step approach to life planning for personal growth and development. Using a workbook format, the authors encourage individual learners to write goals, set deadlines, develop skills, engage in self assessment, translate goals into projects, and build cooperative relationships. Learners are asked to complete a life inventory outlining the things they do and would like to do, their activities, and their values.

14. Hakel, Milton D., Thomas D. Hollman, and James H. Ohnesorge, "Relative Influence of Prestige as a Determiner of Intelligence Judgments for Occupations." *Journal of Vocational Behavior*, 1, No. 1 (1971), 69-74.

    Examines how well students can discriminate among occupations based on average intelligence of various occupational group members. The authors constructed a forced-choice test, which takes occupational prestige into account and represents 24 combinations of intelligence and prestige differences. Results indicate that subjects' accuracy in identifying the occupation with the higher than average intelligence was significantly less than chance, because they made their choices based exclusively on prestige.

15. Hall, Mary H. "A Conversation with Peter F. Drucker." *The Personnel Administrator*, 13, No. 6 (1968), 18-25.

    Drucker responds to questions on career choice, second careers, life long education, job-related pressures, philosophy of work and careers, and what to look for in an employer.

16. Harmon, Lenore W. "The Life and Career Plans of Young Adult College Women: A Follow-Up Study." *Journal of Counseling Psychology*, 28, No. 5 (1981), 416-427.

    Examines the process of career choice by women in a follow-up study of 391 women six years after entering college. These women had considered an average of nine occupations, had liberal attitudes towards women's roles and an awareness of sex discrimination, and had maintained an interest in the traditional vocations which were popular when they entered college (housewife, nurse, teacher) but also had developed interests in nontraditional jobs (physicist, college professor).

17. Harren, Vincent A. "A Model of Career Decision Making for College Students." *Journal of Vocational Behavior*, 14, No. 2 (1979), 113-119

    Presents a model of career decision making applicable exclusively to undergraduate college students. Restricting the conceptualization in this way results in a model which includes: enumeration of immediate or anticipated environmental factors influencing decision making, specification of the internal psychological processes of decision making, and identification of important developmental and personality characteristics of the decision maker. The model provides a framework for developing empirically verifiable hypotheses, assessing student needs, and designing counseling and educational strategies.

18. Hart, Darrel H., Keith Raynor, and Edwin R. Christensen. "Planning, Preparation, and Chance in Occupational Entry." *Journal of Vocational Behavior*, 1, No. 3 (1971), 279-285.

    Develops a model for classifying the degree of preparation, planning, and chance in occupational entry, and tests it using career histories of 60 men. Findings indicate a relationship between planned determinants of occupational entry and occupational level. Most professional men entered their occupations mainly through preparation and planning; however, some skilled men entered their occupations through planning, while chance events were primarily influential for others. Entry into occupations by semi-skilled men generally involved unplanned chance events. Unplanned situational events should receive greater emphasis in occupational theory and vocational counseling.

19. Hoyt, Daniel R., and J.D. Lewis. "Planning for a Career in Human Resource Management." *Personnel Administrator*, 25, No. 10 (1980), 53-54; 67-68.

    Students who are interested in planning for a career in human resource management are given advice on appropriate academic coursework, the need for experience in non-classroom activities, and the importance of carefully planned job search activities.

20. Hummel, Dean L., and Carl McDaniels. *How to Help Your Child Plan a Career*. Washington, D.C.: Acropolis Books, 1979.

    Designed to help parents assist children with career planning. Up-to-date information is presented on occupations, usable resources, career games, future career opportunities, and career exercises. Chapter 12 provides a 16-page annotated bibliography on general and special career development concerns.

21. Karpicle, Susan. "Perceived and Real Sex Differences in College Students Career Planning." *Journal of Counseling Psychology*, 27, No. 3 (1980), 240-245.

    Examines sex differences in the motive to avoid success, home-career conflict, and influence on career planning by members of the opposite sex. Sex differences in counselor's perceptions regarding these variables are also studied. Results show female students report more home-career conflict and success avoidance than their male counterparts. Male and female counselors perceived that female students experienced more of all three dependent variables than were actually reported by female students.

22. Klegon, Douglas. "The Sociology of Professions: An Emerging Perspective." *Sociology of Work and Occupations*, 5, No. 3 (1978), 259-283.

    Discusses the shortcomings of the traditional sociological approaches to studying professions and then explores an alternative approach. He contends that the ability to gain and sustain professional status is related to specific occupational strategies and to broader social forces and distributions of power. This approach entails giving attention to the social meaning of occupational tasks as well as the causes and consequences of professionalism.

23. Kotter, John P., Victor A. Faux, and Charles McArthur. *Self Assessment and Career Development*. Englewood Cliffs, N.J.: Prentice-Hall, 1978.

    A text/workbook designed to help people manage their own careers. The first part of the book explores the techniques and uses of self assessment. Information generating devices include the written interview, AVL Study of Values, the 24-hour diary, the Strong-Campbell interest inventory, life style representations, and background fact sheets. The second part focuses on career development and challenges at different career stages. Illustrative cases, exercises, and worksheets are provided along with examples of written self assessments and career plans.

24. Kroll, Arthur M., et al. *Career Development: Growth and Crisis*. New York: John Wiley and Sons, 1970.

    Examines the interrelations between the concept of self in career development theory with emphasis on the development of cognitive decision making abilities. The authors draw on self theory, cognitive theory, social psychology, and career development theory in their attempt to collect, synthesize, integrate, and extend existing elements of theory. Self evaluation, vocational interests, career choice, decision making models, and coping with career crises are addressed.

25. Krumboltz, John D., Jane F. Becker-Haven, and Kent F. Burnett. "Counseling Psychology." *Annual Review of Psychology*, 30 (1979), 555-602.

    Reviews the literature on career transitions published during the years 1974 through 1978. Special attention is devoted to decision making skills, career maturity, nature and quality of vocational choices, employment seeking, and occupational adaptation. Research is summarized on these and other topics relevant to counseling psychology.

26. Lippitt, Gordon L. "Integrating Personal and Professional Development." *Training and Development Journal*, 34, No. 5 (1980), 34-41.

    Suggests five steps for achieving personal and career integration: (1) take charge of your own life; (2) engage in mind, body, and spirit stretching; (3) inventory your life; (4) develop an action plan; and (5) plan for support, review, and evaluation.

27. Meir, Elchanan I. "The Structure of Occupations by Interest—A Smallest Space Analysis." *Journal of Vocational Behavior*, 3, No. 1 (1973), 21-31.

    An interest questionnaire was administered to 220 boys and 296 girls in the final grade of Israeli high school. An identical circular field structure for both sexes was produced based on Smallest Space Analysis of the responses. The fields were ordered as follows: Service-General-Cultural-Organization-Business-Technology-Science-Outdoor-Arts and Entertainment. The occupational levels were organized in hierarchical order within each field. Results were explained using facet analysis.

28. Meir, Elchanan I., and Nehemia Friedland. "The Relationship Between Intrinsic-Extrinsic Needs and Occupational Preferences." *Journal of Vocational Behavior*, 1, No. 2 (1971), 159-165.

    Five occupations were ranked according to the individual preferences of 80 girls and boys attending the 12th grade of high school in Israel. The sample was divided into four groups of 20 and given five questionnaires, consisting of extrinsic and intrinsic needs. Each questionnaire dealt with one of the five occupations and included a different combination of needs for each group. Findings showed a positive correlation between the occupational preference ranking and the intrinsic needs, but not the extrinsic needs.

29. Mitchell, Anita M., G. Brian Jones, and John D. Krumboltz. ed. *Social Learning and Career Decision Making*. Cranston, R.I.: Carroll Press, 1979

   Thirteen essays which address the relationship between education and work and the contribution of education to individual career choice. The volume seeks to develop "a comprehensive orientation to career decision making which could explain its lifelong process and have practical implications for influencing that process." (p. 3)

30. Montana, Patrick J., and Margaret V. Higginson. *Career Life Planning for Americans*. New York: AMACOM, 1978.

   Explores career life planning (CLP) from both an individual and an organizational perspective. Among the concerns addressed are the factors affecting CLP in early, middle, and later years; the problems, issues, and processes of CLP; and activities/programs developed by organizations and for individuals to promote CLP. Agendas for the future are recommended to improve the environment for career life planning and development.

31. Moore, Charles G. *The Career Game*. New York: National Institute of Career Planning, 1976.

   Advises the post-high school student on how to formulate career preferences, how to analyze and evaluate career opportunities, and how to develop reliable career information upon which to base career decisions. The subjects of career economics and strategic analysis are introduced to help readers anticipate market changes and develop strategies to adjust to these changes. Practical advice on "how to market yourself" and on "women at work" is included.

32. Moore, Donna J. *Take Charge of Your Own Career*. Seattle: Belieu Lithograph and Printing, 1979.

   A simple do-it-yourself guide on individual career planning. The author presents a step-by-step approach for self assessment of a person's skills and strengths to find the right job where those skills and strengths can be used. Readers are encouraged to examine their need for career guidance, determine their skills, match their skills to the job market, plot their route to the career they want, and market themselves.

33. Mortimer, Jeylan T. "Occupational Value Socialization in Business and Professional Families." *Sociology of Work and Occupations*, 2, No. 1 (1975), 29-53.

    Examines family relationships and male college seniors' vocational values. Findings show different patterns of association in business and professional origin groups. When four socioeconomic measures were controlled, there was a positive relationship between familial closeness and communication and the businessmen's sons' assessment of intrinsic rewards. These variables were positively related to sons' intrinsic concerns in the professional families. In the business origin group, relationships between sons' values and family relationships depended on the functional emphasis of the fathers' work.

34. Okosky, Charles E. "Career Planning--Or How to Succeed in Business by Really Trying When the Other Way Doesn't Work." *Personnel Journal*, 52, No. 11 (1973), 955-961.

    Employees often feel inadequate to the task of career planning and managers often feel equally uncomfortable in the role of career counselors. To ensure that correct career decisions are made, employees should evaluate their past, present, and possibly future jobs to determine whether their goals are consistent with their abilities.

35. O'Neill, George, and Nena O'Neill. *Shifting Gears*. New York: M. Evans and Co., 1974.

    Each person needs to learn how to shift gears in a world of constant change and how to integrate this change on a personal basis. The authors encourage individuals to assume responsibility for self-determination by formulating and integrating a life strategy.

36. Osipow, Samuel H. *Theories of Career Development*. New York: Appleton-Century Crofts, 1973.

    Describes various career development theories, assesses their adequacy, examines research relevant to the theories, synthesizes the various approaches that currently exist, and considers their implications and utility for career counseling. Developmental approaches and personality models are discussed in detail; psychoanalytic, sociological, and trait-factor approaches to career choice are also considered. The author considers the implications of his analysis for research and for practice.

37. Pinto, Patrick, et al. *Career Planning and Career Management: Perspectives of the Individual and the Organization: An Annotated Bibliography.* Minneapolis: Industrial Research Center, University of Minnesota, 1975.

    Contains 291 annotated references dealing with career planning and management.

38. Reif, William E., and John W. Newstrom. "Career Development by Objectives." *Business Horizons*, 27, No. 5 (1974), 5-10.

    Presents a Contingency Planning Model for career development which places career responsibility in the hands of the individual. The model incorporates concepts of management by objectives, contingency planning, force field analysis, and the psychological contract. A career plan which encompasses an assessment of the situation, setting objectives, developing plans, and reviewing progress will increase the likelihood of a satisfying and productive career.

39. Reissman, Frank, and Hermaine I. Popper. eds. *Up From Poverty: New Career Ladders for Non-Professionals.* New York: Harper and Row, 1968.

    This collection of 23 essays considers: (1) new careers for disadvantaged non-professionals; (2) new career occupations in social welfare, education, health services, corrections, police, civil service, and industry; and (3) guidelines for training non-professionals and designing new careers.

40. Rothstein, William G. "The Significance of Occupations in Work Careers: An Empirical and Theoretical Review." *Journal of Vocational Behavior*, 17, No. 3 (1980), 328-343.

    Contends that most people do not make stable occupational choices initially in their work careers, nor do they evidence a strong commitment to a specific occupation over the course of their careers. High rates of occupational mobility are partially explained by individuals responding to opportunities which unfold during their work careers. Careers can be more accurately viewed as a "series of responses to a succession of opportunity situations than the effort to realize a predetermined occupational goal." (p. 328)

41. Saltoun, Jane. "Fear of Failure in Career Development." *Vocational Guidance Quarterly*, 29, No. 1 (1980), 35-41.

Studies the (1) fear of failure as one constraint on career planning efforts, and (2) the relationship between the fear of failure and immaturity in vocational development. Results show students (N=75) with high levels of fear of failure were less vocationally mature (on five of eight measures) and devalued career planning more than those with low levels of fear of failure.

42. Sidwell, P. Philip. "Career Planning for the Younger Manager." *SAM Advanced Management Journal*, 46, No. 1 (1981), 59-64.

    Career planning means more than just managing one's professional life. It has to include every aspect of life, including one's family, professional goals, education, and emotional needs. The author outlines an approach to developing a personally relevant career strategy.

43. Staats, Elmer. "Career Planning and Development: Which Way is Up?" *Public Administration Review*, 37, No. 1 (1977), 73-76.

    Reports the views of the Comptroller General of the U.S. on the myths and truths of career planning and development. The myths are: there is room at the top; the key to success is being in the right place at the right time; good salesmen make good managers; and career planning and development is a function of the personnel department. The truths include: the best opportunity is the one you have; all development is self-development; all development is individual; and opportunity for development should be universal.

44. Stahl, O. Glenn. "A Developing Concept of Careers." *Public Personnel Review*, 27, No. 1 (1966), 25-27.

    Identifies five factors relating to a concept of careers: (1) seeking out and cultivating the person best suited to do the work; (2) controlling the kinds of careers possible through public education; (3) the conditions of relative mobility in the population; (4) the impact of technology on manpower needs; and (5) the effects of social purposes associated with government programs. These factors will lead to: the end of single-occupation, single-organization, single-location careers; modifications in retirement and tenure systems; increased diversification in subject matter, objective, and locale of work; education becoming a way of life; and careers becoming more responsive to planning.

45. Storey, Walter D. "Which Way: Manager-Directed or Person-Centered Career Pathing." *Training and Development Journal*, 32, No. 1 (1978), 10-14.

   In these turbulent times, workers must learn to make and remake career plans and choices and chart a direction for their careers. This article reviews the state-of-the-art of career-pathing by contrasting the features of manager-directed approaches with person-centered approaches. The two approaches are contrasted by purpose, concept, assumptions, practice, benefits, and problems.

46. Super, Donald E., and Martin J. Bohn. *Occupational Psychology*. Belmont, Cal.: Wadsworth, 1970.

   Integrates what psychologists have discovered about occupations and careers. The author examines the relevance of occupational psychology; explores the role of abilities, interests, values, and personality in occupational choice and development; analyzes careers by contrasting the developmental approach with the differential approach to occupational psychology; and considers the applications of occupational psychology in personnel work and in vocational psychology.

47. Tiedeman, David V. *Career Development: Designing Our Career Machine*. Cranston, R.I.: Carroll, 1979.

   Discusses the philosophical, procedural, and technical problems associated with the design and construction of the Information System for Vocational Decisions (ISVD), or career machine. The ISVD seeks to improve career decision making through the use of a computer-based training system. It was designed to relate knowledge about students to data about education, training, and work as an aid in making career decisions.

48. Tuckman, Bruce W. "An Age-Graded Model for Career Development Education." *Journal of Vocational Behavior*, 4, No. 2 (1974), 193-212.

   Identifies three components in defining career development (self awareness, career awareness, and career decision making) and develops a framework to assist educators in choosing learning experiences which are most beneficial for youth of differing ages. Child development is described in eight stages. For each stage, the author suggests career development themes, as well as sample experiences and activities for each theme. Recommendations are made for instructional media at each stage and related to the previously suggested activities and themes.

49. Wood, S. "A Simple Arithmetical Approach to Career Planning and Recruitment." *British Journal of Industrial Relations*, 3, No. 3 (1965), 291-300.

    Presents a model of planning recruitment and careers based on the British Civil Service. Planning careers is a continuing process which helps you to know when to alter course and how to avoid being forced by events into hurried decisions.

50. Yankelovich, Daniel. "Turbulence in the Working World: Angry Workers, Happy Grads." *Psychology Today*, 8, No. 7 (1974), 80-89.

    Explores the changing perceptions of college students, young blue collar workers, and women toward the world of work. The author discusses five new cultural trends which are transforming the American work ethic.

51. Zenger, John H., et al. *How to Work for a Living and Like It: A Career Planning Workbook*. Reading, Mass.: Addison-Wesley, 1975.

    A brief self-assessment workbook for career planning. Readers are encouraged to complete career profile forms and career planning forms. Career counselors are given advice on how to use the book when working with participants in a one-to-one relationship or in more structured group workshops.

CAREER INFORMATION/VOCATIONAL INTERESTS

52. Bartling, Herbert C., and Albert B. Hood. "An 11-Year Follow-Up of Measured Interest and Vocational Choice." *Journal of Counseling Psychology*, 28, No. 1 (1981), 27-35.

    Reports on a follow-up analysis of 408 university graduates 11 years after they had taken the Strong Vocational Interest Blank; the American College Testing Examination; and the Opinion, Attitude, and Interest Survey. Results show that "expressed choice" was a more accurate predictor of future occupation than "measured interest". The accuracy of both was highest when they were congruent. However, the congruence of either expressed choice or measured interests was not related to job satisfaction.

53. Beachley, Catherine. "Careers via Closed Circuit Television." *Vocational Guidance Quarterly*, 7, No. 2 (1959), 67-70.

    Plans for a program of telecasts over closed circuit television were formulated by high school counselors, classroom teachers, and specialists working on topics related to their phase of education. Telecasts included such fields as occupational information, curriculum choices, and personal problems. Following the completion of more than 100 of these telecasts, the author assessed the value of the program and speculated on television's future as a way of dealing with careers and related occupational information.

54. Blank, Jeff R. "Jobs-Career Key: A Test of Occupational Information." *Vocational Guidance Quarterly*, 27, No. 1 (1978), 6-17.

    Describes the Jobs-Career Key which is an occupational information test. There is a one-to-one correspondence between the occupational titles and Holland's (143) personality and vocational typology. Item responses are referenced to the Dictionary of Occupational Titles and Occupational Outlook Handbook.

55. Blau, Peter M., and Otis D. Duncan. *The American Occupational Structure*. New York: John Wiley and Sons, 1967.

   Analyzes the American occupational structure and the variables that influence social mobility in it. Generalizations are based on a broad-scale empirical survey of over 20,000 working men in the United States. The authors examine status in careers, models of occupational mobility, geographical and social mobility, inequalities of opportunity, stratification systems, and various influences exerted on careers of family members. In the final chapter the authors relate their findings to comparative data on mobility in different industrial societies.

56. Borgen, Fred H., and Mark J. Seling. "Expressed and Inventoried Interests Revisited: Perspicacity in the Person." *Journal of Counseling Psychology*, 25, No. 6 (1978), 536-543.

   Assesses the validities of "inventoried interests" vs. "expressed choice" for predicting college major and career choice outcomes. Expressed choices were found to have superior predictive validity to the Strong Vocational Interest Blank's (SVIB) inventoried interests. Predictive accuracy was highest when the person's expressed choice matched the SVIB prediction.

57. Bureau of Labor Statistics. *Exploring Careers*. Washington, D.C.: G.P.O., 1979.

   Provides career education guidance for junior high school age youngsters. Career awareness is fostered by means of occupational narratives, evaluative questions, activities, and career games organized in 14 occupational groupings.

58. Career Information Center. *The Career Information Center: A Working Model*. Boston, Mass.: Career Information Center, 1969.

   To aid the process of career choice, the model program of career information services was developed for junior and senior high school students. Informational assemblies, conferences, radio and television programs, filmstrips, and tape recordings are included as services. Each type of service is described in detail including its objectives, rationale, and process of development. The Career Information Center at Northeastern University serves teachers, guidance counselors, youth workers, club advisors, students, and the general public.

59. Carnegie Commission on Higher Education. *College Graduates and Jobs*. New York: McGraw-Hill, 1973.

    Explores the connection between higher education and employment. The preferred place of the college graduate on the job market is now being threatened. The Commission assesses the seriousness of the situation and presents the future outlook for college graduates in general, for teachers, for health professionals, and for other selected professionals. Issues such as the changing job market for college graduates and for doctoral recipients are examined along with potential adjustments in demand and supply.

60. Cooper, Jacqueline F. "Comparative Impact of the SCII and the Vocational Card Sort on Career Salience and Career Exploration of Women." *Journal of Counseling Psychology*, 23, No. 4 (1976), 348-352.

    Examines the effects of the Strong-Campbell Interest Inventory (SCII), the Vocational Card Sort (VCS), and the Auxilliary Information Material (AIM) on career options, information seeking, career salience, and satisfaction with career exploration. Findings show the VCS to be more effective than the SCII in increasing career options and increasing exposure to occupational information. AIM increased the career salience of women subjects (N=120).

61. Diamond, Esther E. "Sex-Typical and Sex-Atypical Interests of Kuder Occupational Interest Criterion Groups: Implications for Counseling." *Journal of Counseling Psychology*, 28, No. 3 (1981), 229-242.

    Examines the degree of similarity between scores on female-normed and male-normed scales for Kuder Occupational Interest Survey criterion groups. The author's analysis provides hints on "sex-typical and sex-atypical interests of these groups." (p. 229)

62. Epperson, Douglas L., and D. Corydon Hammond. "Use of Interest Inventories with Native Americans: A Case for Local Norms." *Journal of Counseling Psychology*, 28, No. 3 (1981), 213-220.

    Examines the utility of Kuder's General Interest Inventory (Form E) with a Native American population (N=134). Results suggest that items on Kuder's E may be inappropriate for this population and the author recommends use of local norms for interpretations with such homogeneous groups.

63. Forrester, Gertrude. *Occupational Literature.* New York: H.W. Wilson, 1964.

    In the increasingly complex world of career opportunities, bibliographic compilations can be useful in acquainting youth with sources of information. This bibliography lists approximately 6,000 selected references to occupational literature making it a valuable resource for students, teachers, counselors, and librarians. Brief annotations indicate the major topics and general content of the publications.

64. Gale, Barry, and Linda Gale. *The National Career Directory: An Occupational Information Handbook.* New York: Arco, 1979.

    Provides addresses of organizations which distribute free information about current careers. The authors also summarize information concerning entrance and training requirements for a career, detail specific duties in a variety of positions, estimate earnings in different jobs, outline growth opportunities within a given career field, show the linkages among careers, and highlight the attractions of a host of careers.

65. Ginzberg, Eli. "Career Prospects for Managers-To-Be: A Look at the 1980s." *SAM Advanced Management Journal*, 42, No. 4 (1977), 50-60.

    Offers career planning advice to young managers-to-be who are still in school and identifies factors which will influence the job market for the next four years. Adaptability in career aims will be required of future managers as they witness pronounced shifts in the demand for and supply of managerial talent.

66. Grotenant, Harold T., and Mary E. Durrett. "Occupational Knowledge and Career Development in Adolescence." *Journal of Vocational Behavior*, 17, No. 2 (1980), 171-182.

    Studies the extent to which (1) late adolescents (N=6029) choose occupations whose educational requirements are consistent with their stated educational objectives, and (2) the extent to which students' vocational interests match their occupational choices. Correlations of .41 or less were found between educational plans and educational requirements of the selected occupations. Students were also found to lack knowledge of the vocational interests associated with occupational choices.

Career Information/Vocational Interests

67. Hall, Richard H. *Occupations and the Social Structure.* Englewood Cliffs, N.J.: Prentice-Hall, 1969.

    The purpose of this book is three-fold: (1) to analyze the relationship between the occupational system and the social system; (2) to describe and analyze the types of occupations in the social system; and (3) to serve as a text in occupational sociology or as a supplemental work for related courses. Brief attention is given to career patterns.

68. Harrington, Thomas F., and Arthur J. O'Shea. "Applicability of the Holland (1973) Model of Vocational Development with Spanish-Speaking Clients." *Journal of Counseling Psychology*, 27, No. 3 (1980), 246-251.

    Assesses the applicability of vocational development theories and interest inventories for Spanish-speaking individuals. Findings indicate that the six Holland personality types were present in the Chicano, Puerto Rican, Cuban, and South American subcultures. These types fit the Holland hexagonal model. The construct validity of the Harrington/O'Shea System for Career Decision Making was also confirmed.

69. Hopke, William E. *The Encyclopedia of Careers and Vocational Guidance.* Chicago: Ferguson, 1978.

    This reference book is designed for youths and adults who are making career-related decisions. It covers specific career opportunities and provides information on major occupational groupings. Volume 1 in this two-volume set contains ideas, guidance, and background on a number of areas of work; volume 2 provides specific information about careers.

70. Hoppock, Robert. *Occupational Information: Where to Get It and How to Use It in Counseling and Teaching.* New York: McGraw-Hill, 1976.

    Discusses basic theories of career choice and development and the use of occupational information in counseling. The author identifies the kind of occupational information that counselors and clients need and suggests where to get it and how to evaluate, classify, and file it. General recommendations are made of ways in which occupational information may be presented to groups of all kinds.

71. Mallett, Sheldon D., Arnold R. Spokane, and Forrest L. Vance. "Effects of Vocationally Relevant Information on the Expressed and Measured Interests of Freshman Males." *Journal of Counseling Psychology*. 25, No. 4 (1978), 292-298.

    Examines the effects of a vocational information treatment on the "congruence" of expressed and measured interests of 46 freshman males while controlling for differences due to private and public school background and living environment (home vs. boarding). Findings indicate that private boarding school students were less congruent than public school or private day school graduates. Counseling implications are considered.

72. Perham, John C. "Executive Jobs: A Banner Year." *Dun's Review*, 108, No. 5 (1976), 41-50.

    Dun's annual survey of the executive job market is presented. In 1976 the market for executives expanded with great demand for general managers, active recruiting for financial managers, more opportunities for older executives (50 years or older), and fewer opportunities on the foreign job market for American executives.

73. Perham, John C. "The Boom in Executive Jobs." *Dun's Review*, 110, No. 5 (1977), 80-87.

    There was a considerable increase in executive job openings in 1977. The author explains why so many companies are looking for executives at all levels, identifies the most active industries, and assesses the progress of women in management.

74. Perham, John C. "Update on Executive Jobs." *Dun's Review*, 112, No. 5 (1978), 84-105.

    Dun's 1978 job survey, compiled from lists of management openings provided by 20 of the leading U.S. search firms, shows more companies than ever are looking for more executives. The author identifies the industries most active in hiring.

75. Perham, John C. "Surprising Boom in Executive Jobs." *Dun's Review*, 114, No. 5 (1979), 58-60.

    The executive job market is holding up remarkably well despite the recession. Many staff jobs are available and executive salaries are escalating. Companies are increasingly emphasizing recruitment of operations personnel--in engineering, manufacturing, and materials handling.

Career Information/Vocational Interests 21

76. Perham, John C. "Executive Jobs: Best Year Ever." *Dun's Review*, 116, No. 5 (1980), 52-54.

   Executive recruiters report that there are more job openings for executives than ever before. Neither wage/price guidelines nor recession have slowed the rise in executive jobs and salaries. High housing costs have made some executives reluctant to relocate.

77. Slaney, Robert B. "Expressed and Inventoried Vocational Interests: A Comparison of Instruments." *Journal of Counseling Psychology*, 25, No. 6 (1978), 520-529.

   Compares subject responses (N=84) to the Strong-Campbell Interest Inventory (SCII), a measure of inventoried interests, and the Vocational Card Sort (VCS), a measure of expressed interests. Findings indicate that results from both measures were related, there were no significant differences between the SCII and the VCS in internal consistency, the VCS themes predicted expressed choices better than the SCII themes, and subjects detected sex bias in the SCII but not in the VCS.

78. Slaney, Robert B., and Joyce E.A. Russell. "An Investigation of Different Levels of Agreement Between Expressed and Inventoried Vocational Interests Among College Women." *Journal of Counseling Psychology*, 28, No. 3 (1981), 221-228.

   Examines whether college women (N=175) who had different levels of agreement between expressed and inventoried vocational interests would differ on vocationally relevant dependent variables. Results show there were significant differences between vocational preference inventory scores and college majors, between expressed choice and college major, on Holland's construct of differentiation, and on Holland and Holland's Vocational Decision Making Difficulty Scale.

79. *Standard and Poor's Register of Corporations, Directors, and Executives*. New York: Standard and Poor, 1981. Volumes 1-3.

   These volumes provide information on 37,000 corporations with details on names, titles, annual sales, number of employees, etc. This directory is expensive for the annual subscriber, but it is usually available in libraries and placement centers.

VOCATIONAL GUIDANCE AND COUNSELING

80. Atanasoff, George E., and Robert B. Slaney. "Three Approaches to Counselor-Free Career Exploration Among College Women." *Journal of Counseling Psychology*, 27, No. 4 (1980), 332-339.

    Compares the effects of the interpretive format of the Strong-Campbell Interest Inventory (SCll), the Self-Directed Search (SDS), and the Vocational Card Sort (VCS). Results of treatments on 140 undergraduate women show that the SDS and VCS themes were closer to the expressed choices of participants than were the SCll themes.

81. Bank, Ira M. "Children Explore Careerland Through Role Models." *Vocational Guidance Quarterly*, 17, No. 4 (1969), 284-288.

    Boys and girls need experiences during the elementary school years which provide substantial opportunities for vocational inquiry. During these maleable years in the lives of elementary school students a broader base for vocational choice can be provided. An expanded careerland can be developed by counselors who can expose children to the world of work and to workers at an early age. The effectiveness of such exposures during the formative years may enhance the individual's choice of alternatives in the later years of development.

82. Bartlett, Willis E. "Vocational Maturity: Its Past, Present, and Future Development." *Journal of Vocational Behavior*, 1, No. 3 (1971), 217-229.

    Reviews and critically analyzes various approaches to studying vocational maturity. While the viability of vocational maturity was generally supported, the author points to the conflicting results of research on this subject and to the infrequent application of these results to counseling. Vocational maturity development is conceptualized as being similar to and not separate from personality development. The author suggests future research studies which would examine the relationships between vocational maturity development and aspects of personality development.

83. Bartlett, Willis E., and Destry Oldham. "Career Adjustment Counseling of 'Young-Old' Women." *Vocational Guidance Quarterly*, 27, No. 2 (1978), 156-163.

    Reviews the literature concerning the vocational adjustment problems experienced by some "young-old" women. Special attention is given to female employees with suggestions offered for vocational and personal counseling intervention alternatives.

84. Bolles, Richard N. *The Quick Job-Hunting Map.* Berkeley: Ten Speed Press, 1975.

    Assists job hunters and career changers in a self-directed search to identify the skills they have and enjoy, how to identify the places they would like to work, and how to get hired in such a place.

85. Bolles, Richard N. *What Color Is Your Parachute?* Berkeley: Ten Speed Press, 1980.

    Provides practical step-by-step instructions for job hunters and career changers. Topical coverage includes: a description of the way an average person goes about job hunting; the effectiveness of various job hunting methods; kinds of help available to the job hunter and prescriptions for successful job hunting; career and life planning; how the hiring process operates; and how to get the job you want. Useful exercises and instruments are included to assist persons in undertaking new careers as well as for life planning.

86. Boocock, Sarane S. "The Life Career Game." *Personnel and Guidance Journal*, 46, No. 4 (1967), 328-335.

    One way vocational counselors can overcome the discrepancy between the adolescent and the adult world is to use games with simulated environments. The author describes an example of such a game where students plan the life of a fictitious student and receive information on the likely consequences of their decisions. Results of field testing with the game show that it can disseminate factual information about career decision making, arouse student interest, and give students a realistic, though vicarious, glimpse of aspects of the adult world.

87. Borrow, Henry, ed. *Man in a World at Work*. Boston: Houghton Mifflin, 1964.

   Contains 24 essays which examine the nature of vocational guidance, the significance of the human work experience, the role of the individual in the labor force, and research and professional practice in vocational guidance.

88. Bradley, Richard W., and R. Douglas Smith. "Studies and Projects to Improve Vocational Guidance Services." *Vocational Guidance Quarterly*, 19, No. 4 (1971), 281-288.

   School counselors who design and conduct research projects appropriate to their own schools can contribute to the improvement of counseling and guidance. Prospective counselors have been encouraged to engage in research projects while in graduate school so that once on the job these applications can continue with their own students. The article details the preferences of practicing counselors in terms of the types of vocationally-related research they would like to see done.

89. Campbell, Robert E., et al. *Career Guidance: A Handbook of Methods*. Columbus: Charles E. Merrill, 1973.

   Discusses over 600 current techniques for achieving specific career guidance objectives. In addition to organizing, codifying, and synthesizing innovative guidance methods, the authors provide a conceptual framework for selection of methods under varying conditions, provide models and guidelines for developing a total career guidance program, and identify gaps and discrepancies in career guidance methods. Chapter 8 provides 643 abstracts on career guidance methods.

90. Carey, E. Niel. "Vocational Guidance for All: Is Differentiated Staffing the Answer." *American Vocational Journal*, 45, No. 4 (1970), 68-69.

   A differentiated staffing pattern is suggested in an attempt to provide vocational guidance to all students. Four categories of personnel would provide the services for this program: (1) school counselor, (2) guidance teacher, (3) para-professional, and (4) specialist/coordinator.

91. Crites, John O. "A Model for the Measurement of Vocational Maturity." *Journal of Counseling Psychology*, 8, No. 3 (1961), 255-259.

Analyzes and critiques a variety of definitions of vocational maturity. The author suggests a procedure for measuring the degree of vocational development (DVD) and the rate of vocational development (RVD). The DVD refers to "the maturity of an individual's vocational behavior as indicated by the similarity between his behavior and that of the oldest individual in his vocational life stage." (p. 259) The RVD refers to "the maturity of an individual's vocational behavior in comparison with that of his own age group." (p. 259)

92. Crites, John O. *Vocational Psychology: The Study of Vocational Behavior and Development.* New York: McGraw-Hill, 1973.

    Provides an up-to-date review of research and theory in the field of vocational psychology. Unlike earlier texts, the author emphasizes vocational behavior by focusing primarily on vocational choice and vocational adjustment. This work seeks to codify and define vocational psychology as a field of scientific study.

93. Cross, William C. "A Career Guidance Program for Small Rural High Schools." *Vocational Guidance Quarterly*, 19, No. 2 (1970), 146-150.

    The provision of "circuit riding" services to two rural high schools by advanced graduate students in counseling was found to raise substantially the number of graduating seniors who continued their educations.

94. Dixon, David N., and Charles D. Claiborn. "Effects of Need and Commitment on Career Exploration Behaviors." *Journal of Counseling Psychology*, 28, No. 5 (1981), 411-415.

    Tests the impact of (1) perceived need (by the client) for assistance in career decision making, and (2) commitment to career exploration on counselor social power. Results show that perceived need did not significantly affect attitude change or information seeking; however, commitment to change did have a significant effect on information seeking. The implications for counseling are discussed.

95. DuBato, George S. "VOGUE: A Demonstration System of Occupational Information for Career Guidance." *Vocational Guidance Quarterly*, 17, No. 2 (1968), 117-119.

An occupational information utilization survey was a major feature of this New York State study. Guidance counselors responded to questionnaires which were designed to determine: (1) the occupational information needs of counselors, (2) the occupational information resources available and utilized by counselors, and (3) the desires of counselors for changes in occupational information which might make it more useful in career guidance.

96. Egner, Jean R., and Dorothy J. Jackson. "Effectiveness of a Counseling Intervention Program for Teaching Career Decision-Making Skills." *Journal of Counseling Psychology*, 25, No. 1 (1978), 45-52.

Develops a career decision making model and intervention to help students increase career maturity and decision making skills. A pilot program was evaluated and students were shown to have significantly increased their career maturity was significantly associated with decision making. The program was useful to students in evaluating future career options.

97. "Executive Job Hunters Get a Guide." *Business Week*, No. 1898 (1966), 45-48.

Career counseling to place the right person in the right job is a growing service industry today. Recent developments in executive career guidance are briefly traced.

98. Feingold, S. Norman. "Perspectives on Career Guidance: An Administrator's View." *Peabody Journal of Education*, 52, No. 1 (1974), 5-13.

Counselors are more involved than ever before in career guidance and career development. The author provides 22 guidelines for counselors to help them cope with new emerging problems and a changing role.

99. Fitzgerald, Louise F. "Nontraditional Occupations: Not for Women Only." *Journal of Counseling Psychology*, 27, No. 3, (1980), 252-259.

Reports on male and female college students' (N=120) ratings of male counselors who are interviewing either male or female clients considering either a nontraditional or a traditional job choice. Findings indicate that while students regarded traditional job choices as more appropriate than non-traditional choices, this affected neither their ratings of the counselor nor their willingness to work with him.

100. Gelatt, H.B. "Decision Making: A Conceptual Frame of Reference for Counseling." *Journal of Counseling Psychology*, 9, No. 3 (1962), 240-245.

Proposes a theoretical framework for secondary school guidance and counseling services. A "sequential decision making process" is described where a decision maker uses information to select a course of action which may be "terminal" (final) or "investigatory" (calling for more information). The process of deciding requires three information systems: predictive system (i.e., possible alternative outcomes); value system (desirability of outcomes); and criterion system (rules for evaluating appropriate action). The implications of the model for guidance practice are considered.

101. Ginzberg, Eli. *Career Guidance: Who Needs It, Who Provides It, Who Can Improve It.* New York: McGraw-Hill, 1971.

Examines both the socio-economic factors and the psychological processes which help determine how people establish and implement their career plans. The book focuses on educational and vocational guidance. Initial chapters outline the framework by setting forth the historical context and social dimensions of career guidance. The emphasis then shifts to the institutions through which guidance operates. Final sections evaluate and examine the future of the guidance field and present recommendations to improve counseling functions.

102. Hamilton, Jack A., and G. Brian Jones. "Individualizing Educational and Vocational Guidance Designing a Prototype Program." *Vocational Guidance Quarterly*, 19, No. 4 (1971), 293-299.

Individualized career guidance programs should seek to assist each student to formulate educational and vocational goals that will guide his performance both within and outside the school environment. To select and implement both short and long-range goals, each student must possess accurate and useful information to help him relate his own individual characteristics to various vocational and educational options.

103. Helm, Carl. "Computer Simulation Techniques for Research on Guidance Problems." *Personnel and Guidance Journal*, 46, No. 1 (1967), 47-52.

Considers the potential use of computers to aid in the clarification and testing of counseling theory. The author presents test interpretations both by a psychologist and by a computer.

104. Herr, Edwin L. *Guidance of the College Bound: Problems, Practices, and Perspectives*. New York: Appleton-Century-Crofts, 1969.

    Provides counselor research-based aids for assisting young people in selecting among academic alternatives taking into account their personal characteristics.

105. Herr, Edwin L. *Decision-Making and Vocational Development*. Houghton Mifflin, 1970.

    Examines the interrelationships of decision making and vocational development, summarizes the current approaches to understanding decision making, and identifies the specific effects of different personal characteristics on decision making and vocational development.

106. Hilton, Thomas L. "Career Decision Making." *Journal of Counseling Psychology*, 9, No. 4 (1962), 291-298.

    Summarizes five possible models of the career decision making process and then presents the authors' model which is based on complex information-processing mechanisms. The main elements of Hilton's model are premises, plans, and cognitive dissonance. He suggests that "reduction of dissonance among a person's beliefs about himself and his environment" is the primary motivation in career decision making. (p. 298) The author presents a flow chart of career decision making and tests three sets of hypotheses based on the model.

107. Holland, John L., Thomas M. Magoon, and Arnold R. Spokane. "Counseling Psychology: Career Interventions, Research, and Theory." *Annual Review of Psychology*, 32 (1981), 279-305.

    Reviews the career-related literature published during the period 1978-1979. The review groups articles into four categories: career interventions, vocational research, speculation, and theory. Among the subjects covered are forms of career assistance, diagnostic assessments, occupational classification, expressed and measured interests, career patterns and processes, career decision making, and biases/barriers.

108. Ivey, Allen E., and Weston H. Morrill. "Career Process: A New Concept for Vocational Behavior." *Personnel and Guidance Journal*, 46, No. 7 (1968), 644-649.

    Defines and discusses the "career process" concept which stresses the various changes and developmental

tasks in vocational life. Counselors should recognize
that vocational choice is not an end point, but a step
in the developmental process. Two cases of career
process counseling are described.

109. Jepson, David A. "Vocational Decision Making Strategy
Types: An Exploratory Essay." *Vocational Guidance
Quarterly*, 23, No. 1 (1974), 17-23.

Explores the various vocational decision-making
strategies used by adolescents with similar career
goals. The author describes and contrasts 12 distinctive
decision-making patterns using a sample of 59 female
and 59 male high school students. Two strategy types--
the "active planners" and the "singular fatalists"--
receive more elaborate descriptions. The implications
of these vocational decision-making patterns are
discussed.

110. Jepson, David A., and Josiah S. Dilley. "Vocational
Decision-Making Models: A Review of Comparative
Analysis." *Review of Educational Research*, 44, No. 3
(1974), 331-349.

Outlines psychological decision theory; summarizes
eight well-known vocational decision-making models (VDMs);
compares the assumptions and concepts of VDMs; and shows
the applicability of VDMs to different types of decisions.

111. Jones, Lawrence K., and Mary F. Chenery. "Multiple Sub-
types Among Vocationally Undecided College Students:
A Model and Assessment Instrument." *Journal of
Counseling Psychology*, 27, No. 5 (1980), 469-477.

Develops a model of vocational decision status and
constructs an instrument, the Vocational Decision Scale
(VDS), to assess its dimensions. The model's three
dimensions are decidedness, comfort with level of
decidedness, and reasons for being undecided. The
utility of the model and the reliability/validity of
the VDS were examined using data from 224 college
students. Results indicate the utility of the model
and the validity/reliability of the VDS.

112. Katz, Martin. "A Model of Guidance for Career Decision
Making." *Vocational Guidance Quarterly*, 15, No. 1
(1966), 2-10.

Outlines a model of career decision making which
combines three systems of data: a value system, an

information system, and a prediction system. Those making career decisions are assisted in considering the range of values in the culture and encouraged to assess their own values. Appropriate information is conveyed concerning the opportunity or extent of return associated with each option. Predictive data are communicated and guidance counselors show how these three systems come together in a rational process.

113. Kivlighan, Dennis M., and Jon A. Mageseth. "Effects of Matching Treatment Approaches and Personality Types in Group Vocational Counseling." *Journal of Counseling Psychology*, 28, No. 4 (1981), 315-320.

The Vocational Preference Inventory was used to identify participants as either people oriented or task oriented. Vocational counseling using a learning through interaction method (LTI) was given to half of the people-oriented participants; counseling via a learning through individual problem solving method (LTIPS) was given to the other half. Similarly, the LTI and LTIPS methods were used with each half of the task-oriented participants. Results showed that counseling approaches which matched personality types were more effective than those which did not match personality type.

114. Krumboltz, John D., and Wade W. Schroeder. "Promoting Career Planning Through Reinforcement." *Personnel and Guidance Journal*, 44, No. 1 (1965), 19-26.

Student volunteers (54, 11th graders) for vocational and educational counseling received one of three treatments: (1) reinforcement counseling (reinforcement of information seeking responses); (2) model-reinforcement counseling (prior to reinforcement counseling each client hears a tape recording of a male counselee); and (3) control. Findings show that model-reinforcement counseling is more effective than reinforcement counseling for males but not for females.

115. Morrill, Weston H., and David J. Forrest. "Dimensions of Counseling for Career Development." *Personnel and Guidance Journal*, 49, No. 4 (1970), 299-305.

The authors describe four types of career counseling: helping the client with a specific decision via a traditional vocational counseling approach; teaching decision making skills; viewing career development as a process, not an end point; and focusing on creating the ability to use an individual's strength to achieve self-set objectives.

116. Oliver, Laurel W. "Outcome Measurement in Career Counseling Research." *Journal of Counseling Psychology*, 26, No. 3 (1979), 217-226.

    Examines the issues in career counseling outcome measurement including such matters as criteria, instruments, and design and analysis. Recommendations for researchers are provided.

117. Omvig, Chryton P., Rodney W. Tulloch, and Edward G. Thomas. "The Effect of Career Education on Career Maturity." *Journal of Vocational Behavior*, 7, No. 2 (1975), 265-273.

    Assesses the effects of a career education program on students' career maturity. Data were derived from a sample of 480 sixth and eighth grade students, half of whom remained in a regular school program. Higher posttest maturity levels were formed among career education students. Significant differences were found in occupational knowledge of sixth graders, in the attitude scale score for eighth graders, and in occupational planning for both the sixth and eighth graders.

118. Peterson, Elwood R., Fred A. Rowe, and Lorna R. Whiting. "Professional-Paraprofessional Cooperation in Career Development." *Personnel and Guidance Journal*, 52, No. 6 (1974), 413-417.

    Describes how a career development curriculum is systematically developed by professional counselors for use by paraprofessionals and volunteer church workers. The curriculum is developed based on a comprehensive needs assessment. This model is useful to guidance programs because it integrates guidance units into an existing curriculum in a program structure which makes extensive use of paraprofessionals.

119. Prediger, Dale. "Tests and Developmental Career Guidance: The Untried Relationship." *Measurement and Evaluation in Guidance*, 5, No. 3 (1972), 426-429.

    Argues for a reassessment and realignment of the relationship between tests and counseling. The role of tests in career counseling is to: (1) stimulate career exploration, (2) provide predictive information related to career choice options, and (3) stimulate exploration of self in relation to career. Tests must be part of an experiential developmental guidance program if they are going to influence student development.

120. Reardon, Robert C., and Harman D. Burck. *Facilitating Career Development: Strategies for Counselors*. Springfield, Ill.: Charles C. Thomas, 1975.

   This collection of 15 essays emphasizes the media, techniques, strategies, and delivery systems which will be of immediate aid to the career counselor who seeks to help adolescents forming career decisions. The book stresses practice by focusing on the activities which those in the helping professions can engage in to help various clientele become more effective in their careers.

121. Reardon, Robert, and William Kahnweiler. "Comparison of Pencil-and-Paper and Tactile-Board Forms of the Self-Directed Search." *Journal of Counseling Psychology*, 27, No. 7 (1980), 328-331.

   Assesses two forms of the Self-Directed Search (SDS): the paper-and-pencil and tactile board form. Findings indicate that there was no significant difference between subjects' (N=48) preference of one form over the other. Differences were evident when participants' sex and grade point average were considered.

122. Rubinton, Natalie. "Instruction in Career Decision Making and Decision-Making Styles." *Journal of Counseling Psychology*, 27, No. 6 (1980), 581-588.

   Investigates the effectiveness of decision-making styles and decision-making interventions on career choice and vocational maturity. Data from 120 community college freshmen indicate that decision-making style (rational, intuitive, dependent) contributed to both vocational maturity and certainty of career choice. Intuitive decision makers responded better to intuitive interventions, and rational decision makers responded better to rational interventions.

123. Snodgrass, Gregory, and Charles C. Healy. "Developing a Replicable Career Decision-Making Counseling Procedure." *Journal of Counseling Psychology*, 26, No. 3 (1979), 210-216.

   Evaluates the effectiveness of well defined career counseling procedures and reports the benefits identified by clients. Results indicate that clients increased their awareness of career planning and decision making and their satisfaction with career choices. Clients also reported that counseling improved their self awareness, but not their ability to solve career problems.

124. Super, Donald E., and Phoebe L. Overstreet. *The Vocational Maturity of Ninth Grade Boys*. New York: Teachers College, Columbia Univ., 1960.

    Seeks to conceptualize the field of vocational development. The authors' longitudinal study of the vocational maturity of ninth grade boys clarifies educational problems associated with making vocational decisions during the adolescent years. The implications for education are discussed.

125. Warnath, Charles F. "Vocational Theories: Direction to Nowhere." *Personnel and Guidance Journal*, 53, No. 6 (1975), 422-428.

    Argues that vocational psychologists and counselors should consider theoretical models which are broader than vocational choice or vocational development models. These new models should be based on general human effectiveness without requiring a fulfilling job as a necessary concept. More emphasis should be placed on identifying those factors in the work situation which encourage satisfaction and confirm feelings of worth and human dignity.

CAREER CHOICE

126. Allison, Elisabeth, and Pinney Allen. "Male-Female Professionals: A Model of Career Choice." *Industrial Relations*, 17, No. 3 (1978), 333-337.

    Presents evidence suggesting that the behavior of females entering professions may be as economically motivated as males. A model for examining the economic rationality of male and female career choice is developed and related to the professions of nursing, teaching, chemistry, and law. The estimates of male and female "salary elasticities" for new recruits in these fields are roughly equal for both sexes. The implications for career decisions are discussed.

127. Almquist, Elizabeth M. "Sex Stereotyping in Occupational Choice: The Case for College Women." *Journal of Vocational Behavior*, 5, No. 1 (1974), 13-21.

    Studies a class of women over their four years of college. The choice of a female-dominated occupation rather than a traditionally male occupation was the only occupational variable which divided the group. Women in traditionally male occupations differ from women in feminine occupations in terms of work values, work experience, familial influence, role model influence, and selected college activities. With regard to relationship with parents and sociability experiences, the two groups are not appreciably different.

128. Andberg, Wendy L., Charlene V. Follett, and Darwin D. Hendel. "Career Influences, Educational Experiences, and Professional Attitudes of Women and Men in Veterinary Medicine." *Journal of College Student Placement*, 20, No. 2 (1979), 158-165.

    Compares male and female students from a college of veterinary medicine on factors influencing their career choice, their academic experience, gender-role expectations, attitudes, and need for support services. The

ors recommend recruitment of counselors experienced
ocational guidance for women in institutions with
easing female enrollments.

129. Arffa, Marvin S. "The Influence of Volunteer Experience on Career Choice." *Vocational Guidance Quarterly*, 14, No. 4 (1966), 287-289.

    Explores the influence of experience as a psychiatric hospital volunteer on the career decision of high school and college students. The author was interested in any changes in career choice of students after a volunteer-type experience, the direction of such changes, and whether those changes could be attributed to the experience as a volunteer. The results fail to support the hypothesis that volunteer experience in a hospital directly influences a change in career choice.

130. Blau, Peter M., et al. "Occupational Choice: A Conceptual Framework." *Industrial and Labor Relations Review*, 9, No. 3 (1956), 531-543.

    Develops a conceptual framework which attempts to tie together the economic, psychological, and sociological aspects influencing the process of job choice. The authors outline a systematic pattern for empirical research. The conceptual framework identifies four characteristics of individuals and four occupations as determinants of occupational entry. These determinants also affect a person's career satisfaction, mobility, and occupational orientation.

131. Borchard, David C., John J. Kelly, and Nancy Pat K. Weaver. *Your Career: Choices, Chances, Changes*. Dubuque, Iowa: Kendall Hunt, 1980.

    A workbook designed for those people who are searching for a satisfying career. It is organized around four units (the career planning process, career-related talents, career insight and direction, and career choice and planning) which help readers examine their attitudes toward choosing a career, their talents, values, wants, and personality in relation to their career choice. Readers are exposed to a decision-making model designed to help them develop realistic career choices and plans. Examples and practical exercises are provided.

132. Denues, Celia. *Career Perspective: Your Choice of Work*. Worthington, Ohio: Charles A. Jones, 1972.

Provides individuals who seek a place in the world of work with assistance in the process of making career decisions, self analysis, and evaluation. This guide is organized into three sections: (1) the world of work, (2) the basis of choice, and (3) making the choice. Work is viewed as a way of life, not merely a job; and the career path is portrayed as a developmental process, not one single decision.

133. Ekehammar, Bo. "Test of a Psychological Cost-Benefit Model for Career Choice." *Journal of Vocational Behavior*, 10, No. 3 (1977), 245-260.

    Applies a psychological cost-benefit model for career choice to the choice situation occurring after high school graduation. The authors constructed psychological cost, benefit, and profit scales, with regard to continued education. Results indicate a positive relationship between psychological benefit-profit and aspiration-level with respect to continued education. Group differences regarding post high school choice also differed substantially, and in the expected direction, as to psychological cost-benefit-profit. Thus, the model was shown to have high predictive validity.

134. Ellis, Priscilla. *Career Choice and Attitudes Toward Work Among Professionals-in-Training*. Diss., Yale Univ., 1977.

    Examines career choice and the meanings of work for professionals-in-training. Forty law students were interviewed about the experience that led to the decision to go to law school, their expectations regarding future work, and their experience in law school. Study results show the impact of the public world on the individual's private psychological world of work. Major influences were changing attitudes of youth, the women's movement, and new career patterns.

135. Glueck, William F. "How Recruiters Influence Job Choices on Campus." *Personnel*, 48, No. 2 (1971), 46-52.

    Studies a group of 50 seniors at the University of Texas through the experience of interviewing with campus recruiters. The author analyzes preferences and impressions expressed before and after the seniors made their company selection. Three explanations (accidental, economic, psychological) were thought to affect a choice of a company for which to work. The psychological model

fit the students' choices most closely. In evaluating
the company, the "recruiter" was an important "inter-
vening variable"; most students stopped considering the
company if they had a negative impression of the
recruiters.

136. Goodale, James G., and Douglas T. Hall. "Inheriting a
Career: The Influence of Sex, Values, and Parents."
Journal of Vocational Behavior, 8, No. 1 (1976), 19-30.

Examines the mediating impacts of work values and
parental influence as these factors affect the relationship between social origin and plans for college and
career of 437 high school students in the Northeast.
Student perceptions of parental interest in students'
school studies and parents' desires that their child
will attend college did serve as mediators; however,
students' work values were not found to be mediators
of the relationship between parental background and
career aspirations.

137. Gottfredson, Gary D., and John L. Holland. "Vocational
Choices of Men and Women: A Comparison of Predictors
from the Self-Directed Search." *Journal of Counseling
Psychology*, 22, No. 1 (1975), 28-34.

Examines several predictors of occupational choice
based upon a theory of careers. A sample of 894 women
reported their occupational choices one or three years
after taking the Self-Directed Search at entry into
college. The authors found support for the hypotheses
that a person's competencies, activities, self-estimates,
interests, and vocational choices can be organized by
a six-category typology to predict subsequent vocational
choice. The best predictor of later vocational choice
is current choice.

138. Greenhaus, Jeffrey H. "A Factorial Investigation of
Career Salience." *Journal of Vocational Behavior*,
3, No. 2 (1973), 95-98.

After factor analyzing a series of career salience
items, the author relates the factors to several indices
of occupational choice behavior. Emerging from analysis
were three factors: (1) career advancement and planning;
(2) general attitudes toward work; and (3) the relative
priority of a career. General work attitudes were
significantly related to the "ideal" occupational choice
for both sexes and to a congruent occupational choice
for males. Also this factor was most highly related to
self-esteem for both females and males.

139. Harmon, Lenore W. "The Childhood and Adolescent Career Plans of College Women." *Journal of Vocational Behavior*, 1, No. 1 (1971), 45-56.

   A sample of 1,188 freshman women were asked, in retrospect, whether they had ever considered any of 135 occupational titles as possible careers. The study examined the popularity of each occupation, the time frame at which each occupation was considered, and the persistence over time of respondents' preferences. Early in life, a restricted range of occupations were considered. The most persistent preferences tended to be feminine occupations. The early preferences of freshman women who currently plan on careers in either medical technology or social work were contrasted.

140. Harren, Vincent A., et al. "Influence of Sex Role Attitudes and Cognitive Styles on Career Decision Making." *Journal of Counseling Psychology*, 25, No. 5 (1978), 390-398.

   Studies variables affecting college students' choice of a major and satisfaction with their choice. Using path analysis, the authors assess the influence of gender, sex role attitudes, decision making process, and cognitive style on choice of major. Results suggest that "gender influences sex role attitudes; and sex role attitudes and cognitive styles influence progress in the decision making process." (p. 390) The decision making process has a direct influence on satisfaction with choice of college major.

141. Hawley, Peggy. "What Women Think Men Think: Does It Affect Their Career Choice." *Journal of Counseling Psychology*, 18, No. 3 (1971), 193-199.

   Tests the proposition that men's views have an important although often unrecognized influence on women's career choices. The effect of men's attitudes on women's career decisions was found to be significant in this study of 86 women. Women's perceptions of men's view of the feminine ideal differed depending on the women's career group and their perceptions differed according to their marital status.

142. Holland, John L. "Explorations of a Theory of Vocational Choice and Achievement: 11. A Four Prediction Study." *Psychological Reports*, 12, No. 2 (1963), 547-594.

   Tests hypotheses related to a theory of vocational choice and personality types in a four-year longitudinal study. The author analyzed model student types in varying college environments to examine the prediction of vocational choice and its stability. The results support selected hypotheses in the theory. Student achievement and stability in vocational choice and major field are: (1) enhanced where there is congruence between student type and college type, and (2) more closely related to personal attributes than institutional attributes.

143. Holland, John L. *The Psychology of Vocational Choice*, Waltham, Mass.: Blaisdell, 1966.

Relates personal orientation to career choice decisions. Using the Vocational Preference Inventory it is possible to identify an individual's personal orientation and to predict his/her present career aspiration or later career choice. The author discusses six personality types and six matching occupational environments (realistic, investigative, social, conventional, enterprising, and artistic). Holland's theory suggests that artistic people will tend to chose careers in artistic environments.

144. Holland, John L. *Making Vocational Choices: A Theory of Careers*. Englewood Cliffs, N.J.: Prentice-Hall, 1973.

Outlines a theory of personality types and environmental models which organize existing knowledge of vocational choice, vocational interests, and personality. His analysis suggests that some occupational categories (e.g., social-enterprising) are quite similar while others (artistic-conventional) are very dissimilar. Individuals whose vocational preferences fall in two closely related fields (social-enterprising) are more internally consistent than those whose scores fall in two incompatible categories (artistic-conventional).

145. Holland, John L. *The Self-Directed Search*. Palo Alto: Consulting Psychologists Press, 1977.

A self-assessment booklet to aid in educational and vocational planning. Readers are encouraged to engage in occupational daydreaming; to identify those activities which they like and can perform well; to state the occupations which interest or appeal to them; and to rate themselves on a series of traits. Participants are given instructions on how to organize and interpret their responses.

146. Holland, John L., and Joan E. Holland. "Vocational Indecision: More Evidence and Speculation." *Journal of Counseling Psychology*, 24, No. 5 (1977), 404-414.

Seeks to identify the characteristics of students who are decided or undecided about career goals. Both decided and undecided high school (N=1,005) and college (N=692) students were assessed with measures of vocational attitude, personality, interests, and decision making ability. While the two groups of students were alike on most measures, they differed on the Identity and Vocational Attitude scales. The authors interpret some types of indecision as "the outcome of a proposed indecisive disposition." (p. 404)

147. Horton, Joseph A. *The Personality Characteristics of Professional Career Women: A Study of the Concurrent Validity of John Holland's Theory of Vocational Choice.* Diss., Ohio State Univ., 1975.

    Tests the validity of Holland's (143; 144) theory of vocational choice. The four instruments (Vocational Preference Inventory, Holland Scales Sets 1 and 11, and Self-Directed Search) developed by Holland and his associates were given to groups of professional, college educated career women. These women worked in occupations corresponding to Holland's six vocational environments. Results suggest that all four instruments are effective in operationalizing the concepts of Holland's theory.

148. Janis, Irving, and Don Wheeler. "Thinking Clearly About Career Choices." *Psychology Today*, 11, No. 12 (1978), 67-76; 121-122.

    Recommends three strategies for improving career choices: (1) develop a balance sheet grid classifying the anticipated outcomes of contemplated courses of action; (2) provide clear descriptions of the negative consequences associated with a course of action to minimize post-decision stress; and (3) offer decision counseling by a consultant to improve the quality of career decisions.

149. Korman, Abraham K. "Self-Esteem as a Moderator of the Relationship Between Self-Perceived Abilities and Vocational Choice." *Journal of Applied Psychology*, 51, No. 1 (1967), 65-67.

    Predicts and finds that students high in self-esteem are more likely to select occupations which they perceive require high abilities than students low in self-esteem.

150. Mansfield, Roger. "Self-Esteem, Self-Perceived Abilities, and Vocational Choice." *Journal of Vocational Behavior*, 3, No. 4 (1973), 433-441.

Tests the theory that self-esteem is a moderating variable in the process of choosing occupations. When the relationships were examined between self-esteem, self-perceived abilities, and abilities perceived as required in occupations, the above mentioned theory was not supported. Instead, the self-implementation theory of vocational choice was supported. However, results did show that those with low self-esteem were less likely than those with high self-esteem to view themselves as having the abilities they saw as needed in their chosen jobs.

151. McArthur, Charles C. "Career Choice Starts at Home." *Personnel Administration*, 30, No. 4 (1967), 3-5; 12-15.

A long-range study of 200 men designed to determine why they chose particular careers concludes that career choice is the result of a cumulative process called "enculturation" which starts early in a young person's preschool years and family life.

152. Moreland, John R., et al. "Sex Role Self-Concept and Career Decision Making." *Journal of Counseling Psychology*, 26, No. 4 (1979), 329-336.

Tests the hypothesis that "differences in students endorsements of sex-role-related personal qualities are associated with differences in their decision making progress regarding choice of college, choice of major, and choice of occupation." (p. 334) Results show that sex-role self-concept was related to progress on all three decisions for both male and female college students. However, sex role self-concept was related to the use of both rational and intuitive decision making styles for women, whereas it was related only to the rational style for men.

153. Munley, Patrick H. "Erik Erickson's Theory of Psychosocial Development and Vocational Behavior." *Journal of Counseling Psychology*, 22, No. 4 (1975), 314-319.

Compares students classified in different choice-adjustment groups and students scoring at different levels on the Career Maturity Inventory to detect differences among stage-resolution attitudes as measured by the Inventory of Psychosocial Development and the Dignan

Ego Identity scale. Results show students making adjusted vocational choices and developing mature career attitudes were also more successful in resolving the first six psychosocial stage crises.

154. O'Neill, James M., Thomas M. Magoon, and Terence J. Tracey. "Status of Holland's Investigative Personality types and Their Consistency Levels Seven Years Later." *Journal of Counseling Psychology*, 25, No. 6 (1978), 530-535.

Assesses over a seven year period the predictability of Holland's Investigative personality (143) and the three consistency levels (high, middle, low). Results from questionnaire data (N=95) suggest that for male investigative types, the Self-Directed Search is efficient in predicting (seven years later) actual job entry, graduate major, and ideal and projected plans.

155. Ory, John C., and Linda M. Helfrich. "A Study of Individual Characteristics and Career Aspirations." *Vocational Guidance Quarterly*, 27, No. 1 (1978), 43-54.

Investigates two groups of college honor students--one female group and one male group--to determine the interaction of individual characteristics and career aspirations. Results confirm the impact of cultural stereotypes on career selection in men and women.

156. Patchner, Michael A. *The Impact of Doctoral Social Work Upon Career Selection and Professional Activities.* Diss., Univ. of Pittsburgh, 1980.

Examines the impact social work education has had upon the subsequent career selections of this decades social work doctoral education graduates. Doctoral graduates (N=262) who were part of a national sample completed questionnaires the results of which indicated that most of them had established career goals prior to entering doctoral programs.

157. Plotsky, Francis A., and Rosemary Goad. "Encouraging Women Through a Career Conference." *Personnel and Guidance Journal*, 52, No. 7 (1974), 486-488.

Describes a conference on career development at the University of Texas at Austin which was designed to facilitate dialogue on career choices between undergraduate women and professional women from the university or community.

158. Reardon, Robert C., Roy O. Bonnell, Jr., and Michael R. Huddleston. "Self-Directed Career Exploration: A Comparison of CHOICES and the Self-Directed Search." *Journal of Vocational Behavior*, 20, No. 1 (1982), 22-30.

    Compares student reactions to the Self-Directed Search (SDS), a paper/pencil career planning guide, and CHOICES, a computerized career guidance program. While both programs were positively rated, subjects (N=75) showed a preference for CHOICES over the SDS.

159. Roe, Anna. "Early Determinants of Vocational Choice." *Journal of Counseling Psychology*, 4, No. 3 (1957), 212-217.

    Suggests hypotheses about the relationship between early experience and personality factors affecting an individual's vocational choice.

160. Shappel, D.L., et al. "An Application of Roe's Vocational Choice Model." *School Counselor*, 19, No. 1 (1971), 43-48.

    Counselors can apply Roe's (159) vocational choice model to the counseling setting by using occupational inventories and counseling strategies presented by the author. Counselors-in-training might be assisted by practicum supervisors, via small group procedures, using selected items from such an inventory to facilitate counselees' thinking regarding untapped needs.

161. Slaney, Robert B. "Expressed Vocational Choice and Vocational Indecision." *Journal of Counseling Psychology*, 27, No. 2 (1980), 122-129.

    Responses to the Occupational Alternatives Question were used to divide 232 male and female college students into four groups. The author hypothesized that these groups would differ on dependent variables related to career decision making. Results show significant group differences on congruence with college major, satisfaction with college major and career choice, Vocational Preference Inventory responses, and two scales measuring vocational indecision.

162. Slaney, Robert B., Debra Palko-Nonemaker, and Ralph Alexander. "An Investigation of Two Measures of Career Indecision." *Journal of Vocational Behavior*, 18, No. 1 (1981), 92-103.

Compares two scales measuring career indecision, the Career Decision Scale and the Vocational Decision-Making Difficulty Scale. Using scale scores from 857 male and female undergraduates, the authors analyzed the similarities and differences between both measures. Both scales are seen as promising ways to more effectively measure career indecision, select vocational treatments, and evaluate the impact of such treatments.

163. Vroom, Victor. "Organizational Choice: A Study of Pre- and Postdecision Processes." *Organizational Behavior and Human Performance*, 1, No. 2 (1966), 212-225.

    Examines the organizational choice situation by testing three hypotheses dealing with consistency between beliefs, attraction, and behavior. Graduate students who were in the process of selecting an organization in which to start their managerial career rated the attractiveness and instrumentality of organizations for the attainment of their goals.

164. Walsh, W. Bruce. "Consistent Occupational Preferences and Personality." *Journal of Vocational Behavior*, 4, No. 2 (1974), 145-153.

    Examines the differences in personality variables between students making occupational choices which were congruent and incongruent. The main effect of groups was significant for nine personality variables. The test for interaction was significant for three personality variables and the main effect of sex was significant for seven personality variables. Results indicate that better maintenance of vocational and personal stability and greater satisfaction exists among students in the congruent male group than among students in the incongruent female and male groups.

165. Walsh, W. Bruce, and Cynthia A. Barrow. "Consistent and Inconsistent Career Preferences and Personality." *Journal of Vocational Behavior*, 1, No. 3 (1971), 271-278.

    Explores the differences on personality variables between freshman students who made choices on college majors which were congruent or incongruent. The main effect of congruence was not found to be significant, based on analysis of the personality scale scores. Significant findings did emerge in the test for the main effect of sex and the test for interaction on six different personality scales, with one exception. Results show that subjects in the congruent male group have less stable college major choices than subjects in the congruent female group.

166. Wanous, John P. "Organizational Entry: Moving from Outside to Inside." *Psychological Bulletin*, 84, No. 4 (1977), 601-618.

Analyzes organizational entry from an individual perspective focusing on the ways individuals develop preferences and choose new organizations, the accuracy and completeness of information received by outsiders prior to entry, and the effect of recruitment on choice and post-entry attitudes and behavior. Research findings from numerous studies are summarized and the author draws conclusions concerning organizational entry from these studies.

167. Wertheim, Edward G., Cathy S. Widom, and Laurence H. Wortzel. "Multivariate Analysis of Male and Female Professional Career Choice Correlates." *Journal of Applied Psychology*, 63, No. 2 (1978), 234-242.

Studies the background characteristics of male and female graduate students in four professional degree programs in a comparative multivariate analysis of professional career correlates. Findings confirm the hypothesis that "differences across careers for each variable were greater than differences between the sexes within careers." (p. 234) The best predictors of career choice may be pre-existing dispositions. Limitations of the study are noted.

168. Williams, Constance M. "Occupational Choice of Male Graduate Students as Related to Values and Personality: A Test of Holland's Theory." *Journal of Vocational Behavior*, 2, No. 1 (1972), 39-46.

Seeks to determine the relationships among value patterns, personality factors, and occupational choice, as determined by major area of academic concentration of graduate students at the University of North Dakota. Relationships were investigated between major area of concentration and scores attained on the Allport-Vernon-Lindzey Study of Values, the Miller Occupational Values Indication, the Holland Vocational Preference Inventory, and the Cattel and Eber Sixteen Personality Factor Questionnaire. Results show that life values, work values, and personality characteristics were related to occupational choice in a significant way.

5

JOB SEARCH: RESUMES AND INTERVIEWS

169. Allen, Robert E., and Timothy J. Keavney. "The Relative Effectiveness of Alternative Job Sources." *Journal of Vocational Behavior*, 16, No. 1 (1981), 18-32.

    Examines the relationship between job source and subsequent work experiences. Findings reveal that among workers (N=467) initially entering the labor market, those who relied on formal job sources tended to work in higher-level occupations and in jobs more closely linked to their training than did their counterparts who used alternative job sources.

170. Anderson, Richard J. "Memo to Job Seekers: Writing a Professional Resume." *Child Welfare*, 54, No. 2 (1975), 123-125.

    Describes the various parts of a professional resume, including personal characteristics, educational background, employment history, and significant professional contributions (i.e., speeches, articles), offers hints for drafting a supplemental letter.

171. Baxter, James C., et al. "Letters of Recommendation: A Question of Value." *Journal of Applied Psychology*, 66, No. 3 (1981), 296-301.

    Examines the validity and utility of letters of recommendation within the framework of perception. The author studied 80 letters to determine "the levels of agreement found among descriptions organized to reveal the presence of discriminative, consensual, and differentiating patterns of perception." (p. 296) Results show a pattern of "nondiscriminative, nonconsensual, and nondifferentiating descriptions." (p. 296)

172. Berliner, Don. *Want a Job? Get Some Experience. Want Experience? Get a Job.* New York: AMACOM, 1978.

    Provides realistic advice on searching for a first job by pointing out the pitfalls along the job hunting path and how to avoid them. Among the subjects considered are resumes; references; job leads; pre-interview, interview, and post-interview game plans; and the first month on the job.

173. Brady, William F., Jr. "Getting Down to Basics About Landing That Job." *SAM Advanced Management Journal*, 42, No. 1 (1977), 47-54.

   The image projected by a job applicant may have a lot to do with the decision of whom to hire. Effective communication can aid the applicant in focusing on job interests, uncovering job opportunities, and generating employer contacts.

174. Brennan, Lawrence D., Stanley Strand, and Edward C. Gruber. *Resumes for Better Jobs*. New York: Monarch Press, 1981.

   Provides step-by-step tips on preparing a "job-getting" resume. The authors present 83 resumes as guides for resume content and format, explain the essentials of resume writing, and illustrate effective cover letters. Worksheet specimens are included in the appendix.

175. Cohen, Leonard. *Choosing to Work: An Action-Oriented Job Finding Book*. Reston, Va.: Reston, 1979.

   An action-oriented workbook which provides advice on how to identify work-related skills, develop confidence in these skills, and find a job where such skills can be used. The dual focus of the author is on job search (i.e., game plans, job skills, resumes, applications, interviews) and on overcoming biases (i.e., race, over 65, part-time workers, ex-offenders, physically handicapped). Practical illustrations and worksheets are included.

176. Cohen, William A. *The Executive's Guide to Finding a Superior Job*. New York: AMACOM, 1978.

   Contains advice on job-hunting techniques including the following: planning for job hunting, establishing career objectives, taking psychological tests, developing superior resumes, improving interview performance, using "headhunters", and controlling the hiring situation.

177. Crystal, John C., and Richard N. Bolles. *Where Do I Go from Here with My Life*. New York: Seabury Press, 1974.

A life/work planning manual for instructors, counselors, or self-motivated individuals who desire exposure to an effective system of job searching and career mobility. This workbook is designed for use in conjunction with Bolles' book (85) to present a comprehensive systematic approach to occupational decision making. It can be used in different ways by those working with groups, those working with individuals, and individuals working alone.

178. Dayton, Charles W. "The Young Person's Job Search: Insights from a Study." *Journal of Counseling Psychology*, 28, No. 4 (1981), 321-333.

    Examines job search approaches used by young people. Using two cohorts (one about 20 years old, the other in its early 30s) data are reported on the job-seeking approaches being used, the "aids" and "barriers" to job-search success, and the demographic and ability factors which make a difference in job-finding success. A profile of the successful job-seeking youth is provided.

179. Deutsch, Arnold R. *The Complete Job Book*. New York: Cornerstone Library, 1980.

    Provides a working guide to choosing careers, finding jobs, taking advantage of job-related opportunities, switching jobs or careers, and dealing with the challenge of contemporary worklife.

180. Dupree, Flint O. *Your Career in the Federal Service*. New York: Harper and Row, 1980.

    Provides the job seeker with the information needed to decide whether to work in the federal government. The book examines conditions in the competitive service; the way jobs are filled; federal agencies and their functions; career fields; career plans; career training and development; rewards and benefits; and presidential and congressional relations.

181. Fox, Marcia R. *Put Your Degree to Work*. New York: W.W. Norton, 1979.

    A guide for job hunters which gives special attention to career planning during student years, job search activities, the resume, the cover letter, and the interview.

182. Granovetter, Mark S. *Getting a Job: A Study of Contact and Careers*. Cambridge: Harvard University Press, 1974.

   Surveys professional, technical, and managerial personnel (N=282) who had changed jobs within the past five years. Three job-getting techniques were compared: applications directly to the company; use of employment agencies, newspaper advertisements, etc.; and informal contacts. A major finding was the heavy reliance of individuals on personal contacts to get information about jobs, especially for better paying and more satisfying positions.

183. Hawkins, James E. *The Uncle Sam Connection: An Insiders Guide to Federal Employment*. Chicago: Follett, 1978.

   A practical guide for those seeking initial employment in the federal government and for those desiring different or better job in the federal service. The author spells out the steps involved in locating and landing a federal job, including advice on application and qualification procedures. Hints on achieving upward mobility are provided and the merits of "job-hopping" vs. "staying put" are considered.

184. Hollandsworth, James G., Jr., and Beverly A. Sandifer. "Behavioral Training for Increasing Effective Job-Interview Skills: Follow Up and Evaluation." *Journal of Counseling Psychology*, 26, No. 4 (1979), 448-450.

   Assesses the usefulness and effectiveness of an empirically derived model for job-interview skills training. Evaluation results suggest that both trainers and trainees in varied settings judge the model to be a useful and valued approach for developing job-interview skills.

185. Jameson, Robert J. *The Professional Job Changing System: World's Fastest Way to Get a Better Job*. New York: Performance Dynamics, 1977.

   Provides general guidelines and specific advice on changing jobs to move "up" within one's present field or "out" to another field. The author examines such matters as generating interviews, handling references and application forms, dealing with interview situations, developing resumes and cover letters, overcoming liabilities, developing a plan of action, using reference information, and preparing a financial planning guide.

186. Klingner, Donald E., and Anthony J. Davis. *The Job Seekers Guide: A Workbook for Improving Your Career Situation.* New York: Human Sciences Press, 1980.

   Summarizes the ABC's of getting and keeping a job. The book is divided into seven sections addressing the following topics: (1) What kind of person are you? (2) How to get ready for job-hunting; (3) Do you like your job? (4) How to develop your own job strategy? (5) How to prepare for a job interview; (6) Now that you have your job, can you keep it? and (7) Books and articles to consult for additional help. Numerous self-assessment exercises and checklists are provided, along with practical advice on the "how to's" of job hunting.

187. Kryger, Barbara R., and Richard Shikiar. "Sexual Discrimination in the Use of Letters of Recommendation." *Journal of Applied Psychology*, 63, No. 3 (1978), 309-315.

   Tests the hypothesis that the applicant's chance of getting a job would be affected by both the sex of the person writing a letter of recommendation and the applicant's sex. Results, based on 35 questionnaires sent to male personnel directors, show (1) female applicants were more likely to proceed to the interview stage than male applicants; (2) favorable letters for a female were perceived to be more accurate than favorable letters for males; and (3) female applicants were perceived to have more initiative, responsibility, and to be more teachable.

188. Latham, Gary P., et al. "The Situational Interview." *Journal of Applied Psychology*, 64, No. 4 (1980), 422-427.

   Describes the situational interview where job applicants are asked how they would respond to different situations or critical incidents. Interviewers then score answers according to benchmark statements developed by job experts. Favorable reliability, internal consistency, and concurrent validity coefficients are reported.

189. Lathrop, Richard. *Who's Hiring Who.* Berkeley: Ten Speed Press, 1980.

   Gives guidance to college graduates on preparing resumes, cover letters, and follow up thank you notes; tips on dealing with interviews; and advice on building contacts. The auther contends that the key to job finding is to discover what an organization's problems are and to show the organization that you can help solve those problems and fulfill organizational needs.

190. Lederer, Murial. *Blue Collar Jobs for Women*. New York: E.P. Dutton, 1979.

Advises women on how to obtain skills and get hired in well-paid blue-collar jobs. These jobs are grouped into six categories: construction, industrial production, mechanics and repairers, scientific and technical, transportation, and other skilled occupations. Over 80 jobs are categorized and discussed according to such dimensions as pay, training, apprenticeships, job and advancement opportunities, working conditions, and actual job requirements.

191. Lukowski, Susan, and Margaret Piton. *Strategy and Tactics for Getting a Government Job*. Washington, D.C.: Potomac Books, 1972.

The U.S. federal government has a lot to offer in the area of employment opportunities. However, the red tape and inefficiency of the civil service system might discourage job hunters from applying. This book is a guide for navigating the civil service system and the other employment offices within the legislative and executive branches of the federal government as well as those which are outside of government. Suggestions for overcoming problems and delays in the job-hunt process are provided.

192. Medley, H. Anthony. *Sweaty Palms: The Neglected Art of Being Interviewed*. Belmont, California: Lifetime Learning Publications, 1978.

Focuses on how to conduct yourself in a job interview. The author humorously addresses such issues as "how to": allay your fears, present yourself in the best light, control the interview content, parry tough questions, keep from offending the interviewer, counteract the effects of a bad reference, handle salary discussions, and enforce your legal rights. Advice is also provided on how to relax, dress, handle stress, and turn questions to your advantage. A section is included on what the law prohibits an interviewer from asking.

193. Meyer, John L., and Melvin W. Donaho. *Get the Right Person for the Job: Managing Interviews and Selecting Employees*. Englewood Cliffs, N.J.: Prentice-Hall, 1979.

Provides managers and personnelists with information concerning changes and practices in employee selection. Among the topics considered are: preliminary planning and recruiting stages; interpretation and screening of data; management and conduct of job interviews; and hiring, induction, and entry of new employees. Laws and court actions impinging on the selection process are reviewed.

194. Mitchell, Howard M. "What Should You Ask the Company Interviewer?" *SAM Advanced Management Journal*, 42, No. 1 (1977), 58-61.

    Job hunters should consider questions they might ask interviewers as well as questions interviewers might ask them. A first step in determining interests and motives should be self questioning. At campus and initial interviews, questions about industries and firms might be asked appropriately. At final interviews, questions concerning career prospects are legitimate.

195. "Placement Firms: Can They Help?" *Public Relations Journal*, 34, No. 7 (1979), 30-32.

    Placement agencies and executive search firms are of limited value to those seeking entry-level public relations jobs. The author suggests college courses, types of volunteer experience, and extra-curricular activities which would be useful in helping to land that first job. Also suggestions of possible entry-level public relations positions are provided.

196. Reid, Graham L. "Job Search and the Effectiveness of Job-Finding Methods." *Industrial and Labor Relations Review*, 25, No. 4 (1972), 479-495.

    Compares informal methods of job finding with formal methods of job search. Results show the former to be as successful as the latter. Success in job search is defined as satisfaction with the new job, wages, and length of period unemployed.

197. Reynes, Tony. "You Sell Products--Now Learn to Sell Yourself Likewise." *Advertising Age*, 50, No. 1 (1979), 6, 15, 16, 18.

    Discusses six factors to be considered in leaving one's current position: money, responsibility, learning, mobility, qualitative factors, and flexibility. Practical hints on preparing a resume and presenting one's self in an interview are offered.

198. Rosenthal, Beth. "Headhunters." *Across the Board*, 14, No. 8 (1977), 19-23.

Management Woman is the name of an executive search firm exclusively for women. The company was formed to assist women who were having difficulty finding suitable executive jobs. This new business has been aided by recent laws allowing women to take employing organizations to court if discrimination occurs.

199. Rothstein, Mitchell, and Douglas N. Jackson. "Decision Making in the Employment Interview: An Experimental Approach." *Journal of Applied Psychology*, 65, No. 3 (1980), 271-283.

    Assesses the potential of a social perception model for investigating the process of making selection decisions. Results demonstrate that judges were able to make differential evaluations of two contrived job applicants and that group consensus might improve interviewer selection decisions.

200. Rozelle, Richard M., and James C. Baxter. "Influence of Role Pressures on the Perceiver: Judgement of Videotaped Interviews Varying Judge Accountability and Responsibility." *Journal of Applied Psychology*, 66, No. 4 (1981), 437-441.

    Examines "the relative influence of the perceiver versus the perceived on person perception" using mocked videotaped interviews of applicants to graduate school. Results indicate that under conditions of high judge accountability and/or responsibility "a perceptual pattern of high interjudge agreement and low within judge overlap for descriptive characteristics of applicant pairs was obtained..." (p. 437)

201. Salmon, Richard D. *The Job Hunter's Guide to Eight Great American Cities*. Cambridge: Brattle Publishers, 1978.

    Describes effective job hunting techniques and provides useful information for the prospective job hunter and resident of eight American cities--Atlanta, Boston, Denver, Phoenix, Portland, San Diego, San Francisco, and Seattle.

202. Schmidt, Peggy J. *Making It on Your First Job: When You're Young, Inexperienced, and Ambitious*. New York: Avon Books, 1981.

    A job hunter's manual which also explains how to cope with the challenges and problems of a first job and come out on top. Chapters on pre-employment preparation (academics and extracurriculars, internships, career choices, graduate degrees) and job search (employers, job campaigns, interviews) are supplemented by chapters providing on-the-job advice (first jobs, bosses, office politics, co-workers, ethics, discrimination, and moving on).

203. Sigelman, Carol K., Susan F. Elias, and Pamela Danker-Brown. "Interview Behaviors of Mentally Retarded Adults as Predictors of Employability." *Journal of Applied Psychology*, 65, No. 1 (1980), 67-73.

    Assesses the relative influences of nonverbal and verbal behaviors of mentally retarded adults in a simulated job interview on the ratings and hiring decisions of interviewers. Results indicate that verbal behaviors were more influential, with interviewees demonstrating intelligible speech, speaking at length, and responding appropriately to questions more likely to make favorable impressions.

204. Smith, Michael H. *The Resume Writer's Handbook*. New York: Barnes and Noble, 1980.

    Describes the basic elements of a resume, analyzes summary-style formats, examines 29 original sample resumes, and provides worksheets for developing a rough-draft resume.

205. Speas, Carol M. "Job-Seeking Interview Skills Training: A Comparison of Four Instructional Techniques." *Journal of Counseling Psychology*, 26, No. 5 (1979), 405-412.

    Examines whether some types of skill training can improve job-seeking interview skills. Four instructional techniques were examined: model exposure (MP), role playing (RP), model exposure plus role playing (MRP), and model exposure and role playing with videotape feedback (VIDEO). Overall findings indicate that the MRP and VIDEO treatments can increase probability of hire.

206. Traxel, Robert G. *Manager's Guide to Successful Job Hunting*. New York: McGraw-Hill, 1978.

    A "how to" book written for executive job-hunters and aspiring managers. Among the topics addressed are goal setting, self assessment strategies, identification of potential employers, job interviews, references, and negiotiations.

207. Ullman, Joseph C., and George P. Huber. "Are Job Banks Improving the Labor Market Information System?" *Industrial and Labor Relations Review*, 27, No. 2 (1974), 171-185.

   Describes the history and status of job banks, examines their effectiveness, and assesses future uses of job banks. The authors conclude that the job bank fell short of reaching its goals of (1) reducing frictional employment, (2) achieving more efficient job-man matching, and (3) improving services to disadvantaged applicants.

208. Ulrich, Heinz, and J. Robert Connor. *The National Job-Finding Guide*. Garden City, N.Y.: Doubleday, 1981.

   Tells how and why to get a job by providing leads to over three fourths of the jobs available annually in the U.S. Separate chapters cover tips for the job hunter, job prospects for the 1980s, employment agencies, executive recruitment firms, forty plus clubs, special job opportunities (women, minorities, handicapped), trade and professional periodicals, newspaper guide, federal and state job centers and an index to corporations (alphabetical and geographic).

209. Zehring, John W. *Careers in State and Local Government*. Garrett Park, Md.: Garrett Park Press, 1980.

   Discusses career opportunities in state and local government. Specific information is provided on internships, coop study, part-time and summer jobs; occupational information; examinations; applications, resumes, interviews; job listing services; and periodicals, resources, and associations dealing with state and local government.

6

PLANNING TO ADVANCE

210. Baker, H. Kent, and Steven H. Holmberg. "Stepping Up to Supervision: Making the Transition." *Supervisory Management*, 26, No. 9 (1981), 10-18.

Discusses the changes in job duties, attitudes and behavior as a person moves from the technical ranks to a supervisory position. Common reasons for supervisory failure are: (1) lack of training and support, (2) inability to adapt to change, (3) myopic vision, (4) poor interpersonal relationships, and (5) lack of fit.

211. Bell, Robert R., and J. Bernard Keys. "Preparing for a Move to Middle Management." *Supervisory Management*, 25, No. 7 (1980), 10-16.

Advises first-line supervisors on how to prepare for the move up to middle management. Among the changes they will encounter as middle managers are different emphases on functions, extended time outlooks, increased politicization of the job, and requirements for new skills and aptitudes. The Johari Window is introduced as an analytic device used for self assessment of leadership and managerial personalities.

212. Benson, Carl A. "Mobility and Career Development for Black Professionals." *The Personnel Administrator*, 20, No. 3 (1975), 40-43.

Many black professionals would prefer to live in a major urban center with a large black population. However, career advancement in part depends on a willingness to take advantage of opportunities that are open. To advance, black professionals must be willing to accept locations that are available, even if they are in the hinterlands, and to make a change when the opportunity comes. The author discusses the reasons why many black professionals seek the security of large, metropolitan areas.

213. Berardo, Don. "Increasing Upward Mobility--The Stuff Achievement is Made of." *Data Management*, 19, No. 3 (1981), 40-43.

    Discusses the criteria for career growth of information managers. Technical proficiency and personal traits are discussed in relation to career balance sheets. A score card for data processing career direction is provided.

214. Berger, Mike. "The Management Obsolescence Inventory." *Training and Development Journal*, 28, No. 6 (1974), 38-39.

    Describes a brief self-development checklist which can help managers recognize their own lack of self-development and their need for training.

215. Broadwall, Martin M. "Moving Up to Supervision." *Training and Development Journal*, 33, No. 2 (1979), 12-18.

    Offers people aspiring to supervisory positions an opportunity to learn necessary survival skills before they become supervisors. The author identifies basic skills needed by supervisors and shows how these can be learned in the would-be supervisor's present jobs.

216. Carroll, Archie B., and Ted F. Anthony. "An Overview of the Supervisor's Job." *Personnel Journal*, 55, No. 5 (1976), 228-231.

    Outlines five categories of responsibilities assumed by supervisors: (1) to higher management, (2) to employees, (3) to co-workers, (4) to staff departments, and (5) to the union. The article is addressed both to the new supervisor who has just moved up the career ladder and to the experienced supervisor who wants a refresher in supervision.

217. Couch, Peter D. "Learning to be a Middle Manager." *Business Horizons*, 22, No. 1 (1979), 33-41.

    The step upward to middle management often requires a change in relationships, attitudes, performance expectations, and skills. However, new middle managers may get little help in learning their new responsibilities. The author reviews some of the "learning needs" of new middle managers and some of the personal and organizational barriers they must overcome. Recommended steps to be taken by individuals and developers are listed to prepare for movement into middle management work.

218. Friant, R.J., Jr. "Getting Ahead in the Company: How to Keep Track of Where You Are and Where You're Going." *Management Review*, 56, No. 4 (1967), 42-49.

Describes a strategy to help individuals with ten to 20 years experience to get where they want to go in the company. The performance profile worksheet is presented as a useful career planning tool. Use of the worksheet can benefit both the employee and the company.

219. Gleason, Richard D. "Planning the Way to the Top." *Business Horizons*, 14, No. 3 (1971), 60-62.

Identifies five basic routes to the top in any corporation: sales/marketing, personnel/labor relations, manufacturing, engineering, and financial. Personal career planning leads to the attainment of career goals. Career success is facilitated if employees know where they want to go, how they want to get there, and when they should reach their career milestones.

220. Haldane, Bernard. *Career Satisfaction and Success: A Guide to Job Freedom*. New York: American Management Association, 1974.

Describes ways for employees to negotiate for promotions, transfers, and raises: to set goals and accomplish them; and to cope with or overcome job frustrations. It includes a supervisor's guide to cooperation with subordinates. The author describes the System to Identify Motivated Skills (SIMS) which assists employees in identifying their strengths. The first ten chapters are devoted to the individual identification and appreciation of motivated skills; the final two chapters show managers how this knowledge can have beneficial application for an organizational viewpoint.

221. Johns, Ted. "The Efficient Executive." *Management Today*, February 1979, 85-88.

Describes five ways to advance in organizations: (1) sponsorship, (2) informal, unpublicized variables (e.g., club memberships), (3) conformity and subservience, (4) being in the right place at the right time, and (5) attaining your work objectives.

222. Kleinger, Brian H. "Managing Your Career." *Supervisory Management*, 25, No. 3 (1980), 17-23.

Presents the following strategies for persons who are strongly motivated to advance in their careers: develop career competencies; know the formal and informal criteria by which you will be judged; develop alliances; be a top-notch performer; seek feedback; standout from the pack; become crucial to your boss; train your replacement; keep your options open; reassess your career periodically; and leave the company at your convenience and on a good note.

223. Knudson, Harry R., and Wendell L. French. "Planning Your Executive Career." *Management Review*, 50, No. 5 (1961), 35-37.

An executive must do his own career planning by assessing where he is now, projecting where he wishes to go, and determining how to get there. Guidelines are presented to assist the executive in selecting the best course of action for achieving his objectives. Organizational goals and activities should be examined as a framework for evaluating individual goals and activities.

224. Mardon, J., and R.M. Hopkins. "The Eight-Year Career Development Plan." *Training and Development Journal*, 23, No. 11 (1969), 10-15.

Outlines a procedure whereby an employee clarifies his career objectives and the means for achieving them. The authors discuss the elements of plan development, alternative career routes, the benefits to the company and the employee from a career plan, and the preparation of work schedules.

225. McCloskey, Michael. "Goals and Directions in Personal Planning." *The Academy of Management Review*, 2, No. 3 (1977), 454-463.

Identifies the limitations of rational planning and argues for an alternative approach where individuals identify both their "domain" (i.e., the "arena of favored activity and personal commitment") and "direction" (i.e., the "symbolic expression of whom one wants to become"). (p. 457)

226. Meyer, Herbert E. "Remodeling the Executive for the Corporate Climb." *Fortune*, 100, No. 1 (1979), 82-92.

Ambitious executives are attempting to improve their chances for promotion by hiring image consultants who provide advice for clothing, physical appearance, and social graces. Specific examples of successful "packaging" of executives are provided.

Planning to Advance 61

227. Meyers, Thomas K. "Go Abroad, Young Man." *Dun's Review*, 99, No. 2 (1972), 77-78.

   Describes the pros and cons of international assignments for American executives intent on climbing the corporate ladder.

228. Morrison, Donald G., and David C. Schmittlein. "Model of Careers in a Simple Hierarchy: Generalizing the Junior Professionals Decision Rule." *Bell Journal of Economics*, 12, No. 1 (1981), 310-320.

   Discusses a career path model for junior professionals who can decide to leave the organization for an outside employment opportunity or remain and hope for advancement to senior levels. The authors provide simple decision rules for junior executives which can be continuously applied. A weakness of the model, acknowledged by the authors, is its sole concentration on the supply of labor without considering demand for labor.

229. Moses, Knolly. "Networking: Who You Know May Be As Important As What You Know." *Black Enterprise*, 11, No. 2 (1980), 29-34.

   Corporate advancement in one's career path is often less a matter of what you know than who you know. Those who use contacts to further their own career or business ends are "networking." As blacks assume middle management positions, they should activate this networking system to maintain their position and help others to advance. A blueprint for networkers is provided.

230. Murray, Thomas J. "How Not to Become Chief Executive." *Dun's Review*, 111, No. 4 (1978), 57-58.

   Reveals some of the most glaring mistakes made by ambitious executives who inadvertantly bungle their attempts to secure the top job.

231. Orr, Warren G. "A Professional Framework for Self-Development." *SAM Advanced Management Journal*, 37, No. 1 (1972), 25-29.

   A manager's ability to manage himself and his people may determine the frequency of his promotions, the extent of his salary increases, and the challenge of his future job assignments. The author provides hints for improving self-development and management skills.

232. Parker, Robert A. "How to Climb the Communications Ladder to Success." *Public Relations Journal*, 37, No. 3 (1981), 46-50.

Four communications executives discuss the strategies for communicators to employ if they are to advance up the corporate ladder. Public relations professionals should identify top management's objectives and merge their own departmental aims with overall corporate ends.

233. "Plotting the Route to the Top." *Business Week*, No. 2352 (1974), 127-138.

Contains four brief articles on career management. In plotting the route to the top, the authors advise: individual career planning; choose your employer carefully; do not remain a specialist for too long; remain mobile and visible; invest in an MBA; and join the executive team.

234. Porter, Albert. "The Myth of Managerial Tenure." *Management Today*, April 1977, 63-65.

Managers should not assume that they are safe in their jobs so long as they keep performing. Since managers can be dismissed at any time, for any or no reason, they should plan ahead for this eventuality. A manager should discuss alternatives and plans with his family, have sufficient savings to sustain him at a reduced life style, and seek professional assistance through organizations designed to help.

235. Reid, J.N. "The Managerial Growth Selector." *Training and Development Journal*, 33, No. 4 (1979), 22-27.

Describes a tool (the managerial growth selector) designed to help managers identify areas of needed development and develop plans to increase managerial potential. This decision-guide tool allows managers to systematically assess their strengths in 16 areas of managerial potential. Specific instructions on the instrument are provided.

236. Saline, Lindon E. "Understanding and Doing Something About Professional Development." *Training and Development Journal*, 31, No. 8 (1977), 3-10.

Discusses professional development for professionals and managers. Three criteria are presented which describe the state of an individual's professional development: (1) current capability to perform socially, academically, professionally; (2) self esteem; and (3) basic preparation for future personal growth. These criteria are related to six stages of life in a conceptual structure which encourages clarification of professional development goals.

237. Scheele, Adele. *Skills for Success: A Guide to the Top.* New York: William Morrow, 1979.

   Identifies six "critical competencies" for career success. These "competencies" are to: (1) experience doing; (2) risk taking; (3) show belonging; (4) exhibit specializing; (5) use catapulting; and (6) magnify accomplishing. These six competencies can be divided into three different spheres--industrial (1,2), organizational (3,4), and societal (5,6) from the most personal level to a societal one. A chapter is devoted to each of these competencies. The individual process of careering is then examined focusing on four prominant people in diverse fields.

238. Seidenfield, J. Martin. "3 Steps to Supervisory Maturity." *Supervision*, 43, No. 7 (1981), 3-4.

   Identifies and describes three stages in the work history of supervisors: the soft stage (new supervisor is "all heart"), the hard stage (supervisor is hostile, withdrawn), and maturity (supervisor integrates humanistic impulses with supervisory expertise). The new supervisor will be better able to cope by anticipating and recognizing these stages.

239. Stephenson, Harriet. "A Manager's Personal Training and Development Need-Determination Questionnaire." *Training and Development Journal*, 24, No. 6 (1970), 40.

   Presents a 26-item questionnaire as a self-assessment and need-determination guide for a manager's own professional development.

240. Sussman, John A. "Making it to the Top." *Management Review*, 68, No. 7 (1979), 15-21.

   This survey of 1,700 executives in 750 of the largest U.S. corporations provides a composite picture of the successful top executive. The career profile emphasizes concern for results, integrity, and desire for responsibility. Specific findings are reported on success traits, factors affecting success, executive mobility, career aspirations, cash compensation, sex, and ethnic origin and political philosophy.

241. Walter, Verne. "Self Motivated Personal Career Planning: A Break-through in Human Resource Management." *Personnel Journal*, 55, No. 3 (1976), 112-115; 136.

   Questions the current manager-centered approaches to human resource management and employee career development and develops an employee-centered approach to career assessment and planning. The author reviews the major barriers blocking the discovery and development of productive talent before outlining his self-motivated personal career planning approach.

242. Weiss, W.H. "Are You Promotable?" *Supervision*, 42, No. 1 (1980), 3-5.

   Promotion is not automatic, people on the job must work for it. Employees need to examine the qualifications that characterize a good manager and engage in self-assessment to decide whether they possess them. The author reviews factors management might consider in making promotion decisions.

243. Welch, C. William. "An Executive Guide to Getting into Print." *Management Review*, 65, No. 9 (1976), 25-30.

   Authoring articles is one way of gaining visability to help your career. In order for an executive to write a publishable article he must consider the market and the demand for the information on the subject he is addressing. Helpful hints about the writing process, editors preferences, and steps to follow are provided.

244. "What Makes a Successful Executive: An Executive Personnel Consultant's Opinion." *SAM Advanced Management Journal*, 41, No. 2 (1976), 49-56.

   Reports on an interview with R. Randall Irwin concerning basic characteristics needed by a manager to be effective and successful. Among them are integrity, intelligence, willingness to work, enthusiasm, and humanism. Irwin comments on how managers-to-be should plan their careers to achieve success.

7

CONTINUING EDUCATION

245. Butkus, Alvin A. "Should Executives Go Back to School?" *Dun's Review*, 96, No. 3 (1970), 36-38.

   Executives are questioning the value of returning to college for management courses. Many college programs are too elementary for seasoned executives. The benefits of even the strongest academic programs are abstract, making it difficult to justify high corporate costs.

246. Carol, Arthur, and Samuel Parry. "The Economic Rationale of Occupational Choice." *Industrial and Labor Relations Review*, 21, No. 2 (1968), 183-196.

   Challenges the idea that the more formal education a person obtains, the higher paying his occupation may be and, ultimately, the greater his lifetime earnings. The authors conclude that in the case of many occupations, a higher lifetime return would result from foregoing the higher education and investing its cost in a savings account.

247. Crotty, Philip T. "Continuing Education and the Experienced Manager." *California Management Review*, 17, No. 1 (1974), 108-123.

   A survey of students (94 MBA and 117 Management Development Program respondents) in continuing education programs in business explored the perceptions of the students concerning educational objectives, the curriculum, career advancement possibilities, and career effects associated with attending MBA and MDP programs. The implications of findings for the university and for business are discussed.

248. Crotty, Philip T. "Development Programs for Mature Managers." *Business Horizons*, 17, No. 6 (1974), 80-86.

   Discusses management development, adult education, and executive programs. The author emphasizes the important role of universities in reeducating executives and stresses the increasing necessity for such a role to be performed effectively.

249. Johnson, Donald M., and Harold J. Palm. "A Focus on Careers." *Training and Development Journal*, 29, No. 6 (1975), 28-30; 32.

    Describes a summer program which provided graduate credit to elementary, secondary, and post-secondary school educators in Northern Illinois who studied career trends and manpower needs. Summer institutes in 1973 and 1974 brought the education and employment communities together for positive interaction. Educators became more aware of employment opportunities and problems confronting employers; employers developed new insights and perspectives from the educators.

250. Katz, Arthur J. *Education and the Uncommon Wheel: An Analysis of the Views of Thirty American Corporate Leaders of the Role of Educational Experiences in the Development of Successful Managerial Careers*. Diss., Golden Gate Univ., 1976.

    Examines the perceptions of senior executives (N=30) on the role and usefulness of different types of educational experiences as preparation for successful careers in business administration. Findings showed that of the criteria for selecting top executives, educational qualifications were among the least important, and experience and successful management performance were among the most important. A broad liberal arts background and work experience prior to undertaking positions was recommended by the senior executives interviewed.

251. Kaufman, H.G. "Continuing Education and Job Performance." *Journal of Applied Psychology*, 63, No. 2 (1978), 248-251.

    Reports the results of a longitudinal study of continuing education course participation and job performance by engineers who work for three organizations. Results indicate that: (1) graduate courses taken by engineers during the early years in their careers were strongly related to job performance only for those in the R and D organization; and (2) in all three organizations the engineers "who were initially the poorest performers tended to take the most in-house courses during the half life period." (p. 250)

252. Krizian, Adolph. *The Influence of the Certified Administrative Manager Program on Career Development of Certified Administrative Managers*. Diss., Univ. of North Dakota, 1978.

Analyzes perceptions of Certified Administrative Managers (C.A.M.) and their immediate supervisors in the U.S. regarding how the C.A.M. program influenced career development. The study profiles a typical Certified Administrative Manager and details the benefits perceived to be associated with the C.A.M. designation.

253. Lauenstein, Milton C. "Classroom to Boardroom: What You Learned May Not Help You." *Business Horizons*, 21, No. 6 (1978), 74-81.

    This interview between a doctoral candidate in a leading school of business and the head of a management consultant firm explores the relationship between principles taught in the classroom and techniques used in the boardroom. The head of a modern corporation should possess both analytical and operating skills and effective career planning should lead to experience in both line and staff assignments.

254. Lesher, Richard L. "Career Education A Call for Action." *Training and Development Journal*, 31, No. 6 (1977), 14-17.

    The National Chamber of Commerce seeks a stronger partnership between education and business to ensure that potential employees have marketable skills relevant to their future careers. The President of the Chamber discusses the purposes and accomplishments of career education and lists eight suggestions for educators to consider.

255. Murray, Norman J.M. "Competency-Based Learning Packages-- A Case Study." *Training and Development Journal*, 30, No. 9 (1976), 3-7.

    Describes the competency-based learning packages and syllabi used in external degree programs of the Institute for Personal and Career Development at Central Michigan University.

256. Oates, David. "Managers Focus on Planning Their Lives." *International Management*, 28, No. 3 (1973), 47.

    Discusses a "life planning" exercise developed by the Graduate School of Management at the University of California at Los Angeles. Managers assess their life's accomplishments and future goals in preparation for a 20-week course which helps them to launch their own firms.

257. Reha, Rose. "Preparing Women for Management Roles." *Business Horizons*, 22, No. 2 (1970), 68-71.

   How are U.S. and Canadian business schools preparing women for management roles? The author finds that one fourth of the schools responding to her survey offer a course or program dealing exclusively or in part with the special needs or problems of female managers. Recommended revisions in business school curricula are detailed.

258. Rosenberg, Howard R. *The Part-Time MBA: Impacts on Mid-Career Development of Managers*. Diss., Univ. of California, Berkeley, 1980.

   Examines the role of part-time professional education in the career development of full-time employees. Hypotheses about the identity of participants in part-time MBA programs, expected results of their participation, and impacts on their careers were tested against the survey data. Participants valued education more (relative to the degree) and expected less career change as they advanced through their programs. They experienced considerable gains in salary and organizational rank after beginning MBA studies, and their expectations of further career advancement were high.

259. Shimberg, Benjamin. "Mandatory Continuing Education: Some Questions to Ask." *State Government*, 51, No. 4 (1978), 215-219.

   Argues against mandatory continuing education because there is insufficient evidence showing that continuing education ensures continued competence and because learning cannot be legislated. Instead the author urges professionals to strengthen their voluntary professional development activities and to increase the enforcement capabilities of their state boards.

260. Villanueva, A.B. "Community Colleges and Public Service Careers." *Public Personnel Management*, 4, No. 6 (1975), 400-404.

   Examines the rationale, role and functions, limitations, and future of community colleges in promotion and development of public service careers. The author concludes that community colleges can make significant contributions by: (1) training young people for entry-level government positions, and (2) retraining or up-dating skills of inservice personnel.

8
CAREER CHANGES IN THE ADULT YEARS

261. Albee, Lou. *Job Hunting After Forty*. New York: Arco, 1972.

    Provides practical advice for the middle-aged unemployed. The author gives pointers on locating job opportunities, preparing and using resumes, completing employment applications, presenting oneself in interviews, and negotiating for salaries. The role of the Forty Plus Club and other "helping organizations" is described.

262. Bates, George E. "A Fresh Look at Retirement." *Harvard Business School Bulletin*, 47, No. 1 (1971), 14-19.

    A survey of Harvard Business School Class of 1925 reports on retirement experience, opinions, and advice for younger alumni. Among the topics covered are: respondents' background, difficulties and adjustments in retirement, residential location, retirement activities, and advice to future retirees.

263. Brennan, William L. "What Happens When There Are Two of You." *Sales Management*, 95, No. 7 (1965), 57-60.

    As corporate mergers and acquisitions become commonplace, merged organizations may find themselves with two executives for each position. Executives who fail to plan their careers will find decisions concerning their future made by others. It is essential for executives to set goals, assess their strengths and weaknesses, and implement plans to accomplish their goals.

264. Chamberlain, Anne. "Executive Odyssey: Looking for a Job at Fifty-Five." *Fortune*, 90, No. 5 (1974), 192-195; 198; 202; 206; 210.

    Describes the odyssey of a 55-year old unemployed executive who spent two and a half months on the road, travelled 6,800 miles, visited 16 cities, and met 278 people in his search for another executive position.

265. Clarke, John R. "Landing the Right Executive Job." *Management Review*, 64, No. 8 (1975), 31-36.

Eight rules for unemployed executives in their search for a new position are: (1) don't lose your "cool" if you're out of a job; (2) be realistic about time; (3) get permanent visability; (4) tote up your strengths; (5) be the interviewer as well as the interviewee; (6) get what you're worth; (7) keep a positive attitude; and (8) watch that chemistry.

266. Cowle, Jerry. *How to Survive Getting Fired--and Win!* Chicago: Follett, 1979.

A survival manual for the recently terminated worker which contains advice on making deals with your former boss, obtaining your contributions to profit sharing and pension plans, securing a new job, using search firms and employment agencies, avoiding depression, and choosing between competing alternatives.

267. Crites, John O. "Testing for Career Adjustment and Development." *Training and Development Journal*, 36, No. 2 (1982), 20-28.

Describes the Career Adjustment and Development Inventory (CAREER ADI) including its content and construction, reliability and validity, applicability and use, and future directions. The Inventory is appended to the article.

268. Dauw, Dean C., and Alan J. Fredian. "Executive Career Guidance." *Personnel Administration*, 34, No. 2 (1971), 26-30.

Discusses three approaches to seeking a new job: referrals from employment agencies, searches by executive recruiting firms, and career guidance from executive consulting firms. Executive career guidance firms can be useful in helping individuals choose the right employer, change careers, and prepare to advance into upper-level ranks.

269. Dever, Scott. "Relocation--Executive Style." *Personnel Administrator*, 25, No. 9 (1980), 63-64.

Fewer executives are willing to relocate due to higher housing costs, tight loan money, and social uncertainty. Social and cultural amenities are more important factors affecting relocation decisions of executives than of middle managers. Inflation and the economy are playing an increasingly important role in attracting persons to jobs.

270. Dyer, Lee D. *An Analysis of the Job Search Behavior Patterns and Re-Employment Experiences of Unemployed Middle-Aged Managers.* Diss., Univ. of Wisconsin, 1971.

Studies the job search behavior and re-employment experiences of 143 unemployed middle-aged managers. The study describes the behaviors and experience of these managers as they search for and attain re-employment, and identifies personal characteristics and job search behaviors associated with re-employment success. Successful job seekers are those who were under greater financial pressure, held expectations consistent with labor market conditions, and conducted more continuous and aggressive job searches.

271. Dyer, Lee D. "Job Search Success of Middle-Aged Managers and Engineers." *Industrial and Labor Relations Review*, 26, No. 3 (1973), 969-979.

Examines the job hunting experience of middle-aged engineers and managers who have lost one job and found another, but frequently at lower pay and after weeks of unemployment. Those most successful in their job search were more aggressive in their job hunting, were accustomed to earning lower salaries, and surprisingly, experienced less formal education.

272. Entrekin, L.V., and J.E. Everett. "Age, and Midcareer Crises: An Empirical Study of Academics." *Journal of Vocational Behavior*, 19, No. 1 (1981), 84-97.

Examines the midcareer crisis/transition of 672 academic staff members in four universities. Findings provide empirical support for both a general career stage model and for a move specific career stage model of academic staff. Academic staff are shown to be susceptible to the midcareer crisis/transition phenomenon.

273. Erickson, Erik H. *Identity: Youth and Crisis.* New York: W.W. Norton, 1968.

Identifies "eight stages of man": (1) infancy, (2) early childhood, (3) preschool age, (4) school age, (5) adolescence, (6) young adulthood, (7) adulthood, and (8) senescence. Each stage is seen as having two components, one positive and one negative. Failures in early stages may adversely affect development in subsequent stages.

274. Farmer, James A., Jr. "An Educational Strategy for Professional Career Change." *Adult Leadership*, 19, No. 10 (1971), 318-320; 353.

   Presents an educative and supportive model designed to help professionals change their careers. Enumerates the steps a theoretical person would take via adult education to readjust after deciding on a second career.

275. Ford, Robert N. "Redesigning and Reassigning Your Way to a Better Job." *Supervisory Management*, 24, No. 8 (1979), 2-9.

   Discusses five strategies employees should consider before locking themselves into a poor job situation: (1) get out, (2) fix it yourself, (3) get help from the boss, (4) get help from the organization, and (5) a job assignment service.

276. Gould, Roger L. "The Process of Adult Life: A Study in Developmental Psychology." *American Journal of Psychiatry*, 129, No. 5 (1972), 521-531.

   Separates the adult life span into various stages. Results show discrimination among seven age groups: 16-17, 18-21, 22-28, 29-36, 37-43, 44-50, and 51-60. The author identifies major shifts in adult developmental psychology for each stage. In the 30s, for example, there is a sense of the finiteness of time, a decreased interest in social activities, an identification of self with family and a "pealing away" of the "illusions of omnipotence and omnipotential." (p. 530)

277. Hanson, Marlys, and Lynn Allen. "Career Planning for Adults." *Training and Development Journal*, 30, No. 3 (1976), 12-14.

   Describes a pilot program in career planning at Lawrence Livermore Laboratory. The program is designed to assist employees in evaluating themselves and the realism of their career plans. It combines a variety of techniques and resources in a personalized approach which stresses self-assessment as an important element in career planning.

278. Hastings, Robert E. "The Fall and Rise of Harold Ottman." *Business Horizons*, 20, No. 2 (1977), 34-37.

   The current era of recession has led many businesses to apply rigorous cost-benefit analysis to staffing requirements. One way for white collar workers to anticipate impending unemployment is to candidly analyze their jobs. A checklist for this purpose is provided. Unemployed managers should consider alternative professions.

279. "How Retirement Opens Room at the Top." *Business Week*, No. 2052 (1968), 68-69.

It is possible to predict top management changes well in advance due to the corporate trend toward mandatory retirement at a specific age. Seventeen specific individuals are briefly profiled.

280. "How to Survive Your Company's Merger." *Business Week*, No. 2603 (1979), 147-148.

Discusses ways to survive a corporate merger and to work out the best possible separation agreement if one's job is lost after a merger. The article presents appropriate employee responses to a variety of situations which might occur when a takeover unfolds.

281. Jacques, Elliott. "Death and the Mid-Life Crisis." *The International Journal of Psycho-Analysis*, 46, No. 4 (1965), 502-514.

Examines the mid-life crisis giving special attention to changes in the mode of work and the content of work. The author also considers psychological reactions to the mid-life situation.

282. Jindal, Gopi R., and Carl H. Stenberg. "A Marketing Approach to the Professional Hiring Process." *SAM Advanced Management Journal*, 43, No. 1 (1978), 58-64.

The marketing approach to finding a job tells managers how to plan career goals and intermediate jobs, assess skills, determine pay potential, negotiate working conditions, prepare a resume, and perform appropriately in an interview.

283. Kennedy, John J. "What to Do When You Get Fired." *Advertising Age*, No. 4 (1973), 39.

Briefly discusses some of the signals which in retrospect might have alerted a terminated employee to anticipate his fate.

284. Kennedy, Marilyn M. *Career Knockouts: How to Battle Back*. Chicago: Follett, 1980.

Discusses career crises which can impede upward mobility and result in employee termination. The author outlines strategies for survival and prospering in an era of cutbacks, reorganizations, mergers, and closings. The common "career knockouts" are identified (e.g., skills failure, burnout, obsolescence, reverse discrimination, bad references, aging) and suggestions for dealing with them are offered.

285. Kinzel, Robert. "Resolving Executives' Early Retirement Problems." *Personnel*, 51, No. 3 (1974), 55-64.

    Many executives find themselves ill-prepared to deal with early retirement. Often they need help in organizing their financial affairs before standard counseling can take over. After detailing the causes of early retirement and the problems accompanying it, the author outlines a new approach to vocational counseling, which starts with financial planning and follows with a standard vocational guidance approach focusing on preferred functions and fields of interest.

286. Leider, Richard. "Mid-Career Renewal." *Training and Development Journal*, 30, No. 5 (1976), 16-20.

    Life/career renewal issues involve some of the most challenging problems facing business and industry and they will be among the most discussed of society's problems in the next five years. The author traces the challenging expectations of American's towards work and the need to redesign work. Life/career planning is essential in today's changing workplace.

287. Le Shan, Eda J. *The Wonderful Crisis of Middle Age*. New York: David McKay, 1973.

    Contains anecdotes and personal reflections of a middle-aged woman who finds the challenges of mid-life to provide "the greatest opportunity one has ever had to become truly alive and oneself." (p. 2)

288. Levinson, Daniel J., et al. *The Seasons of a Man's Life*. New York: Alfred A. Knopf, 1978.

    Presents a conception of the entire life cycle, with primary attention devoted to development in early and middle adulthood. The authors identify a sequence of four eras each lasting approximately 25 years: (1) childhood and adolescence (age 0-20); (2) early adulthood (age 17-45); (3) middle adulthood (age 40-65); and

(4) late adulthood (age 60-?). The study focuses primarily on eras 2 and 3 with detailed analysis of these phases supplemented by illustrative biographies.

289. Loughary, John W., and Theresa M. Ripley. *Career and Life Planning Guide*. Chicago: Follett, 1976

    Aids people in making career and life changes which will lead to greater satisfaction. The reader is encouraged to make lists, complete exercises, and practice skills. Among the "how to" issues dealt with are: choosing your job, changing your career, managing your life, changing your complaints into goals, learning to cope with unfamiliar situations, and analyzing important patterns in your life. Chapter 9 contains sources of career information including annotated bibliographies of books and directories for those considering career change.

290. Lovelady, Steven M. "Forty Plus: A Self-Help Group for Job-Less Executives." *Management Review*, 59, No. 1 (1970), 17-19.

    Describes the activities of Forty Plus, an organization based on the idea of unemployed executives joining forces to find each other jobs.

291. Mahler, Walter R. "How to Take Career Crossroads Without Skidding." *Personnel*, 48, No. 3 (1971), 26-32.

    Identifies four career crossroads or points at which significant "turns" have to be made which will benefit both the individual and the organization. These are: (1) the first supervisory position, (2) experience managing more than one function, (3) managing several businesses, and (4) managing decentralized corporate leadership.

292. Margerison, Charles. "Highway to Managerial Success." *Personnel Management*, 11, No. 8 (1979), 24-28.

    Between the ages of 27 and 40 many employees make the "cross over" between technical and managerial work. The author identifies five factors important in making the cross over a success: (1) ability to work with a diversity of people; (2) need to achieve results; (3) leadership experience early in one's career; (4) early responsibility for important tasks; and (5) breadth of experience in many functions prior to age 35.

293. Martin, Lee. "Out Where the Grass Looks Greener." *Public Relations Journal*, 37, No. 3 (1981), 51-53.

    Public relations professionals may believe there is a better job waiting for them, but changing jobs can be a difficult transition. The hiring mind-set is one of the biggest obstacles to changing jobs. The author discusses difficulties associated with job switching and strategies for overcoming the hiring mind-set.

294. McGill, Michael E. "Facing the Mid-Life Crisis." *Business Horizons*, 20, No. 6 (1977), 5-13.

    Explores three questions: (1) How common is the mid-life crisis? (2) What are the causes of the mid-life crisis? (3) What can be done to help the individual combat the mid-life crisis? Eight theories of the causes of mid-life crisis are identified; the most likely causes were the achievement-aspiration gap, sense of stagnation, adjustment to life, and limits to life.

295. Mines, Herbert T. "The Unemployed Senior Executive." *Business Horizons*, 22, No. 2 (1979), 39-40.

    Unemployed senior executives need help in coping with personal embarrassment, difficulty in telling family and friends, financial matters, and feelings of being lost. Executives who lose their jobs must think of themselves as entrepreneurs who create their own opportunities. They must be on the lookout for danger signals in evaluating new jobs.

296. "Old Bankers Are Not Written Off." *Forbes*, 118, No. 1 (1976), 71-72.

    Bankers who retire often do not stop working since they are still in demand. Frequently they work as consultants doing work that is similar to what they had been doing yet without the day to day responsibilities.

297. Olson, Richard P. *Midlife: A Time to Discover, A Time to Decide*. Valley Forge, Pa.: Judson, 1980.

    Discusses the "inner reckoning" that occurs at midlife, provides an overview of life stages, and discusses middle adult issues in reference to biblical-theological themes. Among the issues considered are health management, marriage, life planning, alternative life styles, and parenting in the middle years.

298. Phillips, Susan D. "Career Exploration in Adulthood." *Journal of Vocational Behavior*, 20, No. 2 (1981), 129-140.

Examines the extent to which career exploration occurs prior to more terminal career behaviors and the extent to which exploratory and terminal career decision modes are interdependent. Results of analysis of decisions by 95 subjects over 18 years supported the author's expectation that decisions made at earlier stages of development are more likely to be exploratory and decisions made at later stages are more likely to be terminal.

299. Potter, Albert L. "The Pink Slip: A Contingency Plan." *Across the Board*, 15, No. 7 (1978), 62-73.

Discusses the myth of managerial job tenure and due process rights and stresses the need to prepare against the loss of a job. The author specifies some of the reasons why managers might suddenly lose their jobs, what some of their responses will likely be, and what they should do beforehand and after the termination occurs.

300. Quadagno, Jill S. "Career Continuity and Retirement Plans of Men and Women Physicians: The Meaning of Disorderly Careers." *Sociology of Work and Occupations*, 5, No. 1 (1978), 55-74.

Examines three assumptions concerning the relationship of women to work and retirement. The study found that irregular work histories were equally likely among older male and female physicians. Career interruptions for women were associated with their identity as wives and mothers; irregular work histories for men were due to historical circumstances, e.g., war. Ideas about the meaning of work, for both male and female physicians were derived from the medical culture which sees intrinsic rewards as most satisfying. The ability to make realistic retirement plans are affected by physician values.

301. Quay, John G. "Career Planning." *Training and Development Journal*, 22, No. 3 (1968), 14-21.

A career planning process begins with the individual's interests, skills, and ambitions, rather than the job requirements. The author outlines an approach to career planning, sketches six of the most common career patterns with suggestions for handling problems in each, and identifies six key turning points in career development with advice on ways companies can assist managers at each juncture.

302. Roe, Anne, and Rhoda Baruch. "Occupational Changes in the Adult Years." *Personnel Administration*, 30, No. 4 (1967), 27-32.

Thirty persons were interviewed who had recently made or were planning to make significant changes in their occupations. Researchers explored the kind of decision being made; the reasons for a decision; the influence of family, community role, and leisure-time interests have on decisions; and what the employee wants from as well as what he/she can offer to a new employer. Results show few of the subjects had carefully considered alternatives or based their decisions on a thoughtful examination of the situation.

303. Rosen, Benson, and Thomas H. Jerdee. "Too Old or Not Too Old." *Harvard Business Review*, 55, No. 6 (1977), 97-107.

Tests the stereotypes about older workers using data from 1,570 managers who responded to a questionnaire describing incidents involving younger and older persons. Results show that managers have negative stereotypes of older workers (e.g., they are less creative and prone to change) which leads the authors to propose certain policy changes.

304. Rush, James C., Andrew C. Peacock, and George T. Milkovich. "Career Stages: A Partial Test of Levinson's Model of Life Career Stages." *Journal of Vocational Behavior*, 16, No. 3 (1980), 347-359.

Tests Levinson's (288) theory of life and career stages using 758 subjects. While Levinson's theory posits four distinct stages between ages 20 and 45 each with their own developmental tasks, behaviors, and attitudes, findings reported here show only moderate support for Levinson's theory and provide "little or no evidence supporting the age-linked notion of these stages." (p. 347) The authors did find the stages to be discriminable concerning certain atitudes.

305. Schoonmaker, Alan N. "Individualism in Management." *California Management Review*, 11, No. 2 (1968), 9-22.

How can a middle manager control his own career and increase his independence in the organization? The author presents eight recommendations which emphasize the need for managers to set goals, analyze their assets and liabilities, consider opportunities, carefully plan their careers, and periodically assess their progress.

306. Schwartz, Irving R. "The Quadrant Construct: A Conceptual Framework for Midlife Counseling." *Training and Development Journal*, 32, No. 5 (1978), 50-52.

The quadrants comprising career development determinants are: (1) personal resources, (2) environmental concerns, (3) life goals, and (4) work opportunities. The author discusses each quadrant and relates them to three successive stages of career growth.

307. Sheehy, Gail. *Passages*. New York: E.P. Dutton, 1974.

Analyzes the predictable turning points in the lives of adults by examining the inner changes on the way to full adulthood, comparing the developmental life patterns of men and women, and exploring the crises for adult couples. Based on 115 life stories from individuals ranging in age from 18 to 55, Sheehy considers, among other things, career-related problems in the "trying 20s", the "catch-30s", and the "switch-40s".

308. Sofer, Cyril. *Men in Mid-Career: A Study of British Managers and Technical Specialists*. Cambridge: Cambridge University, 1970.

Reports the results of interview research with managers (N=40) at mid-career working for the British subsidiary of an American car maker (Autoline) and the plastics division of a British chemical company (Novoplast). The book reviews behavioral science research on careers and examines the differences between the author's research expectations and his empirical findings.

309. Super, Donald E. "A Life-Span, Life Space Approach to Career Development." *Journal of Vocational Behavior*, 16, No. 3 (1980), 282-298.

Presents a Life-Career Rainbow (LCR) to describe more adequately the many aspects of a career throughout the life span. The LCR portrays nine major life-career roles in schematic life space. The two primary uses of the LCR are (1) to help students and adults see the link between life stages, life space, and life style, and (2) to help counselors assist adolescents and adults to analyze, plan, and develop their own careers.

310. Swenson, Allan A. *Starting Over: How to Recharge Your Life-Style and Career--With Firsthand Accounts of the New Pioneers Who've Done It*. New York: A and W, 1978.

Tells the stories of people who have broken away from stable lives, careers, and places and have created a new life for themselves. The author profiles 15 "new pioneers" who have made such changes as that from teacher to newspaper reporter, from attorney to boat mechanic, from utility company lineman to zookeeper. The process of "starting over" is traced from the time the "itch" begins, through planning and making the move, to settling in to a new life.

311. Thomas, Eugene L. "Causes of Mid-Life Change From High-Status Careers." *Vocational Guidance Quarterly*, 27, No. 3 (1979), 202-208.

    Studies factors accounting for mid-life career changes among middle-and upper-middle classmen. Finds confirmation for the proposition that career change is related to psychological changes occuring at mid-life, with resulting modification of goals and values.

312. Weaver, Peter. *Strategies for the Second Half of Life*. New York: Franklin Watts, 1980.

    Analyzes life after 45 showing that this period does not need to be characterized by inactivity and decline. The author gives tips about work, finances, health, and social issues which he thinks will make the second half of life as enjoyable and productive as earlier years. Coping strategies for older workers are provided.

section II
individual career development

CAREER DEVELOPMENT--GENERAL

313. "A Path Up for Women Bankers." *Business Week*, No. 2487 (1977), 105.

    Describes a program designed by Simmons College for the National Association of Bank Women whereby older women in middle management who face career blockages can earn their bachelors degrees in management through a three-year course.

314. Bailey, John A. "Career Development Concepts: Significance and Utility." *Personnel and Guidance Journal*, 4, No. 1 (1968), 24-28.

    Referred to a pre-selected list of significant career development concepts, trustees of four professional associations determined the relative value of each concept. The author makes comparisons among the trustee groups, reports composite data, provides suggestions for using the rank-ordered concepts in research, and suggests ideas for using the concepts as topics for group guidance classes.

315. Bartol, Kathryn M. "Vocational Behavior and Career Development, 1980: A Review." *Journal of Vocational Behavior*, 19, No. 2 (1981), 123-162.

    Reviews the literature on vocational behavior and career development published in 1980. Studies are reviewed in the following categories: assessment; vocational aspiration-choice; job search, recruitment, and selection; career contingencies and patterns; motivation; work outcomes; occupational/social structure; and interventions.

316. Bernstein, Peter. "Prison Can be Bad for Your Career." *Fortune*, 102, No. 2 (1980), 62-65.

    An examination of the cases of Bernie Cornfield, Billie Sol Estes, and Anthony De Angelis leads the author to conclude that most businessmen who are convicted of crime and incarcerated do not resurface as top executives.

317. Betz, Ellen L. "Vocational Behavior and Career Development, 1976: A Review." *Journal of Vocational Behavior*, 11, No. 2 (1977), 129-152.

   Reviews selected literature published in 1976 on vocational and career development and behavior. It includes both research and theoretical contributions on subjects including career maturity and development, measurement, vocational behavior, vocational choice, stereotyping, and related factors.

318. Buskirk, Richard H. *Your Career: How to Plan It, Manage It, Change It.* New York: Mentor, 1976.

   Provides advice on the actions, activities, and attitudes involved in climbing the career ladder and on ways to avoid pitfalls along the career path. The author examines the many stages in career development from entry level to top ranks and outlines the internal and external forces influencing career outcomes. Specific suggestions are given to aid in career planning, actions on the job, climbing the career ladder, and increasing individual productivity.

319. Crites, John O. "A Comprehensive Model of Career Development in Early Adulthood." *Journal of Vocational Behavior*, 9, No. 1 (1976), 105-118.

   Seeks to further our knowledge of how and why new workers establish themselves in the work world and to address some of the theoretical and research issues related to this area. A model of early adulthood career development is proposed, hypotheses to test the model are suggested, and ways in which the model can be translated into operational terms for future research are outlined. Essential elements necessary for the construction and validation of a career adjustment model are itemized.

320. Dalton, Gene, Paul H. Thompson, and Raymond L. Price. "The Four Stages of Professional Careers--A New Look at Performance by Professionals." *Organizational Dynamics*, 6, No. 2 (1977), 19-42.

   Develops a model of four successive career stages--apprentice, colleague, mentor, sponsor--each with different central activities, different primary relationships, and different psychological issues. The basic primary relationship in Stage 1V, for example, is that of sponsor. The central activity is shaping the organization, while the major psychological issue is to exercise power. Effective professional performance occurs when behavior is appropriate for the specific career stage.

Career Development--General 85

321. Dornan, J.M. "Individual Development Process." *Training and Development Journal*, 26, No. 8 (1972), 28-29.

    An individual development (ID) process is presented which is designed to help managers become more effective in dealing with technical and leadership problems. The purposes, assumptions, competency areas, and implementation steps in the ID process are outlined.

322. Garbin, Albeno P., and Ronald G. Stover. "Vocational Behavior and Career Development, 1979: A Review." *Journal of Vocational Behavior*, 17, No. 2 (1980), 125-170.

    Reviews the literature on vocational behavior and career development summarizing books and articles published in 1979. Relevant to the fields of sociology, organizational behavior, and vocational psychology, the article includes such topics as job seeking and recruitment; occupational careers; vocational aspirations-choice; assessment measures; perspectives on work; worker adjustment; motivations, needs, and goals; interventions; and work and the social structure.

323. Geeting, Baxter, and Corinne Geeting. *How to Listen Assertively*. New York: Monarch, 1976.

    Outlines a step-by-step approach to "assertive listening", examines skills involved in different types of listening, and provides practical applications to various life/job situations. Applications are considered in business and industry and in politics and government. Successful managers have developed assertive listening styles.

324. Gifford, J. Nebraska, and Melvin B. Shestak. *Secrets of Success: A Plan Book for Making It in the 1980's*. New York: Pocket Books, 1980.

    Contains interviews with 24 successful men and women who identify the ingredients leading to the achievement of personal and career goals. The interviews are grouped into four categories of success: social success, business success, lifestyle success, and financial success.

325. Gugielmino, Paul J. "Developing the Top-Level Executive for the 1980s and Beyond." *Training and Development Journal*, 33, No. 4 (1979), 12-14.

    A nationwide survey of training managers, middle managers, and professors of management reveals a hierarchy of management skills. The major portion of top management skills is in the "conceptual" category, the major portion for middle managers skills is "human", and the major portion for entry-level managers is "technical". Conceptual skills can be learned best on the job throughout the career or using the case study approach in an instructional setting.

326. Hall, Douglas T. *Careers in Organizations*. Pacific Palisades, Cal.: Goodyear, 1976.

   Takes an organizational approach to career development. The author examines career choice, career stages, career effectiveness, and career management from both an individual and organizational perspective. Practical cases and exercises are included permitting the reader to apply career concepts. Contemporary career issues are also addressed.

327. Haller, Archibald, and Alejandro Portes. "Status Attainment Process." *Sociology of Education*, 46, No. 1 (1973), 51-91.

   Examines the processes by which educational and occupational positions are attained by comparing two theoretical models. The Blau-Duncan (130) model focuses on the structure of status transmission, and the Wisconsin model explores social psychological and interpersonal influences on individual attainment. Practical and research implications of the two models are discussed.

328. "Here Come the Young Turks." *Forbes*, 119, No. 4 (1977), 93-95.

   Notes the increase of young chief executive officers and profiles seven young CEO's.

329. Holland, John L., and Douglas R. Whitney. "Career Development." *Review of Educational Research*, 39, No. 1 (1969), 227-237.

   Review the literature on career development published from April 1965 to July 1968. The review is limited to publications which were deemed to be useful scientific contributions. The author focuses on "the determinants, predictions, classifications, and patterns of vocational preferences for various intervals of time." (p. 227)

330. "Lessons of Leadership: The Man Who Runs General Motors." *Nation's Business*, 66, No. 3 (1978), 62-71.

The Chairman of General Motors, Thomas A. Murphy, discusses his own particular career with GM and challenges facing the company.

331. Miners, Howard. "Managing Down the Line." *Management Today*, November 1978, 67-71.

    Occupying line positions has become increasingly less attractive to engineers in British industry. Staff positions bring greater rewards and less accountability so the brightest workers are shunning the line.

332. Osipow, Samuel H. "Vocational Behavior and Career Development, 1975: A Review." *Journal of Vocational Behavior*, 9, No. 2 (1976), 129-145.

    Reviews the literature concerning career development and vocational behavior which appeared in 1975. Topical coverage includes life span aspects of career development, racial differences and similarities in career development, trends in interest measurement, women's careers, sex roles and career development, vocational interventions, and trends in vocational theory.

333. Perrone, Philip A. "Vocational Development." *Review of Educational Research*, 36, No. 2 (1966), 298-307.

    Reviews the literature on vocational development from 1962 to 1966. The research findings are briefly reviewed under the following headings: theoretical formulations, psychosocial studies of occupations, meaning of work, women's career development, vocational choice and counseling, and information sources.

334. Pietrofesa, John J., and Howard Splete. *Career Development: Theory and Research*. New York: Grune and stratton, 1975.

    Provides an overview of several career theories and reports research results substantiating these theories. Designed for use in courses on career development, career guidance, or career education, this work provides general historical background, defines career-related terms, develops a general conceptual framework for understanding both psychological and social aspects of individuals, and relates current theory and research on career development to the author's framework.

335. Roe, Anne. *The Psychology of Occupations*. New York: John Wiley and Sons, 1956.

A classic statement on career development which surveys the field of the psychology of occupations. The author explores the role of occupations, how people differ, how occupations differ, occupational choice and progress, and the implications of this material for organizational psychology.

336. Schein, Edgar H., et al. "Career Orientations and Perceptions of Rewarded Activity in a Research Organization." *Administrative Science Quarterly*, 9, No. 4 (1965), 333-349.

Data measuring career orientations of scientists and engineers were categorized into two career-identification dimensions (institutional-noninstitutional and technical-managerial) and three career-style dimensions (active-passive, idealistic-cynical, and task-interpersonal). They were also categorized into four variables with respect to how one advances: technical performance, visibility, personality, and organizational circumstances. Low correlations were found between career orientations and perceptions of rewarded activity, suggesting that these are independent variables.

337. Seligman, Daniel. "Luck and Careers." *Fortune*, 194, No. 19 (1981), 60-66, 70, 72.

Considers the role of good and bad luck in influencing career outcomes. Numerous anecdotes illustrate the importance of chance and timing in careers.

338. Stumpf, Stephen A. "Career Roles, Psychological Success, and Job Attitudes." *Journal of Vocational Behavior*, 19, No. 1 (1981), 98-112.

Investigates Hall's (324) psychological success model of career development using path analysis. Three career roles for faculty members and several performance indices are considered. While findings provide moderate support for the psychological-success model for each role, the author did observe alternative paths from performance to job involvement and satisfaction with promotional alternatives.

339. Super, Donald E. *The Psychology of Careers*. New York: Harper and Brothers, 1957.

A theoretical exposition on career development. Super examines the nature of work; the course and cycle of the working life; factors affecting vocational choice, success, and satisfaction; and the theoretical implications and practical applications of this material.

Career Development--General 89

340. Super, Donald E., et al. *Career Development: Self Concept Theory*. New York: College Entrance Examination Board, 1963.

    Contains five essays dealing with vocational development. The essays include an examination of research on self concepts in vocational development, an analysis of efforts to make self concept theory operational, a model for the translation of self concepts into vocational terms, a description of the formation of self and occupational concepts, and an analysis of vocational development in adolescent and early adulthood.

341. Super, Donald E., and Douglas T. Hall. "Career Development: Exploration and Planning." *Annual Review of Psychology*, 29 (1978), 333-372.

    Reviews the literature on career exploration and planning. The review covers research in educational settings as well as research in work settings. Both sections contain conclusions about the existing literature and suggest needed future research. The authors cite 138 references.

342. Tarnowieski, Dale. *The Changing Success Ethic (An A.M.A. Survey Report)*. New York: American Management Association, 1973.

    Summarizes results of an A.M.A. survey of over 2,800 American businessmen focusing on career advancement and promotion opportunities. Nearly half of the respondents changed or considered changing their occupational field; top management was more "career content" than middle or supervisory management; and middle and supervisory managers doubted that their corporate environment offers them sufficient opportunities for growth. American ideas of success are changing from material objectives to less tangible objectives favoring "self-expression" and "the richness of human experience".

343. Tennyson, W. Wesley. "Career Development." *Review of Educational Research*, 38, No. 4 (1968), 346-366.

    Reviews the literature on career development using the following categories: theory construction and testing, correlates of vocational development, sources of influence on work-relevant behavior, occupational status and performance, and facilitation of career development. The author deals primarily with research published between 1966 and 1968.

344. Tiedeman, David V., and Robert P. O'Hara. *Career Development: Choice and Adjustment*. New York: College Entrance Examination Board, 1963.

Examines career development by "relating personality and career through the mechanisms of differentiation and integration." In the authors' view career development is "self development viewed in relation with choice, entry, and progress in educational and vocational pursuits." (p. 46) A paradigm of the processes of differentiation and integration in problem solving is presented.

345. Walsh, W. Bruce. "Vocational Behavior and Career Development, 1978: A Review." *Journal of Vocational Behavior*, 15, No. 2 (1979), 119-154.

Reviews selected literature concerning career development and vocational behavior published during 1978. Subjects receiving attention include job satisfaction, vocational interests, performance, career development and work adjustment of women, life-span aspects of careers, and interventions in career development.

346. Walz, Garry R. "Vocational Development Process." *Review of Educational Research*, 38, No. 2 (1963), 197-204.

Reviews the published literature on vocational development (1960-1963) under the following headings: career development, occupational psychology, occupational classification, women's career development, and sources of occupational information.

347. Wilensky, Harold L. "Orderly Careers and Social Participation: The Impact of Work History on Social Integration in the Middle Mass." *American Sociological Review*, 26, No. 4 (1961), 521-539.

Examines careers as a source of social integration by comparing men with "orderly" careers to those with "chaotic" careers. Chaotic experience in the economic order leads to a retreat from work and community life, while orderly career experiences are associated with stronger attachments to formal organizations and the community. Those in orderly carrers are more likely to have integrated, wide ranging, and stable contacts.

348. "Young Top Management: The New Goals, Rewards, Lifestyles." *Business Week*, No. 2401 (1975), 56-68.

Dedicated under-40 executives can expect to work a 60-hour week, sacrifice some family life, and earn from $18,000 to $90,000 annually. These young executives are flexible in management style, intent on making money, wedded to work, and concerned about the breadth of their knowledge. Some executives are buying financial independence now in preparation for a second career later. Older executives are being hired by some companies to avoid the restlessness on the job.

349. Zytowski, Donald G. "Vocational Behavior and Career Development, 1977: A Review." *Journal of Vocational Behavior*, 13, No. 2 (1978), 141-162.

Reviews selected books and journal articles concerning vocational behavior and career development published in 1977. Among the subjects covered are vocational choice (theoretical contributions, development and correlates of choice, decision/indecision), assessment (vocational skills and attitudes, interest inventories, sex bias), vocational behavior of adults (satisfaction and performance), and intervention in career behavior.

10

PREDICTION OF CAREER ADVANCEMENT

350. Astin, Helen S. "Career Development During the High
      School Years." *Journal of Counseling Psychology*,
      14, No. 1 (1967), 94-98.

      Using the Project TALENT Data Bank, this study assessed
      the career expectations of male high school seniors (N=650)
      based on both their personal characteristics and on environ-
      mental characteristics of their schools. Career outcomes
      at the 12th grade level were best predicted by the
      students' interests and career expectations at the 9th
      grade level. By adding environmental characteristics
      of the high school students attended, the discriminating
      power of the test battery improved.

351. Astin, Helen S. "Career Development of Young Women
      During the Post High School Years." *Journal of Counsel-
      ing Psychology*, 18, No. 4 (1971), 369-393.

      Using the Project TALENT Data Bank, this study examined
      the career development of 5,387 women during the five-
      year period after high school. The best predictor
      variables influencing career development were educational
      attainment, marital status, scholastic aptitudes, and
      socio-economic status. Brighter women maintained or
      raised their vocational aspirations; women with less
      academic talent planned for less demanding careers.

352. Boynton, Robert E. *Managers' Personal Patterns of
      Management Theory and Policy as Factors in Managerial
      Career Attainment*. Diss., Stanford Univ., 1968.

      Investigates the relationship between managerial
      success and managerial attitudes toward several areas
      of managerial theory and managerial policy. Findings
      show attainers differ from laggards in theory and
      policy scores; firms differ from one another in the
      average theory and policy scores of their managers;
      the importance of several policy areas varies between
      firms; and the manager's preferred policy is positively
      correlated with his perception of firm policy.

353. Bray, Douglas W., Richard J. Campbell, and Donald C. Grant. *Formative Years in Business: A Long Term AT&T Study of Managerial Lives.* New York: John Wiley and Sons, 1974.

   Presents a longitudinal analysis of young managers' career patterns in the Bell System. The progress of young managers is tracked from recruitment through the assessment center and into their career in the company. Determinants of progress are identified; dominant life themes are discussed; and changes in management abilities, motivation, personality, and job attitudes are analyzed. The authors examine the relationships between careers and the personality patterns of those who experience them.

354. Coates, Charles H., and Roland J. Pellegrin. "Executive and Supervisors: Informal Factors in Differential Bureaucratic Promotions." *Administrative Science Quarterly*, 2, No. 4 (1957), 200-215.

   Examines career patterns and vertical occupational mobility. Career advancement was more importantly affected by such factors as family social standing and connections; social, civic, and professional group memberships; recreational activities and hobbies; the influence of movies; the acquisition of attitudes, values, and behavior patterns of successful superiors; judicious consumption; and success in establishing higher-level friendships while retaining lower-level ones. Considerations of national origin, political activity, religion, and membership in secret societies.

355. Collins, Shelia K. *Career Development of Women Administrators in Social Work, Nursing, and Education.* Diss., Univ. of Nebraska-Lincoln, 1980.

   Identifies significant variables faciliting career development of women holding top administrative positions in social work, nursing, and education. Results show women administrators: (1) follow the traditional sex role assignments of women in the culture; (2) experience an androgynous resolution of their sex-role identity; (3) were not immune to sex discrimination and sexism; and (4) have probably not experienced a mentor role themselves and did not play a mentor role with others.

356. Dillard, John M., and N. Jo Campbell. "Influences of Puerto Rican, Black, and Anglo Parents' Career Behavior on their Adolescent Children's Career Development." *Vocational Guidance Quarterly*, 30, No. 2 (1981), 139-148.

   Examines the relationship between Puerto Rican, black, and anglo adolescent children's career maturity, expectations, and aspirations and parents' career values and career aspirations for their adolescent children. Results suggest that career behavior of Puerto Rican, black, and anglo parents has differential effects on their adolescent's career development. The findings only partially support the assumption that parent-child interaction in the adolescent's nuclear family crucially affects their career development.

357. Fisher, John E. "Playing Favorites in Large Organizations." *Business Horizons*, 20, No. 3 (1977), 68-74.

   Examines the problems of favoritism, patronage, and sponsorship found in large organizations dominated by authoritarian executives. Patronage and office politics often play a more significant role than technical qualifications in promotion decisions.

358. Guest, David, and Robert Horwood. "Characteristics of the Successful Personnel Manager." *Personnel Management*, 13, No. 5 (1981), 18-23.

   Examines the personnelist's backgrounds, roles, and successes in contrasting organizations. The most important determinents of a personnelist's effectiveness are social skills, personality, experience, and education. Five career paths for personnel practitioners are outlined. Two models (the rational and the attributes models) of individual career success are presented. The authors question the value of the professional model of personnel management.

359. Heilman, Madeline E., and Richard A. Guzzo. "The Perceived Cause of Work Success as a Mediator of Sex Discrimination in Organizations." *Organizational Behavior and Human Performance*, 21, No. 3 (1978), 346-357.

   Tests and finds support for the hypothesis that sex-role stereotypes produce an uneven distribution of rewards from the organization. Data from 29 male and female M.B.A. students suggest that biases are present in attributing different explanations for success to men and women which can lead to discriminatory distribution of organizational rewards. Directions for future research are suggested.

360. Hofstede, Geert. "Predicting Managers' Career Success In An International Setting." *Management International Review*, 15, No. 1 (1975), 43-50.

Tests the predictive validity of staff and peer ratings for overall career potential using data from 322 managers from five countries. Results confirm previous research findings that peer ratings are more significant indicators of career potential than training staff ratings. The author suggests that promotions based on the election of leaders by their co-workers may bring greater success than the customary selection by supervisors.

361. Howes, Nancy J. "Characteristics of Career Success: An Additional Input to Selecting Candidates for Professional Programs." *Journal of Vocational Behavior*, 18, No. 3 (1981), 277-288.

Studies the elements of career success and their relationship with selected individual and academic indicators. Analysis of data from 96 former doctoral students in educational administration revealed no significant relationships between measures of academic success and career success.

362. Korman, Abraham K. "The Prediction of Managerial Performance: A Review." *Personnel Psychology*, 21, No. 3 (1968), 295-322.

Reviews the literature to determine the efficiency with which various methods predict managerial success, and to determine whether these prediction studies might lead to an adequate theory of leadership behavior in industry.

363. Lipsitt, Laurence, and Frank A. Rodgers. "Career Perceptions of Managerial and Professional Personnel." *Journal of Vocational Behavior*, 17, No. 3 (1980), 320-327.

Reports on a survey of 576 professional and managerial employees who attributed career success to inherent abilities, education, and developmental experiences in the company studied. Responses among three age groups were similar regarding factors they believed enhanced or inhibited career development.

364. Livingston, J. Sterling. "The Troubled Transition: Why College and University Graduates Have Difficulty Developing Careers in Business." *Journal of College Placement*, 30, No. 4 (1970), 34-41.

Addresses the lack of correlation between scholastic standing and business success. The traits developed in college were not those identified to be important in career development and progression in business. The author explains why academic achievement is not transferable to managerial achievement. He calls for curriculum reform in universities as well as new personnel selection and development practices in business.

365. Miner, John B. "The Role of Managerial and Professional Motivation in the Career Success of Management Professors." *Academy of Management Journal*, 23, No. 3 (1980), 487-508.

Tests two limited domain theories of organizational motivation. The author's findings confirmed the hypothesis that the theory of professional inducement more effectively predicts the career success of management professors than the hierarchic inducement theory. Implications for professional organizations and practitioners are discussed.

366. Mines, Herbert T. "Finding and Using Executive Talent." *Business Horizons*, 23, No. 3 (1980), 45-48.

The five characteristics of success identified in this survey of 250 outstanding executives are: singleness of purpose, steady progress, willingness to devote time and energy, stable home life, and commitment to a career choice. Executives were also asked about why they move, the problems they see, and the suggestions they would offer.

367. Morgan, Marilyn A. *The Effect of Job History on Managerial Success*. Diss., Northwestern Univ., 1977.

Considers the impact of various work experiences on career success. Two areas of the research literature are synthesized: career development and job design. A model is developed to explain the way job histories affect career success. Results show that the series of jobs throughout a manager's career affect the level of success, and that ability and job history predict career success in a summative way.

368. Noeth, Richard J., and David A. Jepsen. "Predicting Field of Job Entry from Expressed Vocational Choice and Certainty Level." *Journal of Counseling Psychology*, 28, No. 1 (1981), 22-26.

Analyzes "expressed vocational choice" (EVC) and "confidence in those choices" (CTC) as a predictor of career behavior in a nationwide study of 1,994 high school students' career development. The EVCs accurately predicted actual jobs for 38% of those sampled two years after high school. When CTC was added to EVC the predictions were accurate for 43% of "very sure choosers", 38% for "fairly sure choosers", and 28% for "choosers who were not so sure". The implications of results for research and counseling are considered.

369. O'Donovan, Thomas R. *Contrasting Orientations and Career Patterns of Executives and Lower Managers*. Diss., Michigan State Univ., 1961.

Seeks to establish whether differences exist in the background of individuals which distinguish high achievers from lower achievers while such groups are still in their twenties. Results indicate that executives were characterized by a higher occupational origin of their father and wife's father than were lower managers; that executives attained a higher level of education than lower managers; and, for respondents with military experience, executives were discharged at a higher rank than lower managers.

370. Paul, Carol Ann B. *Personal, Educational, and Career Patterns of Men and Women Administrators in the Massachusetts Community Colleges*. Diss., Boston Univ., 1979.

Explores the personal and educational characteristics and career patterns of men and women holding positions as administrators in Massachusetts community colleges. The study seeks to discover and describe the similarities and differences between men and women pursuing careers in community college administration. Study results showed that men and women administrators were similar in more respects than had been predicted.

371. Pellegrin, Roland J., and Charles H. Coates. "Executives and Supervisors: Contrasting Definitions of Career Success." *Administrative Science Quarterly*, 1, No. 2 (1957), 506-517.

Identifies differential definitions of career success held by top executives and first-line supervisors. The achievement of high position is regarded as essential for success to the executive, who needs esteem and accomplishment. Security, respect, and happiness are regarded as essential for success to the supervisor, who has a lower level of aspiration and less mobility drive. Motivation toward higher achievement is evident for the executive; however, once his modest ambitions have been attained, the supervisor does not establish successively higher goals.

372. Phillips, Susan D. "The Development of Career Choices: The Relationship Between Patterns of Commitment and Career Outcomes in Adulthood." *Journal of Vocational Behavior*, 20, No. 2 (1982), 141-152.

Studies the relationship between patterns of commitment and various career outcomes in adulthood. Minimal support was found for the hypothesis that individuals who display "the pattern of increasing commitment would experience higher levels of desirable career outcomes than individuals who display other patterns." (p. 141) The findings suggest that heightened commitment may not lead to the anticipated desirable outcomes.

373. Piggott, Lucille C.J. *The Social Characteristics and Career Patterns of Women Administrators in North Carolina Colleges and Universities*. Diss., Univ. of North Carolina, Greensboro, 1979.

Identifies the variables instrumental in influencing the positions, academic ranks, and salaries of women administrators in North Carolina colleges and universities. Influential variables included professional work experience backgrounds, duties of positions, biographical data, educational background, and attitudes toward the American sex culture as they relate to prevailing stereotype beliefs about woman's place in society. A profile of the typical woman administrator in North Carolina higher education is provided.

374. Rosen, Hjalmar. "Managers Predict Their Futures." *Personnel Administration*, 25, No. 3 (1962), 49-52, 61.

Four levels of management were asked to predict their occupational futures if they continued to be affiliated with the same employer. Managers at all levels predicted fulfilling work and based their predictions on current job experience instead of personal desires. The predictions of staff personnel differed somewhat from those of other managers.

375. Rosenfeld, Rachel A. "Women's Occupational Careers: Individual and Structural Explanations." *Sociology of Work and Occupations*, 6, No. 3 (1979), 283-311.

The occupational advancement patterns for men and women differ. Men experience increase in status during the course of their work lives; women frequently do not. This difference can be explained in one of two ways: (1) There are differences in opportunity structure by sex; (2) there are individual characteristics which tend to vary by sex, including employment patterns. The author concludes that the evidence is not clear-cut when examining the effect of structural versus individual factors on occupational achievement.

11

MOTIVATION AND NEEDS

376. Betz, Ellen L. "Need Fulfillment in the Career Development of Women." *Journal of Vocational Behavior*, 20, No. 1 (1982), 53-66.

   Tests the utility of needs theory in explaining differences in women's career decisions. Analysis of need-importance scores from 481 women college graduates showed homemakers scoring higher on security-safety and social needs, while professional-managerial and clerical-sales employees scored higher on the self esteem need. The highest ranking need for all groups of women was self actualization.

377. Bowin, Robert B. "Middle Managers Mobility Patterns." *Personnel Journal*, 51, No. 12 (1972), 878-882.

   The Career Orientation Anchorage Scale was administered to 384 middle managers in three industries to determine managerial mobility motivations. Results confirm earlier studies that only a small percentage of middle managers anchor their career orientation to future promotions. An important factor in determining career anchorage is the initial entry level of first permanent employment.

378. Burnstein, Eugene. "Fear of Failure, Achievement Motivation, and Aspiring to Prestigeful Occupations." *Journal of Abnormal Psychology*, 67, No. 2 (1963), 189-193.

   Explores the proposition that as fear of failure increases and achievement motivation increases, individuals begin to avoid tests of their competence by reducing the possibility of meaningful occupational failure. Seven specific hypotheses are tested using data from 67 undergraduate students.

379. Di Marco, Nicholas J., and Charles R. Kuehl. "Winning Ways in Motivating Junior Staff." *SAM Advanced Management Journal*, 40, No. 3 (1975), 12-22.

Identifies 20 key motivators influencing on-the-job behavior of junior staff. Among the most important are constant feedback on the quality of their work, freedom in executing their duties, clear definition of tasks, and greater responsibilities as abilities increase.

380. Goldman, Daniel R. "Career Anchorage: Managerial Mobility Motivations--A Replication." *Sociology of Work and Occupations*, 5, No. 2 (1978), 193-208.

    Focusing on managerial mobility motivations, this research replicates a study of career-anchorage points among middle managers (493) in American industry. The study reveals only one in seven motivated to advance to higher positions. The author examines various measures correlated with career anchorage. Those factors analyzed in relation to career anchorage include age, education, present position, and level of labor force entry. The perspective of career anchorage is common to both the limited and unlimited success orientations toward occupational mobility.

381. Gould, Sam. "Need for Achievement, Career Mobility, and the Mexican American College Graduate." *Journal of Vocational Behavior*, 16, No. 1 (1980), 73-82.

    Analyzes the need for achievement (NFA) and career mobility for 111 Mexican-American college graduates. Findings reveal that those having a moderate NFA have the highest upward mobility and those with either a high or low NFA have lower mobility.

382. Hackman, J. Richard, and Edward E. Lawler. "Employee Reactions to Job Characteristics." *Journal of Applied Psychology*, 55, No. 3 (1971), 259-286.

    Presents a conceptual framework enumerating the conditions under which jobs facilitate the development of employee motivation for effective performance. It was hypothesized and found that when jobs are high on four core dimensions (variety, autonomy, task identity, feedback), employees desiring higher order need satisfaction have high motivation, have high job satisfaction, infrequently absent themselves from work, and receive supervisory ratings indicating high quality work.

383. Hall, Douglas T., and Khalil E. Nougaim. "An Examination of Maslow's Need Hierarchy in an Organizational Setting." *Organizational Behavior and Human Performance*, 3, No. 1 (1968), 12-35.

Tests Maslow's hierarchy of human needs using career data from the first five years of a sample of managers. Results confirm findings from other studies that managerial advancement is accompanied with decreased need for safety and increased need for affiliation, achievement and esteem, and self actualization. The authors argue that results can be explained by a model of sequential career stages.

384. Hall, Douglas T., and Roger Mansfield. "Relationships of Age and Seniority with Career Variables of Engineers and Scientists." *Journal of Applied Psychology*, 60, No. 2 (1975), 201-210.

Investigates career stages by examining the relationships of age and seniority with job attitudes, need-related variables, perceived employee effort and performance, and perceived organizational climate. The authors conclude that three career stages (early, middle, and late) do exist with each stage characterized by different variables.

385. Horner, Matina. "Fail: Bright Women." *Psychology Today*, 3, No. 6 (1969), 36-38; 62.

Explores sex differences in achievement motivation. The author discusses the "motive to avoid success" whereby women fear competitive achievement situations which may lead to unpopularity or loss of femininity. Three hypotheses are tested using standard achievement motivation measures and a sample of 90 girls and 88 boys. The author concludes that psychological barriers do influence the intellectual and professional lives of women.

386. Horner, Matina. "Toward an Understanding of Achievement Related Conflicts in Women." *Journal of Social Issues*, 28, No. 2 (1972), 157-175.

Within the framework of an expectancy-value theory of motivation, the author examines women's motives for avoiding success. Fear of success in otherwise achievement-motivated women is aroused by the expectancy that success via achievement will be followed by negative consequences. This fear then inhibits women's performance and levels of aspiration. The impairments associated with fear of success and its consequences for both individuals and society are discussed.

387. Howard, Ann, and Douglas W. Bray. "Today's Young Managers: They Can Do It, But Will They?" *Wharton Magazine*, 5, No. 4 (1981), 22-28.

The Bell System's younger managers do not seem to have the same drive to succeed as those in previous generations. The new generation neither wants nor expects as much from a managerial career; new recruits are less involved with and concerned about advancement; newly hired women were far less dedicated to a lifelong career with the firm; and the new generation is characterized by more diversity of backgrounds and values. The authors examine some possible solutions to these problems.

388. Illfelder, Joyce K. "Fear of Success, Sex Role Attitudes, and Career Salience and Anxiety Levels of College Women." *Journal of Vocational Behavior*, 16, No. 1 (1980), 7-17.

Explores the relationship between fear of success, career salience, and trait anxiety, and the relationship between fear of success, sex role attitudes, and career salience. Results of multiple regression analysis suggest that fear of success and sex-role attitudes, together, significantly predicted the level of career salience. Women who were higher in fear of success and more traditional were lower in career salience. Fear of success and career salience did not significantly affect trait anxiety levels of women.

389. Lawler, Edward E. "How Long Should a Manager Stay in the Same Job?" *Personnel Administration*, 27, No. 5 (1964), 6-8, 27.

Examines the relationship between job attitudes and time spent in the same job. The author concludes that longer tenure in the same job leads to better job attitudes among upper level managers while it is associated with poorer job attitudes among lower and middle level managers. A policy of frequent job changes for lower and middle level managers is recommended.

390. Levine, Adeline, and Janice Crumrine. "Women and Fear of Success: A Problem in Replication." *American Journal of Sociology*, 80, No. 4 (1975), 964-974.

Uses data from 700 male and female college students to replicate Horner's (385; 386) conclusion that women are motivated to avoid success. Participants were instructed to write stories based on certain cues concerning the success of medical students from both sexes. Their results failed to support the hypothesis and conclusions from Horner's study that women would be more likely than men to express negative attitudes about female medical students. The authors caution readers about methodological problems in their study which make their conclusions somewhat tentative.

391. Mager, Robert F., and Peter Pipe. *Analyzing Performance Problems or You Really Oughta Wanna!* Belmont, Cal.: Fearon, 1970.

    Describes a step-by-step procedure for analyzing and solving performance problems. A flow diagram is presented which lists the causes of "performance discrepancies" and shows solutions for each one. Many performance discrepancies arise in situations where there is "plenty of skill but not enough will." (p. 48) This is because there are disincentives to perform as desired, it is beneficial to perform in ways other than those desired, and/or obstacles prevent performing as desired. The solution to most performance discrepancies is to make "the desired privileges dependent upon the performance wanted." (p. 55)

392. McClelland, David. "Achievement Motivation Can be Developed." *Harvard Business Review*, 43, No. 6 (1965), 6-24, 178.

    Argues that providing more aid to poor areas in the U.S. or to underdeveloped countries is an insufficient approach to reducing unemployment. Another approach--training programs to increase the "achievement motive" of individuals in business--was undertaken in the U.S. and India. These field experiments showed that such courses (lasting 10 to 14 days) increased the achievement motive of trainees.

393. Near, Janet P. "The Career Plateau: Causes and Effects." *Business Horizons*, 23, No. 5 (1980), 53-57.

    All workers experience a career plateau. The number of managers reaching this stage is increasing and the consequence is upsetting. Career plateauing occurs due to organizational, cultural, and individual factors. Likely reactions include denial, withdrawal, or challenge. Effective solutions will have to come from the individual and the organization.

394. Parry, Kirk, and John Burch. "An Instrument for Measuring The 'Need to Work'." *Vocational Guidance Quarterly*, 16, No. 4 (1968), 264-268.

Following the model of the Edwards Personal Preference Schedule, an instrument capable of measuring a person's need to work was constructed, using items corresponding to Super's (339) description of the three basic needs to work. Utilizing several populations, an item analysis and consequent improvement of item discrimination was performed. Investigations of the need to work patterns were demonstrated consistent with Super's hypothesis. Carefully controlled studies can be executed using this instrument.

395. Schein, Edgar H. "How 'Career Anchors' Hold Executives to Their Career Paths." *Personnel*, 52, No. 3 (1975), 11-25.

    Assesses the relationship between personal values and career events of managers. Five common themes, or career anchors, help define what people are looking for in their careers: managerial competence, technical-functional competence, security, creativity, and autonomy and independence. The author examines the relationship between career anchors and intellectual aptitude, school performance, parental background, current jobs, and current income. Organizations should help employees recognize their anchors and channel them toward fulfillment of individual needs and goals.

396. Schrage, Harry. "The R&D Entrepreneur: Profile of Success." *Harvard Business Review*, 43, No. 6 (1965), 55-69.

    The "optimal managerial style" of future executives should reflect high achievement motivation, low power motivation, and high self-awareness and understanding of job-related publics.

397. Tomlinson-Keasley, C. "Role Variables: Their Influence on Female Motivational Constructs." *Journal of Counseling Psychology*, 21, No. 3 (1974), 232-237.

    Contrasts the fear of success in two samples of women-- one an older group of married coeds, the other a younger group of unmarried coeds. The two samples showed different levels of fear of success and responded differently to situationally determined cues. The author's interpretation of results emphasizes the conflict between women's personal aspirations and society's role demands for women.

398. Tresemer, David. "Fear of Success: Popular, But Unproven." *Psychology Today*, 7, No. 10 (1974), 82-85.

Examines the "fear-of-success" concept advanced by Horner (385) which held that women had a "motive to avoid success in intellectual competence or leadership potential." (p. 82) Tresemer argues that this concept has not been proven and that more careful research is needed before Horner's conclusions can be accepted.

WORK OUTCOMES

399. Cheloha, Randall S., and James L. Farr. "Absenteeism, Job Involvement, and Job Satisfaction in an Organizational Setting." *Journal of Applied Psychology*, 65, No. 4 (1980), 467-473.

    Examines the relationship between job satisfaction, job involvement, and absenteeism using data from a sample of 159 state government employees. Results using zero-order correlations show both job satisfaction and job involvement to be inversely related to absenteeism, but job involvement is more consistently related to absenteeism. However, analysis of partial correlation coefficients suggests the variance in the relationship between absenteeism and job satisfaction could be explained by the mediating influence of job involvement.

400. Cherrington, David. "The Values of Younger Workers." *Business Horizons*, 20, No. 6 (1977), 18-30.

    Surveys 3,053 workers in 53 companies to determine the attitude differences between younger and older workers. While the author finds support for the work ethic among all workers, younger workers have more negative attitudes about their jobs, their company, and their bosses than do older workers. The discrepancy in attitudes between different age groups is attributable to differences in maturity, historical events, and values training.

401. Constandse, William J. "A Neglected Personnel Problem." *Personnel Journal*, 5, No. 2 (1972), 129-133.

    Executives past forty who do not see any advancement in their careers, but feel locked into their present jobs, often go through a trying phase of adjustment. They might respond to this frustration by considering early retirement, second careers, or community service. Individuals in this situation must realistically appraise their abilities and re-think their options.

402. Dubing, Robert, Joseph E. Champoux, and Lyman W. Porter. "Central Life Interests and Organizational Commitment of Blue-Collar and Clerical Workers." *Administrative Science Quarterly*, 20, No. 1 (1975), 411-421.

Workers with a central life interest (CLI) in work have more commitment to their work organization and more attraction to individual facets of their organization than workers with other CLI orientations. Workers with a nonjob CLI have less organizational commitment and are selectively attracted to characteristics of their employing organization. Workers having flexible CLIs have no specific level of organizational commitment and show the most variability in evaluating the attractiveness of work characteristics.

403. Fox, Frederick V., and Barry M. Staw. "The Trapped Administrator: Effects of Job Insecurity and Policy Resistance Upon Commitment to a Course of Action." *Administrative Science Quarterly*, 24, No. 3 (1979), 449-471.

Operationalizes the notion of the trapped administrator and measures its effects upon commitment to an action alternative. Through an experimental simulation, the authors manipulated job insecurity and policy resistance and measured their effects upon commitment to a course of action. Findings indicate that as job insecurity and policy resistance increase, so does commitment to a previously selected course of action. Trapped administrators are likely to become committed to policy positions and be inflexible to change regardless of the consequences.

404. Garfinkle, Joan P. *A Study of Holland's Theory of Vocational Choice As It Applies to the Job Satisfaction Among Male and Female Supervisors*. Diss., Univ. of San Francisco, 1978.

Examines the relationship between job satisfaction of male and female supervisors and their vocational interests. Results show minimal support for the relationship between job satisfaction and basic interest patterns based upon Holland's typology. There were no significant differences between males and females in five of the six categories: enterprising, conventional, investigative, realistic, and artistic. The only significant difference was found in the social category.

405. Gibson, James L., and Stuart M. Klein. "Employee Attitudes as a Function of Age and Length of Service: A Reconceptualization." *Academy of Management Journal*, 13, No. 4 (1970), 411-425.

Examines the relationship between employee age, length of service (tenure), and job satisfaction. Findings suggest a positive relationship exists between employee satisfaction and age, and a negative relationship exists between tenure and overall job satisfaction. Explanations for the findings and their implications are discussed.

406. Grosky, Oscar. "Career Mobility and Organizational Commitment." *Administrative Science Quarterly*, 10, No. 4 (1966), 488-503.

Tests two hypotheses: (1) the greater the rewards received the greater the degree of the person's commitment to the employing organization; and (2) the greater the obstacles the person faces to obtain the organization's rewards the greater his commitments. The measure of rewards was a manager's "career mobility," operationalized by comparing first position with present position. Indexes of "organizational commitment" included seniority, identification with the company, attitude toward company administrators, and satisfaction with the company. Results show the first hypothesis was not supported, while the second hypothesis was confirmed.

407. Grupp, Fred W., Jr., and Allan R. Richards. "Job Satisfaction Among State Executives in the U.S." *Public Personnel Management*, 4, No. 2 (1975), 104-109.

Reports on a survey of high level, appointed executives in ten states which reveals high levels of satisfaction with their jobs. Their rankings of current occupation are nearer to "ideal" than those of federal or business executives previously surveyed, and they prefer state government employment to jobs in the federal government or in private business.

408. Hall, Douglas T. "A Model of Coping with Role Conflict: The Role Behavior of Educated Women." *Administrative Science Quarterly*, 17, No. 4 (1972), 471-486.

Presents a model of role conflict coping behavior based upon three levels in the role process. The relationship between coping behavior and satisfaction of college-educated women indicates that the act of coping (as opposed to noncoping) may be more strongly related to satisfaction than the particular type of coping strategies used.

409. Harmon, Lenore W. "Anatomy of Career Commitment in Women." *Journal of Counseling Psychology*, 17, No. 1 (1970), 77-80.

   Ten to 12 years after entering college, 169 women were asked to record their "usual occupation," regardless of whether or not they were currently employed in it. Subjects listing one were called "career committed." Results support that women become committed to careers after entering college.

410. Hofstede, Geert. "Alienation at the Top." *Organizational Dynamics*, 4, No. 3 (1976), 44-60.

   Examines alienation among headquarters managers using data from a company-wide attitude survey. Alienation was found to be greatest for personnel working at international headquarters and least for sales personnel working in the field of a major corporation. To reduce alienation at headquarters, Hofstede recommends periodic organizational-effectiveness surveys assessing headquarters-subsidiary relations, altered recruitment and retention policies, rewards for the support function, and restructuring to keep headquarters groups small.

411. Hulin, Charles L., and Milton R. Blood. "Job Enlargement, Individual Differences, and Worker Responses." *Psychological Bulletin*, 69, No. 1 (1968), 41-55.

   Reviews the literature on job enlargement and published work relating job size to job satisfaction and behavior. The authors conclude that the positive relationship between job size and job satisfaction depends largely on the workers' background. The authors question hypothesized relationships between repetition and monotony, monotony and satisfaction, and satisfaction and behavior. A model is presented relating job size to job satisfaction which introduces "worker alienation from middle-class work values" as a third variable.

412. Korman, Abraham K. "Task Success, Task Popularity, and Self Esteem as Influences on Task Liking." *Journal of Applied Psychology*, 52, No. 6 (1968), 484-490.

   Hypothesizes and finds that a positive relationship exists between task success and task satisfaction for those with high self-esteem but not for those with low self esteem.

413. Korman, Abraham K., Ursula Wittig-Berman, and Dorothy Lang. "Career Success and Personal Failure: Alienation in Professionals and Managers." *Academy of Management Journal*, 24, No. 2 (1981), 342-360.

    Concerns the factors that generate negative attitudes among professionals and managers. Personal and social alienation are hypothesized to be positively related to expectancy disconfirmation, contradictory role demands, sense of external control, loss of affiliative satisfactions, and developmental life changes. Research results generally support these hypothesized relationships.

414. Lodahl, Thomas M., and Mathilde Kejner. "The Definition and Measurement of Job Involvement." *Journal of Applied Psychology*, 49, No. 1 (1965), 24-33.

    Defines job involvement, develops a scale for measuring it, presents evidence of the scale's reliability and validity, and correlates job involvement with other job-related attitudes.

415. Manring, Susan L. *Career Patterns of Technically-Trained Professionals: A Person-Environment Interaction Model.* Diss., Case Western Reserve Univ., 1980.

    Studies the interaction of personal, professional, and organizational factors which affect the career development of engineers in industrial organizations. Using a person-environment interaction model, three adaptive patterns for technical careers are identified: specialized adaptation, integrated adaptation, and polarized mal-adaptation. The latter group experience a lower degree of job complexity and less job satisfaction than the other two groups, as well as higher tension and alienation. Several developmental tasks are outlined to facilitate self-mediated careers and personal-professional integration.

416. Mansfield, Roger. "Career Development in the First Year at Work." *Occupational Psychology*, 45, No. 2 (1971), 139-149.

    Studies career commitment using questionnaire data from 116 graduates working in two large industrial companies. The author concludes that occupational commitment developed during the first year at work is limited even for workers who are highly satisfied with their job. At this early stage of their development many people are not committing themselves to a lifelong career.

417. McKelvey, Bill, and Una Sekaran. "Toward a Career-Based Theory of Job Involvement: A Study of Scientists and Engineers." *Administrative Science Quarterly*, 22, No. 2 (1977), 281-305.

   Seeks to determine the relative importance of 49 factors to job involvement. Career and personality factors are of particular importance. As various conditioning factors (personality, orientation, and professional training) are controlled by breakdowns of the sample, levels of variance explained increase. A career-based theory of job involvement is supported by the findings. The authors suggest a differentiation of three job contexts (personal, job, and organizational) to assist in identifying additional factors which may affect job involvement.

418. Moch, Michael K. "Racial Differences in Job Satisfaction: Testing Four Common Explanations." *Journal of Applied Psychology*, 65, No. 3 (1980), 299-306.

   Identifies and assesses various explanations (structural, cultural, social, and social psychological) for differential job satisfaction by race. Results of regression analysis of questionnaire data (N=466) show "race variables accounting for 21 percent of the variance in satisfaction" beyond the four percent accounted for by all other factors.

419. Morris, James H., and Richard M. Steers. "Structural Influences on Organizational Commitment." *Journal of Vocational Behavior*, 17, No. 1 (1980), 50-57.

   Examines the relationship between organization structure and organizational commitment using multiple regression analysis to analyze data from 262 public employees. Six structural variables (decentralization, formalization, span of control, span of subordination, perceived functional dependence, and work group size), as a set, accounted for over 20 percent of the variation in organizational commitment for the sample.

420. Morrison, Robert F. "Career Adaptivity: The Effective Adaptation of Managers to Changing Role Demands." *Journal of Applied Psychology*, 62, No. 5 (1977), 549-558.

   Studies the relationship between personal characteristics and career adaptivity based on data from 77 subjects. The author develops six managerial roles and defines career adaptivity as "the rated ability to adjust successfully to more than one role." (p. 549) The career adaptive group was found to have: completed more career activities; higher self esteem; a simple decision making process; varied their speed in decision making; and more openness to different ideas than the less adaptive group.

421. O'Reilley, Charles A., III, and David F. Caldwell. "Job Choice: The Impact of Intrinsic and Extrinsic Factors on Subsequent Satisfaction and Commitment." *Journal of Applied Psychology*, 65, No. 5 (1980), 559-565.

Tests the hypothesis that MBA graduates (N=108) who based job choices on intrinsic considerations (i.e., interest in the job) would be more satisfied/committed than those who made choices based on extrinsic considerations (i.e., external pressures). Findings indicate subsequent satisfaction/commitment to be positively related to both intrinsic and extrinsic decision factors.

422. Quinn, Robert P., and Martha S. Baldide Mandilovitch. "Education and Job Satisfaction, 1962-1977." *Vocational Guidance Quarterly*, 29, No. 2 (1980), 100-111.

Examines the relationship between education and job satisfaction by performing secondary analysis on data from 11 national surveys of American workers conducted between 1962 and 1977. The authors found a "positive statistically significant, and fairly well replicated relationship between level of education and overall job satisfaction." (p. 109) This finding is subject to several qualifications.

423. Rabinowitz, Samuel, and Douglas T. Hall. "Organizational Research on Job Involvement." *Psychological Bulletin*, 84, No. 2 (1977), 265-288.

Reviews the literature on job involvement. After clarifying the different definitions of the term, the authors review empirical studies dealing with three theoretical viewpoints: (1) job involvement as an individual difference variable (e.g., age, education, sex); (2) as a situationally determined variable (e.g., participative decision making, job characteristics, leadership behavior); and (3) as a product of individual-situation interaction (e.g., job satisfaction, performances, turnover). The correlates of job involvement are identified and directions for future research are charted.

424. Renwick, Patricia A. et al. "What Do You Really Want From Your Job?" *Psychology Today*, 11, No. 12 (1978), 53-65, 118.

Analyzes survey data on job attitudes from 23,008 readers of *Psychology Today*. The sample overrepresents younger, better educated, and higher paid workers, but it presents interesting data on the changing work ethic. While workers still find much of their identity in work, most want more control over their jobs, think it likely they will change jobs in the next five years, and value co-workers and opportunities for self growth at work. To prevent high turnover managers should improve the quality of work and develop improved training and recruitment programs.

425. Rice, Beryl C. *A Study of Professional Career Satisfaction of Women Social Workers in Relation to Career Patterns, Career Saliency, Professional Role Conception Congruence and Race*. Diss., Catholic Univ. of America, 1980.

Examines the level of professional career satisfaction among highly qualified women social workers. Concepts from socialization, role, and career theory provided the theoretical orientation. The four major independent variables (career pattern, career saliency, professional role conception congruence, and race), plus demographic variables, were assessed for their influence on the dependent variable, level of professional career satisfaction.

426. Seeman, Melvin. "On the Meaning of Alienation." *American Sociological Review*, 24, No. 6 (1959), 783-791.

Examines five separate meanings of the term alienation: powerlessness, meaninglessness, normlessness, isolation, and self estrangement.

427. Seeman, Melvin. "On the Personal Consequences of Alienation at Work." *American Sociological Review*, 32, No. 2 (1977), 273-285.

Tests the hypothesis that job alienation resulting from unfulfilling work has serious social side effects. Analysis of interview data from 558 males ranging from 20 to 70 years of age in Malmo, Sweden, failed to support the hypothesis. While alienation was widespread, the anticipated social consequences were not present. The author concludes that people may be unhappy at work, but still demonstate a relatively high level of adaptability.

428. Sheppard, Harold L., and Neil Q. Herrick. *Where Have All the Robots Gone? Worker Dissatisfaction in the 70s.* New York: Free Press, 1972.

   Documents the discontent among workers and identifies dissatisfaction with the job itself as its principal cause. Findings are based on interviews with 400 white male blue collar union members located in two northern states and 1,553 Department of Labor employees. The five-part book identifies discontented workers, describes the sources of their dissatisfaction, profiles young white collar workers, analyzes opportunities for older workers, and considers possibilities for future changes.

429. Stumpf, Stephen A., and Samuel Rabinowitz. "Career Stage as a Moderator of Performance Relationships with Facets of Job Satisfaction and Role Perceptions." *Journal of Vocational Behavior*, 18, No. 2 (1981), 202-218.

   Studies 102 faculty members across three career stages (establishment, advancement, and maintenance) to determine the relationship between performance and job satisfaction, role ambiguity, and role conflict. General support was found for the hypothesis that "individuals at different career stages will exhibit different job satisfaction-perfomance and role perception-performance relationships because different outcomes are likely to be available and salient to them." (p. 215)

430. Tarnowicski, Dale. "Middle Managers' New Values." *Personnel*, 50, No. 1 (1973), 47-53.

   Describes the discontent among corporate middle managers and the need for a reassessment of the role, opportunities, and rewards offered to them. The author summarizes results from the American Management Association's survey of 2,800 U.S. businessmen. Respondents were asked to identify the predominant characteristics of "success" in terms of the business climate of the 1970s.

431. Van Maanen, John, and Ralph Katz. "Individuals and Their Careers: Some Temporal Considerations for Work Satisfaction." *Personnel Psychology*, 29, No. 4 (1976), 601-615.

   Reports the overtime patterns of work satisfaction for employees at different career stages and compares them across four distinct career categories: administrative, professional, clerical, and maintenance. The results show that work satisfaction patterns differ in measurable and significant ways. Among the most interesting findings was that professional employees were more disenchanted with their government jobs than were administrators; that career satisfaction patterns for clerical employees were similar to those of maintenance workers; and that support for organizations' policies is most likely to be found among experienced administrators.

432. Vroom, Victor H., and Edward L. Deci. "The Stability of Post-Decision Dissonance: A Follow-Up Study of the Job Attitudes of Business School Graduates." *Organizational Behavior and Human Performance*, 6, No. 1 (1971), 36-49.

Examines the attitude change toward employing organizations occuring from the time students choose entry jobs to the period one and three and one-half years after graduation. Findings indicate post-decision disillusionment with the attractiveness of the organization and its perceived utility for the attainment of goals decreasing significantly during the first year and remaining at a low level for the next two and one-half years.

433. Weaver, Charles N. "Job Satisfaction in the United States in the 1970s." *Journal of Applied Psychology*, 65, No. 3 (1980), 364-367.

Examines job satisfaction among American workers over the period 1972 to 1978 using data (N=4,709) from seven annual national surveys. Findings show no substantial changes in job satisfaction levels during this period. Whites showed more job satisfaction than blacks. There were no differences in job satisfaction between men and women. Job satisfaction was positively associated with age, income, education, and occupation.

434. Webber, Ross A. "Career Problems of Young Managers." *California Management Review*, 18, No. 4 (1976), 19-33.

In the first few years at work young professionals confront several common problems. Based on interviews with managers, five frequent problem areas are identified and discussed: (1) early frustration and dissatisfaction due to unrealistic expectations; (2) insensitivity and passivity to the organization's political environment; (3) loyalty dilemmas; (4) personal anxiety about one's integrity and commitments; and (5) ethical dilemmas.

435. Wittebort, Susan. "Is Risk Management a Dead-End Job?" *Institutional Investor*, 15, No. 3 (1981), 169-182.

A majority of risk managers feel dissatisfied with the scope of their responsibilities and their future prospects. While the risk management profession has made strides in recent years, most risk managers feel boxed in professionally. Based on interviews with several successful risk managers, the author outlines the career stresses facing risk managers and reports tips in getting ahead.

436. Yankelovich, Daniel. "The New Psychological Contracts at Work." *Psychology Today*, 11, No. 21 (1978), 46-50.

A "new breed of Americans" hold three major work values which differ markedly from traditional outlooks: the increased importance of leisure, the symbolic importance of the paid job, and the preference for less depersonalized jobs. Attitude data show that for most people leisure is more important than work and that, while work is enjoyable, it is not a major source of satisfaction. Recognition and relationships with co-workers were found to be more important than having interesting and non-routine work. The managerial implications of these attitudes are discussed.

437. Zaleznik, Abraham. "Management of Disappointment." *Harvard Business Review*, 45, No. 6 (1967), 59-70.

Explores the dilemmas of leadership arguing that many outstanding leaders have worked through their disappointments and have emerged as stronger and more capable leaders as a result. The author stresses that it is important for leaders to decide what needs to be done, to work with others to do it, to face disappointments honestly, and to understand one's own emotional reactions. "Constructive introspection" along with individual character, courage, and talent are crucial to personal development.

438. Zaleznik, Abraham, Gene W. Dalton, and Louis B. Barnes. *Orientation and Conflict in Career*. Cambridge, Mass.: Harvard Univ. School of Business Administration, 1970.

Examines the career conflicts experienced by trained specialists who must choose either to continue their career as a specialist or shift to a managerial career. The authors test hypotheses derived from psycho-analytic theory with data from 170 scientists and engineers. The authors assess the effects of career conflict on employees' mental health, self esteem, interpersonal relationships at work, productivity, incentives, and personal development.

BURN OUT/ STRESS/ OBSOLESCENCE

439. "Burn Out--When You Can't Do Your Job--and Don't Know Why." *Supervision*, 43, No. 10 (1981), 10-11.

    Describes the causes and symptoms of burn out and suggests six ways of dealing with the problem.

440. Dill, William R., Wallace B.S. Crowston, and Edwin J. Elton. "Strategies for Self Education." *Harvard Business Review*, 43, No. 6 (1965), 119-130.

    Explores the process of self learning and the ways to facilitate it to counteract the threat of personal obsolescence. Self education provides added knowledge and skills, useful practice in the process of learning, and self confidence to face a changing world. These results help managers to be more effective in their daily jobs.

441. Dubin, Samuel S. "Obsolescence or Life Long Education: A Choice for the Professional." *American Psychologist*, 27, No. 5 (1972), 486-498.

    Discusses the meaning of professional obsolescence, its symptoms and causes, and current efforts at coping with it. The skills of psychologists can contribute to continuing education efforts concentrating on the problems of obsolescence, and psychologists can benefit from new employment opportunities in this area.

442. Edelwich, Jerry, and Archie Brodsky. *Burn-out: Stages of Disillusionment in the Helping Professions*. New York: Human Sciences Press, 1980.

    Provides a portrait of burn out drawn from people who have worked in the human services field. The author describes a process of disillusionment which commonly occurs in four stages: enthusiasm, stagnation, frustration, and apathy. Intervention strategies are described which can break this cycle.

443. Ginsburg, Sigmund G. "The Problem of the Burned Out Executive." *Personnel Journal*, 53, No. 8 (1974), 598-601.

Discusses the causes and cures for the "burned-out executive" phenomenon. Suggestions are given for individuals such as taking non-working vacations, involvement in outside activities, continuing education and variety of job assignments, medical check ups, more family involvement, self-analysis, and goal setting. Organizations should provide psychologists to help reduce executive stress and show understanding to those experiencing burn out.

444. Greenwood, James W., III, and James W. Greenwood, Jr. *Managing Executive Stress*. New York: John Wiley and Sons, 1979.

Uses a systems framework to assess the causes (physiological, psychological, environmental) of stress, the costs and consequences of executive stress, and coping mechanisms for reducing stress levels and managing stress.

445. Harel, Gedaliahu, and Loretta K. Conen. "Expectancy Theory Applied to the Process of Professional Obsolescence." *Public Personnel Management*, 11, No. 1 (1982), 13-22.

Examines the determinents of professional obsolescence using expectancy theory. Individual and organizational variables are identified which influence the decision to engage in professional updating. Performance is viewed as a function of both motivation and ability. Professional updating requires updating motivation and possessing the capacity and aptitude to attain competency.

446. Helliwell, Tanis. "Are You a Potential Burnout?" *Training and Development Journal*, 35, No. 10 (1981), 24-31.

Identifies the stress events leading to burn out and describes three stages of burn out. A series of self-assessment questions is provided to enable executives to determine whether they are a potential burn out or whether they are at the first, second, or third stage of burn out. Sixteen potential solutions to burn out are given.

447. Howard, John, David Cunningham, and Peter Rechnitzer. *Rusting Out, Burning Out, Bowing Out: Stress and Survival on the Job*. Toronto: Financial Post, 1978.

   Examines the causes and consequences of on-the-job stress and stress-related illness among managers and professionals. The behavioral characteristics of "Type A" managers are identified, the health risks to Type A's are described, and stress-reducing interventions are suggested. The authors consider the "how to's" and "how not's" of physical exercise to reduce stress and approaches to modify work behavior which will result in stress reduction.

448. Kaufman, H.G. *Obsolescence and Professional Career Development*. New York: AMACOM, 1974.

   Examines the causes and cures of obsolescence in the knowledge and skills of managerial, technical, and professional employees in business and government. Integrating recent empirical research findings with the practical experience of managers and professionals, the author analyzes the problem of obsolescence and prescribes various techniques of personnel management, continuing education, job design, and organizational development, to combat obsolescence.

449. Levinson, Harry. "What to Do So the Obsolescent Executive Won't Be You." *Management Review*, 57, No. 4 (1968), 18-22.

   Everyone who would pursue a managerial career should be aware of three obvious principles: maximum flexibility, lifelong continuing education, and personal feelings are crucial in combating executive obsolescence.

450. Miller, James E. "Eliminate Your Obsolescence." *Journal of Systems Management*, 27, No. 11 (1976), 34-36.

   Discusses the options available to individuals who want to avoid obsolescence by implementing their own professional development program. Among the alternatives are professional associations, publications, colleges, examinations, continuing education, professional seminars, correspondence courses, and programmed instruction.

451. Morrison, David E. "Stress and the Public Administrator." *Public Administration Review*, 37, No. 4 (1977), 407-414.

Analyzes the obvious and less than obvious pressures facing leaders in business and government. Demands on administrators are categorized as non-personal, interpersonal, and very personal pressures. The author discusses "Type A" characteristics, the qualities underlying these characteristics, suggestions for dealing with stress, and a checklist for understanding responses to human change.

452. Paine, Whiton S. ed. *Job Stress and Burnout: Research Theory, and Intervention Perspectives*. Beverly Hills, Cal.: Sage, 1982.

   This 14-chapter volume assesses the state of the art of burn out and stress management. Essays grew out of the first national conference on this subject. They cover such issues as tools for understanding burn out and job stress; models of the symptoms and processes associated with these phenomena; causes and consequences of job stress; the relationship of job stress to broader social trends; and intervention strategies for individuals and organizations.

453. Pesci, Michael. "Stress Management: Separating Myth From Reality." *Personnel Administrator*, 27, No. 1 (1982), 57-59, 62, 67.

   Seeks to separate fact from fantasy about stress by identifying the causes and "casualties" of stress, the characteristics of stress-prone people, myths surrounding stress, and stress management techniques. Among the tools of stress management are diet, exercise, and developing constructive attitudes.

454. Rothman, Robert A. "Problems of Knowledge and Obsolescence Among Professionals: A Case Study in Dentistry." *Social Science Quarterly*, 55, No. 3 (1974), 743-752.

   Discusses the problem of knowledge obsolescence caused by the rapid growth of new knowledge and the need for professionals to continually update their expertise. The author isolates certain conditions in the professional career of dentists which foster obsolescence.

455. Rothman, Robert A., and Robert Perrucci. "Organizational Careers and Professional Expertise." *Administrative Science Quarterly*, 15, No. 3 (1970), 282-293.

   Examines the relationship between different career patterns and the process of obsolescence using case histories of a national sample of professional engineers. A positive relationship between obsolescence and limited technical activity, extensive administrative responsibility, application rather than research, and organizational situations having relatively constant technologies, was demonstrated for four age cohorts, differentiated on the basis of two types of obsolescence and compared at various points in their career.

456. Shearer, Richard L., and Joseph A. Steger. "Manpower Obsolescence: A New Definition and Empirical Investigation of Personal Variables." *Academy of Management Journal*, 18, No. 2 (1975), 263-275.

Identifies some of the personal factors related to professional and managerial obsolescence. The major contributors to nonobsolescence were found to be high need achievement and high levels of organizational participation. For managers, experience is more important than education in determining relative obsolescence.

457. Vash, Carolyn L. *The Burnt-out Administrator*. New York: Springer, 1980.

Identifies the forces leading to administrator burn out. The author illustrates how administrators often lack the power and autonomy attributed to them, how the rewards are disappearing, and how the irrationalities of the system affect the burnt-out administrator (BO-A). After exploring the result of these pressures on the BO-A, the author presents the way "out of the ashes" from a more hopeful perspective.

458. Veninga, Robert L., and James P. Spradley. *The Work/Stress Connection: How to Cope with Job Burnout*. Boston: Little/Brown, 1981.

Explores the nature of job burn out, its causes, and personal plus organizational strategies for coping with it. The authors trace the effects of stress through five progressive burn-out stages: the honeymoon stage (enthusiasm, job satisfaction, energy depletion); fuel shortage (job dissatisfaction, fatigue, substance abuse); chronic symptoms (exhaustion, physical illness, anger); crisis (pessimism, incapacitating illness, escapism); and hitting the wall (career/life endangerment).

CAREER SWITCHES

459. Armstrong, Janet C. "Decision Behavior and Outcome of Midlife Career Changers." *Vocational Guidance Quarterly*, 29, No. 3 (1981), 205-211.

    Describes the decision approaches (e.g., incremental vs. rational) used by two samples of midlife adults who attended community colleges to prepare for a career change. The author seeks to determine whether decision approaches are related to success or failure in career change. Results indicate that the incremental decision making approach was significantly associated with minor career change goals, while the rational model was significantly related to major career change goals.

460. Bayer, Ann. "Beginning Again in the Middle." *Life*, 68, No. 22 (1970), 50-56.

    Profiles five Americans who chose to change their careers.

461. "Choosing a Second Career." *Business Week*, No. 2501 (1977), 119-124.

    Many middle-aged executives are leaving large corporations to pursue second careers in teaching or small business.

462. "From Executive Suite to Halls of Ivy." *Business Week*, No. 2081 (1969), 122-123.

    The former President of the Ford Motor Company, Arjay R. Miller, discusses his reasons for leaving the executive suite to become the Dean of Stanford University's Graduate School of Business and his plans for the future of the School.

463. Jolson, Marvin A., and Neil B. Holbert. "When Executives Shift to Academic Careers." *Business Horizons*, 22, No. 4 (1979), 21-31.

Examines the reactions of former business executives (XBEs) who have switched careers by moving into academia as professors or administrators. The authors profile the XBEs, summarize their reasons for moving into academeme, report on how they are received by co-workers and students, and speculate about the future. Recommendations are made to executives who seek to prepare for academic careers.

464. Jones, Rochelle. *The Big Switch*. New York: McGraw-Hill, 1980.

    Traces the personal histories and life stories of mid-life career switchers and offers interpretations of this new social phenomenon.

465. Keaveny, Timothy J., and John H. Jackson. "Propensity for Career Change Among Supervisors." *Human Resource Management*, 16, No. 3 (1977), 13-16.

    Contends that the mid-life career change that supposedly occurs around age 40 may be a myth. This research reports a negative relationship between age and the inclination to move. Positive correlations were found between job dissatisfaction and career change. Substantial differences were discovered between white and blue collar workers in their willingness to change jobs.

466. Kremple, Robert J., and Coleman Colla. "Guidelines for Executive Job Changes." *Personnel Journal*, 54, No. 1 (1975), 29-31.

    An executive contemplating changing jobs should carefully consider financial and personal factors. The authors describe a technique for achieving a better match between the executive and the projected position. By tabulating and rating of "job value factors", personal preferences can be injected into the assessment. Specific examples illustrate the utility of this approach.

467. Laserson, Nina. "Profiles of Five Second-Careerists." *Personnel*, 50, No. 1 (1973), 36-47.

    Five executives are interviewed as examples of career-switchers. Each was distinguished in their first career and they took different routes to distinction in their second careers. The five include career switches from: directing research to directing a college, a military general to a business generalist, a company executive to a state executive, a television news reporter to a recreation area entrepreneur, and a civil servant to the head of a civil service union. The author detects no set pattern of motivation in the five cases.

468. Leider, Richard J. "The Second Career." *Burroughs Clearing House*, 58, No. 4 (1974), 30, 61-63.

Summarizes trends in the larger society prompting the emergence of second careers. Nearly four out of ten middle managers surveyed envision an alternate career for themselves. Age, situational factors, and societal factors contribute to the quest for second careers. Education, work, and training must be interwoven in future careers as part of one's life style.

469. McCoy, Vivian R., Carol Nalbandian, and Colleen Ryan. *CREATE: A New Model for Career Change*. Lawrence, Kan.: Univ. of Kansas, 1979.

A two-volume trainer and participant manual provides resource information in conducting eight three-hour workshop sessions for people experiencing the career development change process. The model CREATE, an acronymn for a six-step career decision making process, encourages participants to consider various future-oriented work alternatives. The model is designed to help middle aged people to reassess their lives and career goals.

470. Meyer, Pearl. "Why Executives Change Jobs." *The Personnel Administrator*, 24, No. 10 (1979), 59-64.

The greatest motivating forces behind executive job change are (in rank order): (1) long range opportunity, (2) status improvement by title or responsibilities with possible accompanying earnings increase, (3) job dissatisfaction, and (4) desire for improved compensation. Family commitment, health, climate, and other factors were considered less important.

471. Neapolitan, Jerome. "Occupational Change in Mid-Career: An Exploratory Investigation." *Journal of Vocational Behavior*, 16, No. 2 (1980), 212-225.

Examines factors affecting people (N=25) who make voluntary, radical occupational changes. Among the categories of factors found to be important to mid-career change were characteristics of the first occupation (e.g., dissatisfaction), characteristics of the second occupation (e.g., attractiveness), obstacles to change (e.g., financial), and personal considerations (e.g., beliefs about one's ability to succeed in new areas).

472. Robbins, Paula. *Successful Midlife Career Change*. New York: ANACOM, 1978.

Examines the midlife career change patterns of 91 middle- and upper-class men. The author explores the motivations of career switchers; the effects of career change on psychological development; the relationship of career change and life style, income, and family; the aids available to assist people in the process of career change; and the institutional policy changes which might facilitate career change.

473. Samler, Joseph. "A Second Look at Second Careers." *Vocational Guidance Quarterly*, 20, No. 2 (1971), 112-117.

    A commentary on a three-article symposium dealing with "Second Careers as a Way of Life".

474. Schein, Edgar H. "The First Job Dilemma." *Psychology Today*, 1, No. 10 (1968), 26-37.

    Explores the reasons why college graduates change jobs and corporate strategies for reducing this high turnover.

475. Schwed, Peter. "Change of Life Priorities." *Across the Board*, 15, No. 9 (1978), 28-32.

    Examines the life crisis that business executives may encounter during the transitional period from midlife to old age. Schwed contends that aging executives must be prepared to change their priorities when their authority and status is challenged by younger co-workers. Among the practical steps suggested are that aging executives should avoid resisting all changes in the status quo, give up power gracefully, reestablish positive priorities, and retain those functions that they can still perform well.

476. Thomas, L. Eugene. "A Typology of Mid-Life Career Changers." *Journal of Vocational Behavior*, 16, No. 2 (1980), 173-182.

    Focuses on managers and professionals (N=73 men) who voluntarily changed careers during their middle years. A four-fold typology of career changers (drift-outs, opt-outs, force-outs, and bow-outs) was developed and the four types were found to differ on the following variables: amount of education completed, further schooling connected to career change, radicalness of change, and influence of personal values on decision to leave their previous careers.

477. Vaitenas, Rimantis, and Yoash Wiener. "Developmental, Emotional, and Interest Factors in Voluntary Mid-Career Change." *Journal of Vocational Behavior*, 11, No. 3 (1977), 291-304.

   Investigates three correlates of mid-career change: developmental, emotional, and interest. Vocational choice and adult development theories were sources for deriving hypotheses. A sample of career changers were compared to controls who were vocationally stable. Career changers were found to be characterized by low differentiation and consistency of interest, and high fear of failure, emotional maladjustment, and incongruity. Findings were supportive of vocational choice theory; however, results did not show developmental processes to be involved in mid-career change.

478. "Walking Out on Success--For Many It's Paying Off." *U.S. News and World Report*, 76, No. 14 (1974), 43-44.

   Many Americans at 30, 40, or 50 years of age are giving up promising careers to find new ways of earning a living and finding both happiness and prosperity in their new lines of work.

CAREER MOBILITY

479. Allan, Peter. "Career Planning of Top Executives in New York City Government." *Public Personnel Review*, 33, No. 2 (1971), 114-117.

   This study is based on the careers of 811 executives in New York City. The study has two parts: (1) traces the career paths of executives as they experienced mobility within the system, and (2) analyzes executives' careers to determine whether they demonstrate clear patterns. Findings show that executives have come up through the ranks rather than being hired from outside the city service and that women's career patterns are not as strongly defined as those of men.

480. "Bright Prospects in the Executive Job Market." *Nation's Business*, 65, No. 2 (1977), 30-34.

   Prospects are good for managers who want to make a change in 1977. Executive search firms are optimistic regarding mobility and advancement opportunities for executives. Demand is especially strong for general managers and marketing managers.

481. Bylinsky, Gene. "EDP Managers Put on a Business Suit." *Fortune*, 98, No. 9 (1978), 68-74.

   Data processing managers are likely to be upwardly mobile executives in today's corporation. The rising data processing manager needs to become more of a businessman and less of a technician.

482. Cleckley, Betty Jane. *A Study of New Careers and Upward Mobility of New Professionals in Neighborhood Health Centers*. Diss., Brandeis Univ., 1974.

   Examines new careers as a means for job upgrading and/or upward mobility of new professionals in four neighborhood health centers. Two models of career ladders were identified: one specifying that jobs beyond entry-level be created leading to established professional positions; the other specifying that additional levels be developed from aide to assistant to associate. The model yielded useful dimensions for measuring upward mobility.

483. Cohen, Michael. "The Generalist and Organizational Mobility." *Public Administration Review*, 30, No. 5 (1970), 544-552.

A generalist civil servant is one whose career is characterized by organizational mobility which includes work in more than one major department or independent agency. The specialist, by contrast, is one whose career is confined to a single department and whose experience is often downgraded as narrow. Results indicate that the generalist group contains those in administrative positions acting in staff or management support capacities, while the specialist group tends to contain subject matter professionals who are closely identified with program interests.

484. Costello, John. "The Managerial Job Market: Quality Counts." *Nations Business*, 62, No. 12 (1974), 58-60.

To be a mobile executive it is essential to have a good track record. The job market is likely to consider expertise in management techniques as more important than industry knowledge. "Executrends" in the mid-70's show demand up in the areas of general and defense engineering, manufacturing, and finance; demand is down in marketing, general administration, and personnel.

485. Dye, Thomas R., and John W. Pickering. "Governmental and Corporate Elites: Convergence and Differentiation." *Journal of Politics*, 36, No. 4 (1974), 900-925.

Examines the specialization, recruitment channels, interlocking, and social characteristics of the nation's corporate and governmental elite.

486. "Exploding the Myth of Executive Job-Hopping." *Business Week*, No. 2589 (1979), 127-131.

Women in top management tend to be less mobile than previously thought because their jobs/careers are becoming more like those of men.

487. Ford, John. "The Pros and Cons of Changing Jobs." *Public Relations Journal*, 37, No. 3 (1981), 52-53.

While there may be obvious attractions to a new job, the benefits of seniority and progress in one's present position should not be undervalued. Often mobile professionels find their new jobs hold more frustrations and problems than their previous jobs.

488. Gemmill, Gary, and Donald DeSalvia. "The Promotion Beliefs of Managers as a Factor in Career Progress: An Exploratory Study." *Sloan Management Review*, 18, No. 2 (1977), 75-81.

Examines the promotion beliefs of managers and relates them to actual upward mobility. The 209 managers surveyed believed three basic factors were related to attaining promotions: managerial proficiency, public image, and political proficiency. Upwardly mobile managers have different perceptions of the promotion process than their less mobile co-workers in terms of the relative importance of the three factors. They assign less importance to public image and political proficiency criteria.

489. Gemmill, Gary, and W.J. Heisler. "Fatalism as a Factor in Managerial Job Satisfaction, Job Strain, and Mobility." *Personnel Psychology*, 25, No. 2 (1972), 241-250.

Explores the relationship between differential beliefs in a manager's ability to control the environment and job satisfaction, job strain, and mobility. Results support the basic hypothesis that the greater the belief in one's ability to influence the environment, the higher is the reported positional mobility and job satisfaction and the lower is the reported job strain.

490. Goldner, Fred H., and R.R. Ritti. "Professionalization as Career Immobility." *American Journal of Sociology*, 72, No. 5 (1967), 489-502.

Examines professional career leaders in industry and finds they have been used to provide an alternative definition of success. Professional positions do not provide the status and money of "equivalent" managerial positions because the former lack the power to allocate scarce resources or pursue alternative goals. Professionals cannot move up the main career ladder.

491. Grey, Ronald J., and George G. Gordon. "Risk Taking Managers: Who Gets the Top Jobs?" *Management Review*, 67, No. 11 (1978), 8-13.

Examines risk taking and career mobility of corporate managers. Results suggest that risk takers may advance faster than others because of their enhanced capacity to produce desired end results.

492. Heisler, W.J. "Promotion: What Does It Take to Get Ahead." *Business Horizons*, 21, No. 2 (1978), 57-63.

Compares the views of MBAs as would-be managers (N=200) and corporate executives (N=100) on business promotion practices. Both samples were asked to identify from a list of 50 promotional criteria those which are presently important and those which should ideally be used as promotional criteria. The specific similarities and differences between the two sets of respondents are reported in detail; the general results show that the ideals of the two samples are similar, but their views of currently used criteria are quite different.

493. Idema, Thomas H. "Systems Career Path Development." *Journal of Systems Management*, 29, No. 4 (1978), 30-35.

Describes the various routes of a career program for systems persons and how to move up the ladder. The author presents a useful matrix showing the technical/ professional skills and knowledge, individual skills, interpersonal skills, and managerial/organizational skills required for 15 different systems positions.

494. Jennings, Eugene. "Mobicentric Man." *Psychology Today*, 4, No. 2 (1970), 35-36; 70-72.

The mobicentric executive is one who is mobile because of frequent transfers both within and across organizations and because of preferring a diversity of tasks and using a variety of methods to accomplish those tasks. The author compares the mobicentric executive to the insider and the organization man. He discusses a mobility-centered person in terms of three major areas of life: friendship, career, and marriage. Mobicentrics are increasingly represented in top corporate positions.

495. Lauterbach, Albert. "Executive Training and Productivity: Managerial Views in Latin America." *Industrial and Labor Relations Review*, 17, No. 3 (1964), 357-378.

Deals with the selection and promotion of executives in Latin America, the need for executive training, and worker's reaction to productivity measures. Results indicate that (1) selection and promotion of executives is strongly influenced by kinship, politics, and friendship factors; (2) executive training is haphazard and varies according to the area and managerial generation concerned; and (3) the productivity concept is limited to a minority of Latin American managers.

496. Morrison, Ann M. "Job-Hopping to the Top." *Fortune*, 103, No. 9 (1981), 127; 129-130.

   A survey of Fortune 500 companies shows that less than 40 percent have spent their entire careers at the companies they ended up managing. The rest job-hopped their way to the top. The five top producers of chief executive officers are: General Electric, Westinghouse, Ford, Exxon, and Litton.

497. Nigro, Lloyd G., and Kenneth J. Meier. "Executive Mobility in the Federal Service: A Career Perspective." *Public Administration Review*, 35, No. 3 (1975), 291-295.

   Analyzes career mobility patterns of a random sample of GS 16-18 and equivalent level federal government personnel. Using career as a framework, the authors found executives were a highly mobile class of civil servants who have experienced organizational, occupational, and geographic mobility both in and out of government.

498. Tomeski, Edward A., and Konrad E. Sadek. "Utility Theory." *Journal of Systems Management*, 31, No. 7 (1980), 6-11.

   Uses utility theory to examine the causes of career advancement among managers and how to improve one's mobility. The authors focus on the interplay between upward mobile managers and less upward mobile managers.

499. Veiga, John F. *A Behavioral Model of Middle-Manager Career Mobility: An Empirical Analysis.* Diss., Kent State Univ., 1971.

   Develops and tests a behavioral model of career mobility. Two factors in the model are motivational needs and contextual. The three motivational needs factors are driving forces behind the managers' mobility behavior. The 23 contextual factors are short run in duration and operate only during segments of the managers' career span. These factors are also viewed as retarding mobility and are, thus, responsible for offsetting a manager's motivational needs.

500. Veiga, John F. "The Mobile Manager at Mid-Career." *Harvard Business Review*, 51, No. 1 (1973), 115-119.

   Presents a Career Mobility Phase Matrix that was developed from a study of the job moves of 1,243 middle managers. This Matrix traces mobility phases throughout the typical manager's career, and the primary influences on these phases.

501. Warner, W. Lloyd, et al. "New Light on Lateral Entry." *Personnel Administration*, 26, No. 3 (1963), 17-23.

    Analyzes lateral entry using data on 10,851 civilian executives in high administrative positions in the Federal Government. Six basic findings are presented along with the information leading researchers to these conclusions.

502. Williams, Donald C. "Accelerating Pay Rates for Managers Who Switch Employees." *Harvard Business Review*, 54, No. 6 (1976), 8-12.

    Corporate managers making interorganizational changes during 1975 received substantial gains in salaries and bonuses.

SPECIFIC OCCUPATIONS/ PROFESSIONS/ CAREERS

503. Black, Gordon S. "A Theory of Political Ambition: Career Choices and the Role of Structural Incentives." *The American Political Science Review*, 66, No. 1 (1972), 144-159.

    Examines survey data from 435 city councilmen in 89 cities concerning career alternatives for office holders. The author assumes officeholders employ a "rational calculus" in making such choices as dropping out of political life, seeking reelection, and choosing to run for higher office. Results show that political ambition develops as a product of a politician's investment in his/her political career. Such investments are associated with community size and electoral competitiveness.

504. Carr, James W. *Background Characteristics and Career Development of Personnel Managers*. Diss., Univ. of Georgia, 1980.

    Questionnaires were mailed to 1,600 members of five local personnel associations and the American Society of Personnel Administration; 630 returned useable questionnaires. The study found: (1) the administrative responsibility level of personnel administration/industrial relations practitioners was low and the operative responsibility level was high; (2) the most important development factor was experience; and (3) planned developmental programs for practitioners were not being used.

505. Clement, Ronald W., James W. Walker, and Patrick R. Pinto. "Changing Demands on the Training Professional." *Training and Development Journal*, 33, No. 3 (1979), 3-7.

    Examines results of the American Society for Training and Development's survey to determine the competencies required for effective performance in training and development. Survey findings are reported on changes in training and development activities; changes in the job of training and development practitioners; important skills, knowledge, and behavioral requirements for training and development professionals; and the new requirements that are emerging as important.

506. Fishel, Jeff. "Ambition and the Political Vocation: Congressional Challengers in American Politics." *Journal of Politics*, 33, No. 1 (1971), 25-56.

Studies the role of Congressional challengers in American politics. Tests three hypotheses which posit that the greater the tendency toward career orientations: (1) the greater the tendency of candidates to converge in the ideological center, (2) (among Democrats) the greater the tendency to move toward the center on non-economic issues, and (3) (among Republicans) the greater the tendency to move toward the center on both economic and non-economic issues.

507. Frantzich, Stephen E. "De-Recruitment: The Other Side of the Congressional Career Equation." *Western Political Quarterly*, 31, No. 1 (1978), 105-126.

Examines the de-recruitment end of Congressional careers. Results show members leaving Congress are differentiated both by the sources and consequences of their departure. The factors which help explain whether a member will leave voluntarily or be forced out are described by the concepts of vulnerability, disability, opportunity, and job desirability.

508. Grubel, Herbert G. "The Peter Principle and the Efficient Market Hypothesis." *Financial Analysts Journal*, 35, No. 5 (1979), 72-75.

Investment success with portfolios often presents portfolio managers with opportunities to manage different and larger portfolios. Continued success leads to continual movement from one portfolio to another larger portfolio. Eventually managers will confront portfolios so large their talents are tested to the limit. Once they reach their level of "incompetence", they will be unable any longer to achieve above-average returns.

509. Hacker, Andrew. "The Elected and Appointed: Two American Elites." *The American Political Science Review*, 55, No. 3 (1961), 539-549.

Compares two elite groups--100 U.S. Senators and the Presidents of America's largest industrial corporations--to determine what these elites have in common and what they do not. Career mobility is one dimension considered.

510. Hayano, David M. "The Professional Poker Player: Career Identification and the Problem of Respectability." *Social Problems*, 24, No. 5 (1977), 556-564.

Examines how one deviant occupational group, the career-professional poker player, adapts to labeling and stereotyping. Three factors related to career identification are discussed: (1) interest in professional skills, (2) ideological and moral concerns, and (3) reliance on group support.

511. Heidrick, Garner W. "Career Characteristics of Top U.S. Bankers." *Banker's Magazine*, 159, No. 1 (1976), 19-24.

Key characteristics (educational, social, and behavioral) of current banking leaders are examined and comparisons are made with leaders of five and ten years earlier. The changing role of banking leaders is considered. Seven out of eight bank presidents work 50 hours or more each week. To get ahead bank presidents must possess intelligence, analytical ability, flexibility, resourcefulness, and imagination.

512. Hjelm, Victor S., and Joseph P. Pisciotte. "Profiles and Careers of Colorado State Legislators." *Western Political Quarterly*, 21, No. 4 (1968), 698-722.

Provides a socio-economic and political profile of Colorado state legislators and examines their entry, tenure, and turnover as public officials.

513. Hubbard, Howard G., and Edward C. McDonagh. "The Business Executive as a Career Type." *Sociology and Social Research*, 47, No. 2 (1963), 138-147.

Studies the personal values, job satisfaction, recruitment, mobility, and career goals of business executives. The authors use interview data to support their thesis that "business executives as a career group did not consistently manifest an intermediate occupational type." (p. 145) Findings show that business executives' career goals are primarily economic; they do not view careers as a way to gain entry to higher status positions; their value orientation is toward status and money; they have high rates of career mobility; and they typically make late career decisions.

514. Hutcheson, Peggy, and Neal Chalofsky. "Careers in Human Resource Development." *Training and Development Journal*, 35, No. 7 (1981), 13-15.

Examines the career entry points, career paths, career options, and educational requirements for human resource development (HRD) professionals. The authors suggest that HRD professionals should play a more active role in shaping the growth of the HRD field.

515. Klimoski, Richard J. "A Biographical Data Analysis of Career Patterns in Engineering." *Journal of Vocational Behavior*, 3, No. 1 (1973), 103-113.

    Focuses on the Biographical Data Bank, a useful instrument for job assignment or career guidance purposes. Analysis was based on responses to a life history questionnaire by three groups of engineers: those holding management, research and development, and non-engineering positions. Findings show that group differentiation was possible using response patterns. Furthermore, demands of actual career paths chosen were related to items defining these response patterns.

516. Kopelman, Richard E. "Psychological Stages of Careers in Engineering: An Expectancy Theory Taxonomy." *Journal of Vocational Behavior*, 10, No. 3 (1977), 270-286.

    Using data from 376 engineers, the author derived expectancy and value scores to develop a taxonomy of nine psychological categories which are differentially related to satisfaction and motivation. Significant relationships were discovered between age, organizational reward practices, and prior category, on the one hand, and the distribution and movement of engineers across categories, on the other. Both static and longitudinal analyses (over four years) are used. A three-stage dynamic model of engineering careers is suggested.

517. Lansbury, Russell. "Careers, Work, and Leisure Among the New Professionals." *Psychological Review*, 22, No. 3 (1974), 385-400.

    Reports on research concerning attitudes toward work and leisure among specialists working in the management services department of a large British corporation. Results indicate that patterns of work and leisure are significantly influenced by career orientations.

518. Lyden, Fremont J., and Miller, Ernest G. "Why City Managers Leave the Profession: A Longitudinal Study in the Pacific Northwest." *Public Administration Review*, 36, No. 2 (1976), 175-181.

Using data collected in 1966 and 1974, the authors examined why individual city managers leave the profession. The 1974 data indicated that one-fourth of those surveyed in 1966 had left the profession, excluding those who died or retired. The reasons for leaving were council relationships and salary; they sought jobs offering more challenges, greater opportunities, or better conditions of employment. Of those remaining in the profession in 1974, two-thirds had expressed high job satisfaction in 1966, compared with only one-third of respondents who had left the profession in 1974.

519. March, James C., and James G. March. "Almost Random Careers: The Wisconsin School Superintendency, 1940-1972." *Administrative Science Quarterly*, 22, No. 3 (1977), 377-409.

    Examines the careers of Wisconsin school superintendents from 1940 through 1972. The author suggests reasons for anticipating that both individuals and jobs will be indistinguishable and careers at that level will be random. Findings confirm that the system is nearly random. Where there were deviations from randomness it was due primarily to differences among jobs (districts) and to nonstationarity in exit rates over the duration of a job, not to differences among the individuals involved.

520. Mezey, Michael. "Ambition Theory and the Office of Congressman." *Journal of Politics*, 32, No. 3 (1970), 563-579.

    Develops an opportunity-oriented model of Congressional recruitment based on ambition theory.

521. Ortiz, Flora I. "Midcareer Socialization of Educational Administrators." *Review of Educational Research*, 48, No. 1 (1978), 121-132.

    Examines the socialization process of school administrators, emphasizing the positions most likely to be held by midcareerists. Administrators' attitudes and behavior are affected by the school organization, the service functions schools perform, and the career options available within school administration.

522. Osgood, Donald W. "The Personnel Managers' Front-Line Role in the Marketing Field." *Personnel*, 50, No. 6 (1973), 41-46.

Career development for field personnel is enhanced when home-office personnel people really know what is going on in the district/branch offices. The author describes the career-related benefits which occur when personnelists bridge the gap between the home office and outlying branch locations.

523. Purvis, June. "Schoolteaching as a Professional Career." *British Journal of Sociology*, 24, No. 10 (1973), 43-57.

    Argues that the absence of a professional career in schoolteaching may be related to (1) the occupation's semi-professional nature, (2) structural factors within the profession, and (3) attitudinal factors among the members and general public. Prescriptions for action are offered to accelerate the process of professionalization for schoolteachers.

524. Ruchelman, Leonard I. "A Profile of New York State Legislators." *Western Political Quarterly*, 20, No. 3 (1967), 625-638.

    Traces the background characteristics, career-lines, and de-recruitment of New York State legislators.

525. Salmans, Sandra. "Personnel: A New Route to the Top." *International Management*, 32, No. 5 (1977), 24-26.

    The personnel manager is challenging those from the traditional technical fields for top corporate executive jobs.

526. Smith, Abbott P. "Whither T and D--and You." *Training and Development Journal*, 34, No. 5 (1980), 88-94.

    Discusses changes and career opportunities for professionals and practitioners in the training and development field.

527. Splaver, Sarah. *Paraprofessions: Careers of the Future and the Present*. New York: Julian Messner, 1978.

    Paraprofessional careers are described including the history of the paraprofessional, nature of the work qualifications and preparation for entry and advancement, supply and demand, unions and associations, distribution, opportunities for special groups, and future outlooks for each paraprofession. The categories of paraprofessionals covered are architectural and urban planning, education, engineering and science, legal, library science, medical, mental health and human services, and "other" paraprofessionals.

528. "Why Your Salesman Quit." *Sales Management*, 112, No. 7 (1974), 6;10.

 Providing quick career development opportunities may not be an effective strategy for reducing sales force turnover. A recent study is summarized which shows that companies offering fast promotions actually have a higher turnover rate.

529. Wilders, Malcolm. "The Football Club Manager--A Precarious Occupation." *Journal of Management Studies*, 13, No. 1 (1976), 152-163.

 The managerial capacity and general characteristics of the football club manager are assessed. Based on a survey of 45 club managers in the English Football League, the author discussed the role of club managers, their area of responsibility, pre-management careers, career development, management training, termination of contracts, and courses to improve their performance.

CAREER DEVELOPMENT OF WOMEN

530. Almquist, Elizabeth M., Shirley S. Angrist, and Richard Mickelsen. "Women's Career Aspirations and Achievements: College and Seven Years Later." *Sociology of Work and Occupations*, 7, No. 3 (1980), 367-384.

    Describes the educational, familial, and occupational behavior exhibited by 64 women during the seven years immediately following college graduation. The authors found high congruence between college aspirations and subsequent behavior in some areas (e.g., marriage and graduate school), but less congruence in others (e.g., occupational choice). Women had children less frequently and worked more often than they had projected. They pursue a contingency strategy in structuring their adult lives which affects career aspirations and achievements.

531. Allpander, Guvenc G., and Jean E. Gutmann. "Contents and Techniques of Management Development Programs for Women." *Personnel Journal*, 55, No. 2 (1976), 76-79.

    Compares the training and development needs of male and female executives. The authors stress the need for developing supervisory skills among non-managerial women who aspire to higher positions in their organizations. Tabulations are reported of men and women's perception-of motivators, job functions, relationships between effort and task accomplishment, and relationships between task accomplishment and reward.

532. Angrist, Shirley S., Judith R. Lave, and Richard Michelson. "How Working Mothers Manage: Socioeconomic Differences in Work, Child Care, and Household Tasks." *Social Science Quarterly*, 56, No. 4 (1976), 631-637.

    Examines the differences between higher and middle class women in the ways they manage work, child care, and domestic tasks. Professional-managerial women do differ from clerical-technical women in carrying out their multiple roles as worker, mother, and housekeeper. Sociological explanations as well as economic interpretations are offered to better understand how working mothers manage.

533. Asser, Mary Helen. *Career Patterns of Women Administrators in Higher Education: Barriers and Constraints.* Diss., Southern Illinois Univ., 1975.

Identifies positive and negative influences on the career advancement of women administrators; analyzes differences in life styles, professional qualifications, and career attitudes of women in prestigious administrative positions and those in lower administrative positions; and examines women administrators' career aspirations.

534. Baron, Alma S. "New Data on Women Managers." *Training and Development Journal*, 32, No. 11 (1978), 12-13.

A nationwide survey of 6,300 women in management positions asked "What aspects of your jobs are the most difficult for you to perform?" and, "What do you find to be your biggest management problem?" Responses show women identified general management problems such as time management, which were unrelated to sex.

535. Baron, Alma S. "Selection, Development, and Socialization of Women into Management." *Business Quarterly*, 42, No. 4 (1977), 61-67.

Reports that from 1965 to 1970 the percentage of women in management changed very little. To better integrate women into management the author suggests tangible rewards for male managers who develop female managers, selection of mentors to help women move into management, and separation of women from such role-related jobs as coffee making.

536. Bartol, Kathryn M., and Robert A. Bartol. "Women in Managerial and Professional Positions: the United States and the Soviet Union." *Industrial and Labor Relations Review*, 28, No. 4 (1975), 524-553.

Compares female employment in managerial and professional positions in the United States and the Soviet Union. Findings indicate that Soviet women have made much more progress than American women in attaining professional positions, but differences are less pronounced in managerial occupations. The authors suggest that Soviet women workers face many employment problems and that the Soviet Union is overrated as a model of equality in employment.

537. Betz, Nancy E., and Gail Hackett. "The Relationship of Career-Related Self-Efficacy Expectations to Perceived Career Options in College Women and Men." *Journal of Counseling Psychology*, 28, No. 5 (1981), 399-410.

Investigates the applicability of self-efficacy theory to the process of career decision making. Responses from a sample of 235 male and female undergraduate students indicate significant sex differences in self-efficacy regarding traditional vs. nontraditional (for females) occupations. Females reported higher self efficacy regarding traditional occupations and lower self efficacy for nontraditional occupations, while males reported equivalent self-efficacy regarding the two occupational classifications.

538. Bird, Caroline. *Everything a Woman Needs to Know to Get Paid What She's Worth*. New York: Bantam Books, 1974.

Deals with subtle obstacles facing working women as they attempt to demonstrate their competence in a male-oriented job force. Tips are provided on how to get paid what you are worth, identify injustices facing women, detect sex discrimination, advance on the career ladder, and enjoy volunteer work. The last section is a listing of resources--books, newsletters, counseling services, and the names and addresses of people and agencies to contact for help.

539. Brumfield, Peggy D. "Women and the Workplace: A Corporate Perspective." *Journal of Public and International Affairs*, 3, No. 1 (1982), 54-61.

Reviews some of the major government regulations as they affect corporate women, e.g., the Equal Pay Act of 1963, Title Vll and Executive Order 11246, Sex Discrimination Guidelines, and Uniform Guidelines on Employee Selection Procedures.

540. Chenoweth, Lillian C., and Elizabeth Maret. "The Career Patterns of Mature American Women." *Sociology of Work and Occupations*, 7, No. 2 (1980), 222-251.

Identifies three major life-career patterns for mature American women--home, labor force, and mixed careers. Seven hypotheses are explored pertaining to the influence of women's familial resources, familial investments, and capital investments on their career patterns. The hypotheses are generally supported by the findings. However, the observed career patterns of mature women are more strongly related to husbands' attitudes toward wives working outside the home, previous earning levels, and number of children than to marital status, husbands' income, respondents' education, and respondents' attitudes about working women.

541. Cole, Mary E., Barbara S. Swanson, and J. Richard Porter. "Women in Management." *Journal of Public and International Affairs*, 3, No. 1 (1982), 48-53.

    Compares successful female and male managers and finds that successful female managers are very much like their male counterparts but very different from women in general. The authors' evidence suggests that "management skill is not related to gender" and that "very few of either sex actually have the abilities, motivation, and values that typify successful managers." (p. 53)

542. Cooney, Rosemary S. "A Comparative Study of Work Opportunities for Women." *Industrial Relations*, 17, No. 1 (1978), 64-74.

    Examines whether changes in the rate of women's labor force participation are reflective of changes in sexual equality in the labor force. Long-term and short-term trends are discussed based on cross-national data. Results of longitudinal analysis show female participation in nonagricultural activities increasing, sexual segregation declining, and women's work status increasing. However, short-term changes in participation were not reflective of changes in work status or sexual segregation.

543. Cooperman, Irene G. "Second Careers: War Wives and Widows." *Vocational Guidance Quarterly*, 20, No. 2 (1971), 103-111.

    Women workers are responding to the changing demands of a turbulent economy by seeking retraining and reemployment in new and different kinds of jobs. While we lack an adequate base in both data and theory for understanding the career development of women, the author examines new factors affecting working women's lives, problems wives and widows face, aid available to them for second careers, and recommendations for vocational counselors who work with female clients.

544. Darian, Jean C. "Factors Influencing the Rising Labor Force Participation Rates of Married Women With Pre-School Children." *Social Science Quarterly*, 56, No. 4 (1976), 614-630.

Investigates factors influencing the rising labor force participation during the Sixties of married women with pre-school children. Two factors received attention: (1) those reducing the constraint on the working mother, and (2) the age distribution of mothers with pre-school children. The second factor had the greater influence on rapid participation increase of mothers with pre-school children.

545. Deitch, Cyntia H. "The Sociology of Second Place: Social and Cultural Constraints on the Advancement of Women." *Journal of Public and International Affairs*, 3, No. 1 (1982), 1-7.

Argues that women occupy "second place" in the business world in terms of the kinds of jobs they hold and their earnings. Four demographic patterns are discussed: (1) women earn substantially less than men do; (2) men with high-paying careers are less likely than men in lower-paying jobs to have employed wives; (3) women are more likely than men to be in dual-career marriages; and (4) the career advancement of women continues to be curtailed by having children.

546. Douglas, Priscilla D. *An Analysis of Demographic Characteristics and Career Patterns of Women Administrators in Higher Education*. Diss., Univ. of Connecticut, 1976.

Analyzes the demographic characteristics and career patterns of women administrators in higher education. Survey data (N=425) provides the basis for describing the modal administrator, analyzing differences between academic and non-academic administrators, and comparing traditional and non-traditional academic administrators.

547. Epstein, Gilda F. *Women's Place: Options and Limits in Professional Careers*. Berkeley: Univ. of California Press, 1971.

Contends that American women have not adequately exploited their rights and talents. The author focuses on socialization processes which help shape individuals' self identity and their sense of personal limits and choices. Six major categories of role conflict are discussed, each originating from uncertainties associated with being both a professional and a female. Approaches to reconciling such conflicts are described. Women's participation in different professions is shaped by behavioral norms, structural factors, and changing developments in each field.

548. Epstein, Gilda F., and Arline L. Bronzaft. "Female Modesty in Aspiration Level." *Journal of Counseling Psychology*, 21, No. 1 (1974), 57-60.

    Analyzes educational and occupational aspirations of college freshmen by sex and ability level. The findings reported no significant differences between traditional and "open admission" college students in educational and occupational aspirations. Female students tended to favor careers traditionally acceptable to women and to desire fewer years of higher education.

549. "Executives vs. the Career Women." *Psychology Today*, 9, No. 8 (1976), 22.

    Summarizes findings from a survey of 1,500 male executives which showed that they were less confident of a women's ability to satisfy both employer and family than they were of a man's ability.

550. Farmer, H.S. "Helping Women to Resolve the Home Career Conflict." *Personnel and Guidance Journal*, 49, No. 10 (1971), 795-800.

    Vocational counselors can no longer avoid the special demands of vocational decision making posed by women. Factors involved in the vocational choice process with female high school and college students can be clarified by counselors and educators. Exposure to these factors need not be delayed until women seek this counseling; such clarifications should be a regular part of high school and college guidance programs for females. If women select careers at a level equivalent to their potential, society will benefit.

551. Ferrari, Sergio. "The Italian Woman Executive." *Management International Review*, 17, No. 1 (1977), 13-21.

    Profiles the Italian woman executive; describes her career difficulties and potential solutions; examines the management style of woman employees; and considers women's capacity to succeed in management.

552. Finkelhor, Marian K. "From Barriers to Ladders." *Journal of Public and International Affairs*, 3, No. 1 (1982), 8-12.

    Assess the "barriers and ladders" facing working women from 1920 to 1981. Brief attention is given to the laws (e.g., 19th Amendment, state laws, Title Vll) and court decisions (County of Washington v. Alberta Gunther, et al.) affecting women in the workplace.

553. Fitzgerald, Louise F., and John O. Crites. "Toward a Career Psychology of Women: What Do We Know? What Do We Need to Know?" *Journal of Counseling Psychology*, 27, No. 1 (1980), 44-62.

Reviews what is known about the career psychology of women in the areas of theory (career choice, career maturity, achievement motivation), knowledge (sociopsychological, psychometric, reliability), attitudes (counselor bias, client socialization), and counseling techniques (career choice process, career choice content). Specific recommendations for training and practice are offered.

554. Foster, Lawrence W., and Tom Kolinko. "Choosing to be a Managerial Woman: An Examination of Individual Variables and Career Choice." *Sex Roles*, 5, No. 5 (1979), 627-634.

Data from male and female MBA students and from male and female MA candidates in elementary education were examined focusing especially on female MBA students. Female MBA students perceived themselves to be more self assured, higher in initiative, and more creative than did the others. While earlier literature on women entering nontraditional careers suggested possible fear-of-identity or sex-role-inappropriateness problems, there is no evidence of this according to this study.

555. Hackett, Gail, and Nancy E. Betz. "A Self-Efficacy Approach to the Career Development of Women." *Journal of Vocational Behavior*, 18, No. 3 (1981), 326-339.

Presents a conceptualization of women's career development based on self-efficacy theory. The model suggests that due to women's socialization experiences they lack strong expectations of personal efficacy and develop strong internal barriers which restrict the range of career options and prevent full realization of their capabilities in career pursuits. The authors propose four avenues by which self-efficacy can be enhanced.

556. Hall, Douglas T., and Francine E. Gordon. "Career Choices of Married Women: Effects on Conflict, Role Behavior, and Satisfaction." *Journal of Applied Psychology*, 58, No. 1 (1973), 42-48.

Studies the conflicts, satisfactions, and pressures facing married women engaged in either full-time employment, part-time employment, or full-time work as a housewife. It was predicted that satisfaction would be related to the extent to which women actually did what they ideally aspire to do. This hypothesis was confirmed for housekeeping and volunteer activities, but not for part- and full-time employment. Full-time workers were more satisfied than the other two groups.

557. Hall, Francine S., and Douglas T. Hall. "Dual Careers: How Do Companies and Couples Cope with the Problems." *Organizational Dynamics*, 6, No. 4 (1978), 33-50.

Examines the impact of career couples on the organization and corporate strategies for coping with the two-career couple. Using interview data (N=300) the authors discuss such strategies as dual career audits, special recruiting techniques, revision of relocation and nepotism policies, offering supervisory training and seminars for dual-career couples, provision of flexible work environments, easing the strain of unavoidable two-career relocations, and evaluations of program effectiveness.

558. Hall, Francine S., and Douglas T. Hall. *The Two Career Couple*. Reading, Mass.: Addison-Wesley, 1979.

Examines the pitfalls and pleasures of two-career couples. The authors stress the importance of compromise, flexibility, and mutual adjustment in dual-career relationships. Among the issues covered are: career and family stages, coping with multiple roles and stress, dual-career life styles, home-career conflicts, and alternatives for both couples and corporations.

559. Hansen, L. Sunny, and Rita S. Rapoza, eds. *Career Development and Counseling of Women*. Springfield, Ill.: Charles C. Thomas, 1978.

Contains 37 essays which tie together the literature concerning the psychological development of women as it relates to their careers. The volume describes women's careers over the life span; analyzes variables related to female career decision making, aspirations, motivation, and identity; explores socialization processes; considers the economic aspects of women's lives; discusses changing life roles and career patterns; and offers prescriptions on facilitating female development. An annotated bibliography is provided.

560. Hardesty, Sarah A., and Nancy E. Betz. "The Relationship of Career Salience, Attitudes Toward Women, and Demographic and Family Characteristics to Marital Adjustment in Dual-Career Couples." *Journal of Vocational Behavior*, 17, No. 2 (1980), 242-250.

   Investigates predictors of marital adjustment in dual-career couples. Data from 42 dual-career couples show that both wives and husbands report relatively high levels of marital adjustment, moderate levels of career salience, and relatively profeminist attitudes toward women. Career interests were ranked as less important than were family interests. Attitudinal differences between males and females in dual career couples are also reported.

561. Harrison, Evelyn. "The Working Woman: Barriers in Employment." *Public Administration Review*, 24, No. 2 (1964), 78-86.

   Examines the prejudices and barriers which prevent American women from fully participating in American life. The author summarizes some conventional and faulty assumptions concerning comparative employment characteristics of women and men. One of the areas of comparison is career advancement. President Johnson's insistence on a larger role for women in government resulted in an improvement in the employment status of women in the federal service and focused attention on the issue of working women in other sectors of the economy.

562. Hay, Christine. "Women in Management: The Obstacles and Opportunities They Face." *Personnel Administrator*, 25, No. 4 (1980), 31-39.

   Upward mobility for women is partially dependent upon changing the attitudes of men and women--especially those of women toward women. Women need to become involved in management training, career planning, and mentor relationships.

563. Herbert, Theodore T., and Edward B. Yost. "Women as Effective Managers: A Strategic Model for Overcoming Barriers." *Human Resource Management*, 17, No. 1 (1978), 18-25.

   Proposes a strategic model for overcoming obstacles to the utilization of women managers. Among the obstacles to the development of women are college programs which have traditionally prepared males only, informal mentoring networks excluding women, societal expectations and socialization patterns, and women's aspirations and assessments of their managerial potential.

564. "Is There Enough Room at the Top for Women Managers." *International Management*, 36, No. 4 (1981), 17-19; 21-22.

    Opportunities for female executives are better than ever, but many feel stifled by continued prejudices. Exerpts from interviews with women managers are presented summarizing their successes, problems, insights, frustrations, and experiences competing in a male-dominated market.

565. Jacques, Philip F. "Women Working Within the System: Possibilities and Constraints." *Journal of Public and International Affairs*, 3, No. 1 (1982), 27-32.

    Career-motivated women can deal with the "male management barrier" by working within the system, using a women's networking approach, and establishing an effective relationship with a mentor. Women who follow these recommendations may still encounter obstacles impeding their professional advancement.

566. Jarman, Betty Jane. *The Effect of Parental Messages on the Career Patterns of Professional Women*. Diss., California School of Professional Psychology, Fresno, 1976.

    Examines parental effects on womens' career patterns. The sample includes women in the final stages of advanced professional training. Results show that subjects had higher potency scores for fathers and higher attitudes Toward Women Scale (AWS) scores for mothers when comparing scores between parents. Subjects also had higher AWS scores compared to undergraduate women and positive Semantic Differential Scores for both parents. The study concludes that career-oriented women have a positive, enriching relationship with their parents.

567. Kahne, Hilda. "Women in the Professions: Career Considerations and Job Placement Techniques." *Journal of Economic Issues*, 5, No. 3 (1971), 28-45.

    Examines the problems of career choice and job placement for women in professional occupations. Remedies are proposed which would increase the range of career choice and improve job placement procedures so they are more tailored to women's life styles and work requirements.

568. Lee, Nancy. *Targeting the Top*. Garden City, N.Y.: Doubleday, 1980.

   Advises women who seek to develop a successful business career. This four-part book provides: (1) self-assessment guidance to help women identify what they want from work and what they are willing to sacrifice to get it; (2) advice on planning and managing careers; (3) information on useful resources and how to obtain them; and (4) suggestions on when and how to make strategic career moves. Information on dual career couples, time management, and mentoring is included.

569. Levitt, Eleanor Sosnow. "Vocational Development of Professional Women: A Review." *Journal of Vocational Behavior*, 1, No. 4 (1971), 375-385.

   Reviews research examining women's background, personality, interest, value, and current life situation variables as these factors relate to their vocational behavior and development. Results were inconsistent in many instances. This inconsistency may be due to the fact that many studies have centered on college women who had not yet experienced marriage or regular employment, or to inadequate definition of the concept of "career orientation".

570. Lopata, Helena Z. "The Life Cycle of the Social Role of Housewife." *Sociology and Social Research*, 51, No. 1 (1966), 5-22.

   Analyzes the life cycle of the social role of the housewife relying upon interviews with 1,000 Chicago housewives. The housewife's social role peaks early in the woman's life cycle, preceding the necessary socialization, training, and identification.

571. Loring, Rosalind, and Theodore Wells. *Breakthrough: Women into Management*. New York: Van Nostrand Reinhold, 1972.

   Offers guidelines to managers in implementing equal employment opportunity legislation and in dealing with the problems of integrating women into management. The nine chapters cover issues such as the legal, social, and economic factors leading to changes in the Seventies; action guidelines for implementing affirmative action programs; the managerial climate in a male-dominated society; the sex-role culture in the U.S.; relationships and issues with women at work; and predictions for the future.

572. Lunnebord, Patricia W. "Sex and Career Decision-Making Styles." *Journal of Counseling Psychology*, 25, No. 4 (1978), 299-305.

Reports on three studies which test the hypotheses that women put greater reliance on the Intuitive style and men on the Planning style in making career decisions. Findings indicate no sex differences in the participants (N=116) stage or style of decision making, self-assessed vocational decisiveness, or vocational self-concept crystallization. The author sees no need for differential career counseling for the sexes.

573. Mahoney, Thomas A. "Factors Determining Labor Force Participation of Married Women." *Industrial and Labor Relations Review*, 14, No. 4 (1961), 563-577.

Studies a sample of women in St. Paul, Minnesota, to determine the influence of a set of variables on labor force participation of women. The most important predictor of labor force participation was previous employment experience, but this was modified by such factors as age and presence of young children in the home.

574. Munley, Patrick H. "Interests of Career and Homemaking Oriented Women." *Journal of Vocational Behavior*, 4, No. 1 (1974), 43-48.

A sample of 90 undergraduate women was separated into two groups: career and homemaking oriented. On occupational scales, these two groups attained significantly different scores. Significant correlations existed between career orientation and academic achievement interest and homemaking basic interest scales, but such correlations were not present with a masculinity-femininity scale. Findings are analyzed in terms of the interest pattern of homemaking and career-oriented students.

575. O'Hara, Paula. "Women in Business: Great Expectations." *Journal of Public and International Affairs*, 3, No. 1 (1982), 37-43.

Discusses six factors affecting career success of women in business: a success plan, ability, commitment, corporate style, credibility, and power.

576. O'Leary, Virginia E. "Some Attitudinal Barriers to Occupational Aspirations in Women." *Psychological Bulletin*, 81, No. 11 (1974), 809-826.

Reviews the literature on attitudinal barriers inhibiting women workers from engaging in achievement-oriented behavior leading to promotions into management. Both external factors (e.g., societal sex role stereotypes) and internal factors (e.g., fear of failure) are discussed.

577. Orth, Charles D. III, and Frederick Jacobs. "Women in Management: Patterns for Change." *Harvard Business Review*, 48, No. 4 (1971), 139-147.

Identifies barriers to women's career (i.e., inflexible attitudes, unclear career patterns, unequal salaries, and outdated notions) and suggests a plan of action including appraisal of past successes and failures, recruiting, training, promoting, sponsoring, and retaining qualified women. Day care facilities and appropriate programs should be designed.

578. Papanek, Hanna. "Men, Women, and Work: Reflections on the Two-Person Career." *American Journal of Sociology*, 78, No. 4 (1973), 852-872.

The "two-person career" pattern refers to the American middle class woman's career involvement being expressed through "vicarious achievement" in her husband's job by a "combination of formal and informal institutional demands which is placed on both members of a married couple of whom only the man is employed by the institution." (p. 852) Papanek discusses the stereotypes perpetuated by this practice, the duties the wives assume in a "two-person career", the consequences of this pattern for women's careers, and the differences between this American practice and patterns in sex-segregated societies in South Asia.

579. Peterson, Candida, and James Peterson. "Issues Concerning Collaborating Careers." *Journal of Vocational Behavior*, 7, No. 2 (1975), 173-180.

Asks male and female college students to respond to stories about married physicians whose total income was greatest when (1) the wife was responsible for child care; (2) the husband earned more than the wife; or (3) the wife earned more than the husband. A bias supportive of maternal child care was found in situations (1) and (3), while in situation (2), most females favored paternal responsibility for child care and males selected mother and father with equal frequency. Results did not show an aversion to the wife's earning more than the husband.

580. Picker, Ann M. *Women Educational Administrators: Career Patterns and Perceptions*. Diss., Univ. of California, 1979.

   Studies how women educational administrators function in a predominantly male environment, how their career patterns differ from those of men, and how they perceive their roles. Survey results show that younger men and younger women spent approximately the same time teaching before entering administration; women received more instances of sponsorship than men; women administrators perceived discriminatory practices in recruitment qualifications; and women administrators, more often than men, aspired beyond the position of principal as their ultimate career goal.

581. Pinkstaff, Marlene A., and Anna B. Wilkinson. *Women at Work: Overcoming the Obstacles*. Reading, Mass.: Addison-Wesley, 1979.

   Examines the problems facing working women and offers techniques for solving them. Separate chapters explore such issues as self image, guilt, work-family conflicts, networks, achievement, sexism, power, politics, stress, and resentment. The authors emphasize the ways women can overcome or cope with problems in the workplace.

582. Powell, Gary N. "Career Development and the Woman Manager--A Social Power Perspective." *Personnel*, 57, No. 3 (1980), 22-32.

   Presents several alternative career development strategies open to women managers with an appraisal of how each makes use of social power. Each strategy is analyzed in terms of the power base (e.g., expert, coercive, reward) emphasized and its advantages and disadvantages. The author suggests factors to be considered in evaluating the relative merits of each strategy available to women.

583. "Profile of a Woman Officer." *Personnel Administrator*, 25, No. 4 (1980), 80-81.

   An executive search firm, Heidrick and Struggles of Chicago, surveyed women executives over a three-year period. Among the topics covered are compensation, working time, education, job opportunities, and career satisfaction. There are a growing number of women executives, but their development is a slow process.

584. Rand, Lorraine M., and Anna L. Miller. "A Developmental Cross-Sectioning of Women's Careers and Marriage Attitudes and Life Plans." *Journal of Vocational Behavior*, 2, No. 3 (1972), 317-322.

    Concludes that "marriage and a career" is a new cultural imperative that is emerging. Attitudinal data from a sample of women drawn from college, high school, and junior high showed striking consistency on matters such as life plans, education, marriage, and occupation. At age 12, the cultural imperative "to marry" was present, but by adulthood, career emerged as an important element in a life pattern. As young women develop they liberalize their desires and attitudes about work, which are now more easily fulfilled due to relaxed cultural prohibitions against careers for married women.

585. Rapoport, Robert, and Rhona Rapoport. *Dual Career Families*. New York: Penguin Books, 1971.

    Reports research findings on dual career couples based on three types of data: questionnaires from 200 dual career couples; intensive interviews with 16 dual career families; and multiple interviews, observations, and notes of five dual career families. The author describes the particular characteristics of dual career families which distinguish them from traditional families. Most of the book is devoted to the five dual career families who were most intensively studied.

586. Rapoport, Robert, and Rhona Rapoport. *Working Couples*. New York: Harper and Row, 1978.

    Nineteen authors contributed to this twelve-essay collection analyzing working couples. Topical coverage includes cross cultural comparisons of working couples; socio economic differences among working couples; analysis of such problems as commuting, child rearing/care, divorce/separation, work sharing/job sharing, interdependence, and accommodation; assessments of the present and future status of working couples; and suggestions of coping strategies for working couples.

587. Roland, Alan, and Barbara Harris. *Career and Motherhood*. New York: Human Sciences Press, 1979.

Explores the dual-role identity of women who try to combine career and motherhood. The authors, along with five other contributors, examine such issues as female identity, career-children conflicts, women and career goals, and changing women's roles. Contributors seek to integrate socio-historical and psychoanalytic perspectives on career and motherhood.

588. Rosen, Benson, and Thomas H. Jerdee. "Sex Stereotyping in the Executive Suite." *Harvard Business Review*, 52, No. 2 (1974), 45-58.

   Reports survey findings showing that managers often make personnel decisions using traditional male/female concepts. Sexual discrimination occurs when managers show greater concern for the careers of men than for women and when there is skepticism about women's abilities to balance work and family demands. This differential treatment could adversely affect the self image and career progress of female employees.

589. Schein, Virginia Ellen. "Relationship Between Sex Role Stereotypes and Requisite Management Characteristics Among Female Managers." *Journal of Applied Psychology*, 60, No. 3 (1976), 340-344.

   Reports results of a survey of 167 female middle managers which examines sex role stereotypes and requisite management characteristics. Findings suggest that women perceive successful middle managers to possess qualifications and characteristics more frequently identified with men than with women.

590. Schissel, Robert F. "Development of a Career-Orientation Scale for Women." *Journal of Counseling Psychology*, 15, No. 3 (1968), 257-262.

   Develops and presents a Career-Oriented Scale that discriminates between career- and non-career-oriented women on the basis of interests.

591. Shockley, Pamela S., and Constance M. Staley. "Women in Management Training Programs: What They Think About Key Issues." *Public Personnel Management*, 9, No. 3 (1980), 214-225.

   Examines the attitudes and behaviors of women in management training programs. The article reports responses in the following general categories: organizational knowledge, organizational role, female organizational role compared to male role, risk taking, power, goal development, communication behavior, mentors, perception of other women in the organization, and supervisory responsibilities.

592. Simmons, Judy. "Struggle for the Executive Suite: Blacks vs. White Women." *Black Enterprise*, 11, No. 2 (1980), 24-27.

   White women are becoming corporate managers more rapidly than black women or men. Citing Equal Employment Opportunity Commission statistics, the author demonstrates that white women are doing better than blacks under affirmative action. The inaccessibility to quality education continues to be a major barrier of black executive advancement.

593. Simpson, Janice C. "The Woman Boss." *Black Enterprise*, 11, No. 6 (1981), 20-25.

   Black women are climbing the corporate ladder despite the obstacles of racism and sexism. Career planning techniques, strategies for winning the corporate game, and the relationship between personal needs and career needs are discussed.

594. Smith, Elsie J. "The Working Mother: A Critique of the Research." *Journal of Vocational Behavior*, 19, No. 2 (1981), 191-211.

   Critiques research on working mothers, including studies on the effects of maternal employment on both preschool and school age children, and on the identity development and life satisfaction of working mothers. Results of the literature review provide few answers concerning the effects of a mother's employment on her children, family, and herself.

595. Smith, Ralph E. ed. *The Subtle Revolution: Women at Work*. Washington, D.C.: The Urban Institute, 1979.

   Contains a collection of essays which explore issues evolving from the changing patterns of female participation in the labor force. The essays review female unemployment trends, problems and opportunities of women within the job market, home-work conflicts, and government policies affecting the economic status of working women.

596. Stake, Jayne E. "Women's Self Estimates of Competence and the Resolution of the Career/Home Conflict." *Journal of Vocational Behavior*, 14, No. 1 (1979), 33-42.

Investigates the relationship among women's role factors self-perceptions of competence, and career commitment. Two scales (the Performance-Self Esteem Scale--PSES-- and the Attitudes Toward Women Scale) and questions concerning home and career choices were completed by 80 female business students and 111 business alumni. Career commitment was negatively related to family involvement and positively related to non-traditional sex-role attitudes, among high PSES subjects. A weaker relationship was formed between career commitment and women's role factors, among low PSES respondents.

597. Stringer-Moore, Donna M. "Impact of Dual Career Couples on Employers: Problems and Solutions." *Public Personnel Management*, 10, No. 4 (1981), 393-401.

Examines difficulties facing employers of dual career or dual worker families by focusing on hiring procedures (i.e., interviewing, anti-nepotism rules), working conditions (i.e., traveling, working hours, relocation), and personal considerations (i.e., child care, time for errands). The author analyzes the problems, offers solutions, and suggests future research topics.

598. Taylor, Mary G., and Shirley F. Hartley. "The Two-Person Career." *Sociology of Work and Occupations*, 2, No. 4 (1975), 354-372.

Tests and finds support for two hypotheses using survey data from 448 minister's wives: (1) respondents were accepting of the principle of vicarious achievement, i.e., fulfillment through the husband and his work; (2) respondents who more actively participate in ministry-related activities were less likely to participate in the work force. There was no support for the hypothesis that the educational system helped to socialize respondents into the vicarious achievement of the two-person career.

599. Thal, Nancy L., and Philip R. Cateora. "Opportunities for Women in International Business." *Business Horizons*, 22, No. 6 (1979), 21-27.

Women with long term career aspirations in multi-national corporations will pursue career paths involving both domestic and international experience. However women who need overseas assignments in order to climb the ladder in international companies may encounter obstacles in their career path due to cultural biases of their own firms or of foreign businesses.

600. Theodore, Athena. ed. *The Professional Woman*. Cambridge, Mass.: Schenkman Publishing Co., 1971.

    Using a sociological framework, the author brings together fifty-three articles/essays, which summarize recent research on the role of professional women in America. Selections deal with such issues as the sexual structure of professions, cultural definitions of the female professional, career choice processes, career commitment, career patterns and marriage, the marginal position of professional women, and female professionalism and social change.

601. Tully, Judy C., Cookie Stephen, and Barbara J. Chance. "The States and Sex-Typed Dimensions of Occupational Aspirations in Young Adolescents." *Social Science Quarterly*, 56, No. 4 (1976), 638-649.

    Considers the importance of status and sex-typing as dimensions of occupational aspirations using data from 1,688 sixth, seventh, and eighth graders. The differential occupational aspirations of adolescent males and females are documented and the importance of the sex-typed dimension of aspirations is demonstrated.

602. Turecamo, Dorrine A. "I'll Never Work for a Woman Supervisor Again." *Supervision*, 42, No. 5 (1980), 6-8.

    Discusses some of the stumbling blocks facing women managers and strategies they can use to gain respect of their superiors and subordinates.

603. "Up the Ladder." *Business Week*, No. 2408 (1975), 58-68.

    Women are moving into the mainstream of corporate management after a decade of agitation and legislation. In examining the movement of women up the corporate ladder, various authors examine such issues as where women start, what constitutes success, does sex matter, marriage vs. job, how to get along, women on trial, falling barriers, and female earning power.

604. Vance, Carmen L. *Comparison of the Career Development of Women Executives in Institutions of Higher Education With Corporate Women Executives*. Diss., Indiana Univ., 1978.

Examines the background and career development of
women in top level administrative positions in higher
education and compares them to corporate women executives.
Among the conclusions were: business women made clear-cut
career decisions when they chose their majors, educational
executives did not plan for their careers; educational
executives were younger and represented a wider range of
ages; the educational level of parents of corporate
women was higher; and women in both groups were high
achievers.

605. Watley, Donivan J., and Rosalyn Kaplan. "Career or
 Marriage? Aspirations and Achievements of Able Young
 Women." *Journal of Vocational Behavior*, 1, No. 1 (1971),
 29-43.

 Female winners of National Merit Scholarships during
the period 1956 to 1960 were questioned in 1965 concerning their career and/or marriage plans. There were
considerable differences in the career-field and educational aspirations of these subjects, however, and those
who were without career plans or who planned to delay
entering a career field scored lower on scholastic
ability tests than those seeking an immediate career.
Differences were also found in the expression of problems
encountered in formulating and implementing plans and
of problems experienced due to being a female.

606. Welch, Susan. "Recruitment of Women to Public Office: A
 Discriminant Analysis." *Western Political Quarterly*,
 31, No. 3 (1978), 372-381.

 Tests the hypothesis that a significant reason for
female exclusion from public office is their underrepresentation in the "eligible pool" of the population from
which candidates are drawn. Educational and occupational
status primarily determine the composition of this
"eligible pool."

607. "When Mothers Are Also Managers." *Business Week*, No.
 2479 (1977), 155-158.

 Mothers who are also corporate executives have to
trade off both family and career. Success in combining
the two depends on accommodations made by corporations
and made by families. The network of outside help
required can absorb one fourth of a mother's take-home
pay. Most mothers who are executives agree that children
can interfere with a woman's upward mobility.

608. Williams, Gregory. "Trends in Occupational Differentiation by Sex." *Sociology of Work and Occupations*, 3, No. 1 (1976), 38-62.

Examines occupational differentiation for the period 1900-1960. The author found a slight decline in occupational differentiation by sex using comparable occupations and controlling for occupational size. The study raises questions concerning the adequacy of measures of differentiation used to analyze occupational differentiation over time.

section III
organizational career management

CAREER MANAGEMENT--GENERAL

609. Aplin, John C. "Issues and Problems in Developing Managerial Careers and Potential." *Business Quarterly*, 43, No. 2 (1978), 22-29.

    Describes the issues and problems associated with implementation of a comprehensive professional manpower development system. The author identifies the factors affecting the system's success and the circumstances likely to bring about successful integration of individual career goals and organizational manpower requirements.

610. Austin, David L. "Must the Past Be Prologue? Or, Why Can't We Do Things Differently?" *Personnel Journal*, 54, No. 5 (1975), 261-265.

    Proposes a new way of organizing and administering a personnel department by eliminating traditional departmental segmentation and organizing around three new positions--value systems manager, information systems manager, and control systems manager. Career development, leadership development, and motivation systems would come under the responsibilities of the value systems manager.

611. Berger, Lance A. "The Staffing Grid: An Integrated Approach to Organizational Development." *Personnel Journal*, 58, No. 8 (1979), 544-546.

    Career planning and team building are two methodologies which can support a single organizational development theme. Establishment of an organizational system of staffing can lead to improved allocation of human resources within companies. The author discusses the process of developing a staffing grid, sharing and integrating the grids, and getting organizational feedback.

612. Davidson, Jeff. "How to Tell When a Good Employee is Job Hunting." *Supervision*, 43, No. 2 (1981), 12-14.

Presents several significant clues which supervisors can use to recognize when valuable employees are actively seeking jobs with another company. Among the clues are a change in dress, avoidance of eye contact, increase in clerical activities, increase in use of telephone, and the office grapevine.

613. Eng, Jo Ellen, and Josephine S. Gottsdanier. "Positive Changes From a Career Development Program." *Training and Development Journal*, 33, No. 1 (1979), 3-7.

    A career development program was developed at the University of California (Santa Barbara campus) to increase the awareness of career possibilities, to increase knowlege of how to reach these possibilities, and to develop the self-confidence required to translate thinking into action. An evaluation after the first year shows significant changes in attitudes and in actual changes of careers for those in the training group.

614. Epstein, Jack. "Career Management Programs." *Personnel Journal*, 53, No. 3 (1974), 191-195.

    Reviews current concepts and basic assumptions in career management. The author questions the validity of development concepts based on the premise that everyone needs to be developed in the same way. After examining civilian career programs in the Department of the Air Force, the author recommends that organizations contemplating developing career programs first should undertake comprehensive studies of their current situations. Once career development programs have been implemented they should be reviewed for effectiveness, adequacy, and utility on a three to five-year cycle.

615. Evans, Martin G. "The Effects of Supervisory Behavior on the Path-Goal Relationship." *Organizational Behavior and Human Performance*, 5, No. 3 (1970), 277-289.

    Examines the impact of leadership behavior on subordinates' "path-goal instrumentalities". Six hypotheses are tested using questionnaire data from respondents working in a public utility and a general hospital. While findings generally support the hypotheses, results differ for the two samples.

616. Ferguson, Lawrence . "Better Management of Managers' Careers." *Harvard Business Review*, 44, No. 2 (1966), 139-152.

Considers the utility of a comprehensive simulation model of business careers as a way to give coherence to the personnel processes of recruitment, selection, training, motivating, and promotion. As science replaces intuition in managerial career planning, reliable predictive patterns of career progress will emerge. Intelligent application of such a model will involve use of computers and a truly participative career planning process.

617. Foster, Mary Sue. "Moving Women Into 'Male' Jobs." *Supervisory Management*, 26, No. 6 (1981), 2-9.

   Offers guidelines for supervisors who are confronted with large numbers of women employees. The author gives suggestions on how to develop these female employees in nontraditional jobs.

618. Foulkes, Fred K. "The Expanding Role of the Personnel Function." *Harvard Business Review*, 53, No. 2 (1975), 71-84.

   Personnel departments need to be more active, progressive, and worthy of respect if they are to respond to changes in the workplace and become active members of the top management team. If companies are going to meet new demands and problems in the workplace, personnel staffs must develop expertise in six areas: (1) attitude surveys, (2) changing work week and worklife, (3) job design, (4) career planning/development, (5) pay and benefits, and (6) supplemental uses of the workplace.

619. Gannon, Martin J., Brian A. Poole, and Robert E. Prangley. "Involuntary Job Rotation and Work Behavior." *Personnel Journal*, 51, No. 6 (1972), 446-448.

   Analyzes the relationship between involuntary job rotation and several measures of work behavior. Concludes that involuntary job rotation is significantly related to increased absenteeism and accidents, but is not significantly related to overtime and tardiness.

620. Granick, David. "International Differences in Executive Reward Systems: Extent, Explanation, and Significance." *Columbia Journal of World Business*, 13, No. 2 (1978), 45-55.

   Tests the hypothesis that differences in executive behavior are tied to wide dispersion of national patterns of reward for corporate executives. Data and illustrative information are presented showing the similarities and differences in managerial behavior in the United States, England, France, and Algeria.

621. Hall, Douglas T. "Potential for Career Growth." *Personnel Administration*, 34, No. 3 (1971), 16-29.

Organizations can deal with the "syndrome of unused potential" and establish a positive success cycle for employees by providing initially challenging job assignments, developing a sense of "supportive autonomy", creating a work planning and review program, matching individual and organizational goals, and clarifying the performance which is expected/rewarded.

622. Hall, Douglas T., and Francine S. Hall. "What's New in Career Management." *Organizational Dynamics*, 5, No. 1 (1976), 17-33.

Reviews three human resource management problems and offers solutions: (1) Problem: Reducing turnover among new employees. Solutions: challenging first jobs, job enrichment, realistic job previews, assigning new recruit to demanding boss. (2) Problem: How to quickly develop potential candidates for top positions. Solutions: assessment centers, job pathing, in-service training. (3) Problems: What to do about promotion in a stable or contracting organization. Solutions: cross-functional moves, fallback positions, downward transfers, corporate tenure.

623. Hall, Francine S. "Gaining EEO Compliance With a Stable Work Force." *Personnel Journal*, 56, No. 9 (1977), 454-457.

Discusses three problem areas organizations encounter when they try to implement EEO with the existing work force: career track barriers, resistance among minorities and women, and attitudinal barriers.

624. Haskell, M.A. *The New Careers Concept: Potential for Public Employment of the Poor*. New York: Praeger, 1969.

Examines labor supply and demand factors in the health field and in the municipal hospital system to explain the reasons for persistent vacancies in both skilled and professional positions. The "new careers" concept is set forth and related to the health services area. Three recommendations are presented: (1) redesign jobs--break complex tasks into simpler ones; (2) create job ladders--enable individuals to "move up" into increasingly better jobs depending on their abilities and skills; and (3) increase on-the-job training.

625. Jongeward, Dorothy, and Dru Scott. *Affirmative Action for Women*. Reading, Mass.: Addison-Wesley, 1977.

Contains 13 essays which describe courses of action organizations could take to implement affirmative action programs for women. Included among the selections are essays interpreting laws affecting organizations and women; the problems of black women employees; counseling services for women; and the place of women in government service and organized religion. The obstacles to women in management are discussed and a strategy for change is presented.

626. Kay, Janice. "Career Development for Women: An Affirmative Action First." *Training and Development Journal*, 30, No. 5 (1976), 22-24.

Suggests the State of Washington's pilot project of career development for women as a model program. The steps involved in setting up the programs are discussed along with program objectives, course content, and trainer's sessions. Results will be determined based on the number of women in government who advance to managerial positions.

627. Kay, M. Jane. "Career Women: The 'Revolting Minority'." *The Personnel Administrator*, 15, No. 1 (1970), 3-6.

Discusses the current status of women, their career opportunities, and the liklihood of their achieving equality. Personnel managers have an important role to play in removing barriers of equal opportunity and insuring that all employees receive rewards commensurate with their contributions. The author considers the implications for the role of management, personnel administration, and career women of changes in workforce composition, organizational structures, and leadership styles.

628. Kellog, Marion S. *Career Management*. New York: American Management Association, 1972.

Describes and recommends improvements in career advancement systems and provides proposals for joint employee-management decision making in the promotion process. The author examines the individual's role and the manager's role in career management. Individual chapters are devoted to the unique career development needs of four categories of workers: young, women, minority professionals, and senior employees. Final chapters provide real-world applications of concepts with cases, and consideration of a manager training program, and a sample career discussion between manager and employee.

629. Kirkhart, Larry, and Neely Gardner. "Symposium on Organizational Development." *Public Administration Review*, 34, No. 2 (1974), 97-140.

This five-article symposium on OD includes: (1) a summary of events, theories, and circumstances pre-dating the emergence of OD as a field; (2) a description of action research and training; (3) an argument for human resource development as a component of OD; (4) an explanation of how training enables people to develop the ability to facilitate team development programs; and (5) an exploration of the potential and limitations of OD as a theory and practice of social change. The articles show where the field of OD has been, summarize new developments, and point out future directions.

630. Koehn, Hank E. "Attitude: Success Element for Women in Business." *Journal of Systems Management*, 27, No. 3 (1976), 12-15.

The advancement of women into management is challenging to the attitudes of both women and men. The author proposes a management development program where both sexes can learn about the changing attitudes, roles, and expectations of the other. Such a program should help women by (1) exposing stereotypes, (2) illuminating irrelevant sex qualifications, (3) insuring objective performance goals, (4) developing team building skills, (5) assisting with career planning, (6) training in conflict management, and (7) emphasizing understanding of corporate structure.

631. Landau, Samuel B., and Gerald S. Leventhal. "A Simulation Study of Administrators' Behavior Toward Employees Who Receive Job Offers." *Journal of Applied Social Psychology*, 6, No. 4 (1976), 291-306.

Examines factors affecting an administrator's pay allocation to an employee who has received a job offer from another firm. Variables affecting an administrator's counter offer were thought to include the employee's productivity, the attractiveness of the job offer, organizational personnel policies, and the administrator's sex. The authors acknowledge several limitations of the study which restrict the generalizability of results.

632. Lee Dore, Russell. "The Colleges." *Training and Development Journal*, 22, No. 8 (1968), 20-24.

What are colleges doing to prepare students for a business career? Two comprehensive studies of business education, one financed by the Ford Foundation and the other by the Carnegie Foundation are discussed with emphasis on what the effectiveness of business education is likely to be after the studies' recommendations have been implemented.

633. Loeb, Stephen E., and Martin J. Gannon. "Educational Factors, Professional Activity, and Job Tenure Among Public Accountants." *Journal of Accountancy*, 141, No. 4 (1976), 88-89.

Reports results of a study of educational factors and professional activities as they relate to employee turnover in national CPA firms. The authors suggest policy implications for personnel strategies.

634. March, James C., and James G. March. "Performance Sampling in Social Matches." *Administrative Science Quarterly*, 23, No. 3 (1978), 434-453.

Views the match between jobholders and jobs as a voluntary social pairing. A general performance sampling model is elaborated, and its utility in understanding careers in organizations is discussed. The authors show how a system of careers might evolve from decisions regarding job exits, and they connect a theory of organizational careers with theories of other social pairings.

635. Margulies, Newton. "Organizational Development and Changes in Organizational Climate." *Public Personnel Management*, 2, No. 2 (1973), 84-93.

Examines the results of monitoring the effects of an OD program over time on organizational climate. The author shows how OD can be used to alter an organization's less open, restrictive culture to produce a more open and functional culture. He reports data at various time intervals: before the OD program, after six months, and after 12 months. OD is a gradual process, requiring commitment from top management if it is to succeed.

636. McCord, Bird. "Identifying and Developing Women for Management Positions." *Training and Development Journal*, 25, No. 11 (1971), 2-5.

The success of women in managerial positions depends upon organizational attitudes and effective development programs. The author identifies factors contributing to underrepresentation of women in management; analyzes early career and college training opportunities for women; and discusses selection, promotion, and training policies in relation to women's entry into managerial positions.

637. McEwan, Bruce. "Professionalizing the Workforce." *SAM Advanced Management Journal*, 46, No. 1 (1981), 53-58.

   Distinguishes between job-oriented employees and career-oriented employees and shows how management can create a motivated workforce which performs at the top of its potential by following a four step career-oriented approach to employee development.

638. Miller, Delbert C., and William H. Form. *Industrial Sociology*. New York: Harper and Brothers, 1951.

   Surveys the field of industrial and occupational sociology. The authors trace the rise and scope of industrial sociology; examine the social organization of the work plant; consider the problems in the workplace and the social adjustment of workers; and explore the relationships of industry, community, and society.

639. Mirides, Ellyn, and Andre Cote. "Women in Management: Strategies for Removing the Barriers." *Personnel Administrator*, 25, No. 4 (1980), 25-28; 48.

   Assesses the status of women in management. After reviewing sex-role stereotyping and other organizational barriers which complicate women's advancement to management, the authors stress the need for current managers to confront their biases and examine their behavior through role playing, seminars, and other participatory exercises. A workplace climate supporting equality for all is needed, if effective women managers are to be developed.

640. Murray, Thomas J. "The Coming Glut in Executives." *Dun's Review*, 109, No. 5 (1977), 64-65; 69.

   With the post-war baby boom and the assembly line production of MBAs we will witness a large surplus of management talent in the next ten years. Patterns of recruitment, compensation, and executive career development will be affected by this "glut" of executives.

641. Ott, Fred L. "Creating Successful Career Development Programs." *Training and Development Journal*, 36, No. 2 (1982), 30-37.

   Employee-assistance personnel (e.g., those helping "troubled employees" deal with drug and alchohol problems) can be an important source of creative ideas for career development personnel.

642. Patton, Arch. "The Boom in Executive Self Interest."
     Business Week, No. 2433 (1976), 16-20.

   Executive self interest is a growing problem since executives in expanding companies are committed first to their specialties, and they question corporate decisions in light of their own interests. As the old loyalties decline young executives may soon form unions that will speak for their career interests and engage in collective bargaining.

643. Patton, Arch. "The Coming Flood of New Executives."
     Harvard Business Review, 54, No. 5 (1976), 20-38.

   Managing executive talent is made more difficult with the surplus of young people entering the job market. Maintaining a high quality staff will not be easy when chances for promotion are slim, starting salaries decrease, and self interest becomes more important to young people than company loyalty. To cope with these challenges managers need to rethink their motivation, compensation, and promotion policies.

644. Perham, John C. "Coming: the Great Executive Exodus."
     Dun's Review, 102, No. 5 (1973), 53-57.

   Middle managers have been hurt by tighter compensation controls. Managerial mobility has been extremely high and may increase with earlier vesting of pension rights. Companies need to devise strategies to hold on to valued executives.

645. Presthus, Robert. "Decline of the Generalist Myth."
     Public Administration Review, 24, No. 4 (1964), 211-216.

   Challenges conceptions of the generalist administrator, emphasizing the inadequacy of generalists in making the sophisticated fiscal decisions necessary in the contemporary industrial state. The British administrative class, who are influenced in their performance and attitudes by traditional education and motivation, are characterized by the author as technically innocent, resistent to scientific management approaches, and casual in their attitude toward research. The generalist myth should be modified, in the author's view, to allow for an equal partnership between amateur-generalists and specialist-experts.

646. Roff, Harry. "Britain's Management Squeeze." *Management Today*, June (1977), 59-61, 129.

Many British companies have overqualified executives because responsibilities to high level jobs have been decreasing at the same time candidates for managerial positions have become increasingly more qualified. Simultaneously, the managerial role is changing from exclusive preoccupation with a company's profit performance to concern also for the managers acceptance by employees, the community, and government. Managerial concerns now involve concerns other than work, such as leisure time and family life.

647. Sarachek, Bernard. "Career Concerns of Black Managers." *Management Review*, 63, No. 10 (1974), 17-24.

    Top management must be aware of the special needs and motivations of blacks who are entering managment's ranks. Management policies need to insure equity in career development, discover ways by which management talent can be recognized and developed, and provide opportunities for both job rotation and sponsorship for would-be black managers.

648. Sasser, W. Earl, Jr., and Frank S. Leonard. "Let 1st-Level Supervisors Do Their Job." *Harvard Business Review*, 58, No. 2 (1980), 113-121.

    First line supervisors have to perform delicate balancing act responding to the demands of management, the demands of unions, and the demands of workers while completing the tasks at hand. In performing this precarious balancing act, supervisors risk losing their sense of identity. Too frequently supervisors have responsibility without commensurate authority. Higher level managers should allow supervisors to exercise the influence inherent in their positions.

649. Schein, Edgar H. "How to Break in the College Graduate." *Harvard Business Review*, 42, No. 6 (1964), 68-76.

    The needs and expectations of college graduates often fail to coincide with the needs and expectations of organizations. This can lead to a self-defeating pattern. The author suggests that careful selection and training of supervisors for new college graduates will help alleviate this problem.

650. Schein, Edgar H. "The Individual, the Organization, and a Career: A Conceptual Scheme." *The Journal of Applied Behavioral Science*, 7, No. 2 (1971), 401-426.

Career Management--General

Presents a set of concepts concerning the nature of the individual, the organization, and the career. The author introduces concepts which will aid empirical researchers in relating the "career" variable to organizational and psychological variables. The concepts include career stages, labile and stable "social selves", transitional processes, and "organizational boundaries". Hypotheses are generated about individual influences on the organization and about organizational influences on the individual.

651. Schein, Edgar H. *Career Dynamics: Matching Individual and Organizational Needs.* Reading, Mass.: Addison-Wesley, 1978.

    Explores career development and human resource planning as crucial individual and organizational improvement programs. The book is divided into three parts: (1) the individual and the life cycle, (2) the individual-organization interaction, and (3) managing human resource planning and development (HRPD). In this latter section, a useful model of a total HRPD system is presented and discussed. A Career Anchor Self Analysis Form is included in the appendix.

652. Scott, William A. "Career Management A Career?" *The Personnel Administrator*, 14, No. 1 (1969), 23-26.

    The enterprising personnelist may wish to make a career of career management. The author describes the planning and implementation of a career management program designed for the Defense Contract Audit Agency. The components of the program are outlined (e.g., career progression plan, training and development plan, performance standards, performance appraisal) and the implications for personnel managers and nonpersonnelists are considered.

653. Seybolt, John W. "Career Development: The State of the Art Among the Grassroots." *Training and Development Journal*, 33, No. 4 (1979), 16-20.

    Seeks to discover whether practitioners are in tune with trends in career development found in the literature by surveying the 59 largest employers in a western metropolitan area of 500,000. Conclusions are that formal career development programs are not pervasive among their employers. Management researchers need to speed up the diffusion-of-innovation process by making visible the benefits of career development to practitioners.

654. Sneath, Frank. "Keeping Up With Organizational Change." *Personnel Management*, 6, No. 1 (1974), 44-48.

Discusses ways the personnel manager might respond during periods of rapid organizational change. Too often the personnelist is frustrated by organizational turbulence because of insufficient influence with top management or inadequate techniques. Personnelists need to be aware of recent advances in group methods, counseling, career development, analytic and diagnostic techniques, and they need to be able to improvise as conditions change.

655. Tsaklanganos, Angelos A. "Sabbaticals for Executives." *Personnel Journal*, 52, No. 5 (1973), 363-366.

Extended leaves of absence for executives have become more commonplace. This article presents arguments in favor of sabbaticals from both the executive and the industry viewpoints. Elegibility factors and suggestions for what to do during sabbaticals are discussed.

656. Van Maanen, John. ed. *Organizational Careers: Some New Perspectives*. New York: John Wiley and Sons, 1977.

An edited book of essays, mostly based on original research, written by authors associated with the Sloan School of Management at M.I.T. The book is divided into three parts: (1) the meaning of careers and socialization, (2) understanding organizational careers and individual differences, and (3) the individual's orientation toward work across a career. The chapters stress both psychological and sociological perspectives and address four distinct issues: "contemporary value shifts, alienation from work, organizational effectiveness, and adult development." (p. 163)

657. York, Reginald O. *The Association of Managerial Style and Worker Job Change Receptivity in Varying Situations*. Diss., Tulane Univ., 1973.

Explores whether there is an identifiable managerial style that is uniformly effective in leadership situations that vary in task structure and group atmosphere. The study concludes that worker job change activity is not significantly associated with the managerial style of the line supervisor, the atmosphere of the work unit, or the task structure of the work position.

Career Management--General

658. Walker, James W. "Human Resource Planning: Managerial Concerns and Practices." *Business Horizons*, 19, No. 3 (1976), 55-59.

   Managers today are concerned about human resource planning practices that are practical, job-related actions likely to yield visible results. Job performance is likely to improve by clarifying the work required for each corporate position, providing well-conceived training for employees, and developing relevant performance appraisals.

659. Walters, Roy H. "How to Develop Managers for the Future--A Systems Approach." *Personnel Administrator*, 25, No. 8 (1980), 42-52.

   Presents a systems model which integrates the functions of manpower planning, recruitment, initial training and development, and monitoring/appraising performance. If these four functions are properly developed and well implemented, they will give any organization an adequate supply of high quality managerial talent.

660. Williams, Cortez H. "Employing the Black Administrator." *Public Personnel Management*, 4, No. 2 (1975), 76-83.

   Black administrators in the United States find a limited number of corporate and government jobs available and face constraints on their mobility. They are likely to encounter a wide diversity of socio-political administrative problems which are inadequately addressed in business and public administration schools. These problem areas are discussed along with employers' reactions to black administrators, blacks in top-level government jobs, training of black administrators, and federal EEO/AA laws.

661. Wolff, Michael F. "Companies and Careers." *Research Management*, 23, No. 4 (1980), 8-9.

   The President of Bell Northern Research responds to eight questions concerning career management of research professionals. Among the issues covered are performance appraisal, dual ladder approaches to career planning, performance and the "average person," and outplacement.

662. Zaleznik, Abraham, Manfred F.R. Kets de Vries, and John H. Holland. "Stress Reactions in Organizations: Syndromes, Causes, and Consequences." *Behavioral Science*, 22, No. 3 (1977), 151-162.

Examines stress reactions of 2,000 high status employees in a large Canadian organization. Stress symptoms were analyzed across three groups--operations, staff, and management. Results show the management group to be relatively free of stress symptoms. Differences among groups were explained largely in terms of bureaucratic role and power which helped the management group avoid or minimize organizational stress.

19

ORGANIZATIONAL CAREER PLANNING

663. Bowen, Donald D., and Douglas T. Hall. "Career Planning for Employee Development." *California Management Review*, 20, No. 2 (1977), 23-35.

    Reviews behavioral science research and theory on career planning, describes alternative career planning techniques, and assesses each technique in light of research and theory. A comparison of do-it-yourself approaches, counseling or coaching options, and career planning workshops, leads the authors to favor workshops. A useful chart listing the characteristics of various career planning activities and the probable contribution of each to career success is appended.

664. Drossel, Margaret. "How Syntax Helps Its Professionals Plan their Careers." *Management Review*, 63, No. 10 (1974), 55-56.

    Syntax Corporation's Career Development Center encourages management candidates to set their own goals and plan their own careers. The Center's staff makes a diagnosis of management candidates by measuring behavioral traits in eight skill areas considered crucial to effective managerial performance. This is done at a series of week-long seminars. These "diagnoses" become the basis for an action plan which candidates can follow to overcome their weaknesses and strengthen their assets.

665. Feldman, Howard S., and Robert P. Marinelli. "Career Planning for Prison Inmates." *Vocational Guidance Quarterly*, 23, No. 4 (1975), 358-362.

    Tests the hypothesis that a career planning experience for a prison inmate population would be useful in raising their vocational maturity. The sample included 90 inmates in a Massachusetts prison facility. The Vocational Development Inventory (VDI) was used as a measure of vocational maturity. Results show that VDI scores for those exposed to a short, individualized vocational training program were significantly higher than for two comparable groups that did not have treatment.

666. Jones, William S. "The Manager's Role in Developmental Planning." *Training and Development Journal*, 30, No. 7 (1976), 3-9.

Managers should follow three key steps in helping people develop: (1) introduce realism into career goals, (2) write a developmental plan which builds upon strengths, and (3) provide emotional support and remove organizational roadblocks.

667. Kaye, Beverly L. "Crystallizing Career Goals." *Supervision*, 42, No. 9 (1980), 10-14.

Describes the role of a manager in helping subordinates to formulate career goals. Career goals should be specific, time-bound, measurable, publicly stated, and relevant to both the employee and organizational needs.

668. Klingner, Donald E. "Career-Life Planning and Development Management." *Public Personnel Management*, 8, No. 6 (1979), 382-390.

Examines three questions related to career-life planning: (1) What is its theoretical base? (2) What techniques are used in career planning approaches? and (3) What factors are critical to success and failure? Two aspects of career planning--a model career pattern and an individual development plan--are included as illustrations. The author concludes that pressure for career-life planning will continue as personnel managers attempt to match employee expectations for personal growth with employers' need for increased organizational productivity.

669. Leider, Richard J. "Emphasizing Career Planning in Human Resource Management." *The Personnel Administrator*, 18, No. 2 (1973), 35-38.

Career planning programs are based on the premise that the employee who knows where he/she is going and how to get there can better harness energy to accomplish both individual and organizational goals. Management has the responsibility to design challenging career opportunities and to communicate information on career opportunities in the organization. A systematic approach to career planning might include three elements: personal growth and career planning workshops, communication of career information, and a manpower information or planning system.

670. Lippitt, Gordon L. "Developing Life Plans." *Training and Development Journal*, 24, No. 5 (1970), 2-7.

   Organizations should help employees examine their life goals and plans as a means of achieving an individual's potential. Organizational training and development personnel should make available individual and group experiences which will help employees to review, evaluate, and examine their life plans. This article examines how their goals are to be achieved and the reasons why organizations should initiate such efforts.

671. Lippitt, Gordon L. "Developing Life Plans." *Training and Development Journal*, 33, No. 6 (1979), 102-108.

   Organizational training and development specialists should make available individual and group experiences designed to assist employees in reviewing, evaluating, and organizing their life plans. Examples of goals, assumptions, and methods to be used in implementing life planning programs are presented with specific activities and cases provided as illustrations. The problems and potentials associated with this new approach to training and development are analyzed.

672. Lopez, Felix E, B. Wayne Rockmore, and Gerald A. Kesselman. "The Development of an Integrated Career Planning Program at Gulf Power Company." *Personnel Administrator*, 25, No. 10 (1980), 21-29.

   Effective career planning programs are built on a foundation of extensive job analysis and sound performance evaluation. The career planning program at Gulf Power Company is described with special attention given to such tools as career plan matrix, job libraries, self-assessment techniques, job analysis, and performance evaluation which assist employees in making appropriate career planning decisions.

673. Montana, Patrick J. "Implementing a Career Life Planning Program." *Personnel*, 56, No. 5 (1979), 66-72.

   A growing responsibility of the human resource manager is the provision of career life planning services. This case study describes a program that can be adapted to either the private or public sector. The setting for the case is the U.S. Department of Labor, which developed a career life planning program for individuals with high potential. The author describes how the program started and methods of implementation. Examples of career planning forms are provided. The author concludes that the success of career programs depends upon the climate, attitudes, and efforts of top management.

674. Moore, Lynda L. "From Manpower Planning to Human Resources Planning Through Career Development." *Personnel*, 56, No. 3 (1979), 9-17.

Traces traditional approaches to manpower planning and more recent pressures for career planning. Moore outlines four basic techniques for career planning (workshops, one-on-one counseling, self-assessment and planning workshops, and communication of job opportunities) and identifies six elements of good programs (clear objectives and responsibilities, confidentiality of information, voluntary participation, performance appraisal and feedback, specification of the organization's responsibility, and audit against objectives).

675. Moravec, Milan. "A Cost-Effective Career Planning Program Requires a Strategy." *Personnel Administrator*, 27, No. 1 (1982), 28-32.

Discusses the steps organizational leaders should follow in implementing a top-down system for career planning. Fifteen key questions are raised and answered as a guide to designing and implementing an effective career planning system.

676. Nemec, Margaret M. "Networking: Here's How at Equitable." *Personnel Administrator*, 25, No. 4 (1980), 63-64.

The Vice President and Personnel Director at Equitable Life Assurance describes the benefits derived from involvement in networking. In this case a small women's discussion group expanded rapidly into a 500-member network for men and women concerned about career planning.

677. Schalders, William N. "Developing an In-House Career Planning Workshop." *Personnel Administrator*, 25, No. 10 (1980), 45-48.

Describes an in-house pilot career planning workshop designed to help employees identify career objectives, to improve the success of an internal promotion system, and to increase employee's use of management skills. The author describes the workshop which was conducted in nine weekly two-hour sessions after working hours for 12 participants. The sessions covered knowledge of the work environment, self-management skills, self-directed processes for planning career and life goals, career paths, career transition, and matching individual goals with organizational goals.

678. Schein, Edgar H. "Increasing Organizational Effectiveness Through Better Human Resource Planning and Development." *Sloan Management Review*, 19, No. 1 (1977), 1-21.

   Examines the role of human resource planning as a determinant of organizational effectiveness and discusses the major components of a human resource planning and career development system. The author stresses the increasing importance of the human element to organizations which adds significance to the personnel manager's job. A conceptual framework for human resource planning is provided and a link with career/life planning is established by showing how organizations can better meet both employee needs and organizational goals.

679. Schwartz, Irving R. "Self-Assessment and Career Planning: Matching Individual and Organizational Goals." *Personnel*, 56, No. 1 (1979), 47-53.

   Self-assessment workshops are a component of career planning. The author organizes factors of career success into four domains: personal resources, work-related needs, values and life goals, and marketplace alternatives. These domains can be used as a checklist of criteria for job satisfaction. He outlines a procedure whereby workshop participants identify their skills and interests, convert these into career themes and job objectives, and test these possibilities on the job or in the job market. An integrated model is presented linking organizational development and career development.

680. Walker, James W. "Individual Career Planning: Managerial Help for Subordinates." *Business Horizons*, 16, No. 1 (1973), 65-72.

   Management needs to do more systematic human resource planning in relation to individual career planning. The career planning process involves occupational/organizational choice, job assignment, performance and development, and retirement. The author offers guidelines to managers for influencing the career planning process.

681. Walker, James W. "Does Career Planning Rock the Boat?" *Human Resource Management*, 17, No. 1 (1978), 2-7.

   Discusses the meaning of career planning, the risks associated with it, strategies for developing realistic employee expectations, and both the positive and negative results of career planning. Company programs can avoid "rocking the boat" by encouraging an "intensive, voluntary, recurring, self-directed process of self-examination." (p. 5) The author outlines a step-by-step approach for implementing a corporate career planning program.

682. Yeager, Joseph C., and Richard J. Leider. "Career Planning: Personnel in the Third Party Role." *Human Resource Management*, 14, No. 1 (1975), 31-35.

   A coherent approach to the delivery of individual career planning has not been implemented on a significant scale. The author discusses the form and substance a career development program would take in modern organizations and outlines the third party role personnel departments could play. Four challenges in the career planning function are: women, minorities, youth, and older workers.

683. Zenger, John H. "Career Planning: Coming in From the Cold." *Training and Development Journal*, 35, No. 7 (1981), 47-52.

   Describes the forces supporting and deterring career planning. The philosophy underlying career planning is considered and both the organizations' and the individuals' responsibilities for career planning are outlined. Managers need to help clarify roles and responsibilities, acquire career discussion skills, and link career planning to the realities of the organization.

ORGANIZATIONAL CAREER DEVELOPMENT

684. Ackerman, Leonard. "Career Development: Preparing Round Pegs for Square Holes." *Training and Development Journal*, 30, No. 2 (1976), 12-14.

    Summarizes the author's misgivings about the underlying philosophy and effectiveness of career development programs. He questions whether we know what skills, experiences, and knowledge will need to be developed. A restructuring of the whole developmental process is needed. Formalized training and education should be restricted to current jobs and possibly for the next job an individual will fill, instead of training for jobs to be filled in the distant future.

685. Bellas, Carl J. "The Dual Track Career System Within the Internal Revenue Service." *Public Personnel Review*, 3, No. 2 (1972), 4-8.

    In 1971, the technical organization of the IRS created the first dual track career system in the federal government. The system was designed to retain valuable technical employees and increase the managerial capabilities of those in supervisory/managerial positions. This article outlines the three phases in the technical career system. The system provides technically qualified supervisors to direct qualified employees and allows advanced technicians to retain such professional components of their job as influence, responsibility, and autonomy.

686. Britten, Robert H. "Unmasking the Career Development Bogeymen." *Personnel Administration*, 24, No. 1 (1961), 33-37; 41.

    Discusses the confusing terminology and air of defeatism associated with career development. The author argues that career development is a "bogeyman" to top management because personnel officials have failed to communicate and demonstrate to top management that it is a worthwhile program. More scientific research is needed as the basis for programs and policies of career development.

687. Connors, John F. "Where Are the Leaders?" *Training and Development Journal*, 30, No. 7 (1976), 10-11.

    Human resource specialists are realizing too few results in their efforts to develop effective leaders for our institutions. Manager and executive development efforts should produce leaders who substantially change the direction, the nature, or the character of organizations.

688. Cook, David R. "Improving Employee Development Programs." *The Personnel Administrator*, 23, No. 7 (1978), 38-42.

    Establishes the need for employee development programs and describes a method for accomplishing long-term objectives and personnel development. Three steps to employee development are outlined: identifying needed skills, analyzing employee skills compared with skills needed, and selecting methods of developing skills. The importance of the employee's participation in implementation is stressed, along with the need for continuous monitoring and evaluation of progress.

689. Cooper, Lloyd G. "HRD--A Professional Manifesto." *Training and Development Journal*, 29, No. 9 (1975), 24-26.

    Lists nine responsibilities of the HRD professional pertaining to career development.

690. Dittrich, John E., and Donald S. Shannon. "Manpower Development." *Management Accounting*, 57, No. 4 (1975), 29-32.

    Describes a manpower development system developed around a Career Development Plan for individual staff members and designed to meet both the employee's career educational needs and the organization's skill requirements.

691. Earwood, Larry. "Employee Satisfaction Through Career Development." *The Personnel Administrator*, 24, No. 8 (1979), 41-42.

    The Singer manufacturing facility in Anderson, South Carolina, provides opportunities for advancement through a "Job Bidding Program". Top management recognized the need to let employees choose the job and gain the training/education required to qualify for the job. The author briefly spells out the guidelines used in the program--including the forms, counseling sessions, and training log sheets--which help insure trained employees fill future vacancies, personal growth for employees, and opportunities for employees to reach job fulfillment.

692. Fazel, Mohammed. "Taking the Mystery Out of Career Development." *Personnel*, 55, No. 2 (1978), 46-53.

Describes the career development activities of the internal audit division of a major bank. The head of the division facilitated employee development by: encouraging employees to work cooperatively on projects in a matrix organization, insuring task openness, providing continuous performance feedback, creating a buddy system, which paired experienced and unexperienced employees, using a team approach to performance appraisal, and implementing a philosophy of management which emphasized the upward mobility of subordinates.

693. Goodson, William D. "Status of Career Planning on College and University Campuses." *Vocational Guidance Quarterly*, 30, No. 3 (1982), 230-235.

Summarizes results of a survey of a sample of college and university career development programs. Six program elements are examined: career counseling, career workshops and seminars, interest inventories, career classes, other services, and evaluation.

694. Grass, Donald. "A Guide to R & D Career Pathing." *Personnel Journal*, 58, No. 4 (1979), 227-231.

Managers must pay more attention to the career development needs of technical professionals. R & D managers should analyze employee's R & D standing, motivational needs, and career stage as an aid in devising career development strategies, training programs, and future initiatives.

695. Guerrier, Yvonne, and Keith MacMillan. "Developing Managers in a Low Growth Organization." *Personnel Management*, 10, No. 12 (1978), 34-38.

Suggests ways of dealing with the absence of opportunity for job change in large corporations in ways that can also help smaller businesses. Several alternative strategies for career development are considered.

696. Haire, Mason. "Managing Management Manpower." *Business Horizons*, 10, No. 4 (1967), 23-28.

Addresses the problem of managerial career development by presenting a matrix including both the characteristics of personnel flow (moving in, out, up, over, and changing) and the optimal responsibilities of the company (recruitment, pay, training, etc.). This model for human resource

development can help management determine the probability
of movement in the organization and the ways in which
the input variables affect personnel flow.

697. Hanson, Marlys C. "Career Development Responsibilities
of Managers." *Personnel Journal*, 56, No. 9 (1977),
443-445.

Discusses theories of adult and career development and
describes how these theories have been used in management training.

698. Hastings, Robert E. "Career Development: Maximizing
Options." *The Personnel Administrator*, 23, No. 5 (1978),
58-61.

Cleveland Trust Bank's Personnel Department has devised
a comprehensive system of career assessment and development. The Bank offers career assessment workshops which
bring employees' interests, potential, and accomplishments into sharper focus. Career planning assistance,
counseling, career pathing, and outplacement services
are provided.

699. Hill, Alfred W. "Career Development: Who Is Responsible?"
Training and Development Journal, 33, No. 5 (1976),
14-15.

Management is responsible for developing and communicating its internal career options to employees and for
showing that there are many different career tracks
within the organization. The rest is up to the individual who has the ultimate responsibility for lifelong
learning and career development.

700. Leach, John J. "Career Development: Some Questions and
Tentative Answers." *Personnel Administrator*, 25, No.
10 (1980), 31-38.

Career development will be a major issue for personnelists in the 1980's. The author examines activities
in career management as they affect employee utilization, organizational effectiveness, improved productivity, and innovation levels. Among the questions considered
are: Why can't employers provide career satisfaction
for employees? Why can't employees better plan their
own careers? Why do people leave the firm? Why do
many career planning programs fail? What form will
new career planning programs take in the future?

701. Life Insurance Agency Management Association. "Career Guidance in the Life Insurance Industry." *Personnel Psychology*, 21, No. 1 (1968), 1-21.

   Describes the Career Analysis Procedure developed by the Life Insurance Agency Management Association to guide and develop promising men and women into the appropriate career path--sales management or career selling.

702. Lippitt, Gordon L. "Developing Professional Skills and Expertise." *Training and Development Journal*, 33, No. 5 (1979), 66-70.

   Presents and discusses the following 11 strategies for the professional development of training and HRD specialists: (1) getting feedback; (2) co-training; (3) documentation; (4) asking colleagues; (5) enrolling in learning opportunities; (6) membership and activity in professional organizations; (7) joining informal colleague groups; (8) personal self-development plans; (9) internship and sabbaticals; (10) consulting, moonlighting, and exchange of experience; (11) reading programs.

703. Marsh, P.J. "The Career Development Workshop." *Training and Development Journal*, 27, No. 7 (1973), 38-45.

   A career planning workshop for managers was designed to support and accelerate the process of individual development without organizational manipulation or coercion. The three student-centered learning objectives of workshops were: (1) improved self understanding and directing, (2) improved understanding of group and organizational dynamics, and (3) a working understanding of the developmental process. These workshops were geared to younger managers working in large operating units.

704. Moment, David. "Career Development: A Future Oriented Historical Approach." *Personnel Administration*, 30, No. 4 (1967), 6-11.

   Calls for a "future-oriented historical approach" to career development which goes beyond the customary question "How does this individual's life fit into the organization?" and asks "Where and how does this current work situation fit into the life cycle of the individual?" As employees experience change in their orientations towards work, training opportunities should be available in the dynamics of choice and individual responsibility to aid in coping with these changes. Career guidance should take into account emotional as well as intellectual factors affecting career choices.

705. Moment, David, and Dalmar Fisher. "Managerial Career Development and the Generational Confrontation." *California Management Review*, 15, No. 3 (1973), 46-55.

Discusses the manager's career development problems and contemporary approaches to managerial career development. The elements of an effective managerial career development program are: (1) deal with the individual's total life space; (2) concentrate on the middle level behavior alternatives; and (3) focused interaction on mutual career development. The dynamic approach outlined by the authors is intended to provide better personal integration in one's career.

706. Morgan, Marilyn, Douglas T. Hall, and Alison Martier. "Career Development Strategies in Industry: Where Are We and Where Should We Be?" *Personnel*, 56, No. 2 (1979), 13-31.

Explores the do's, don'ts, and state of the art in career development. Career programs are grouped into seven categories: career counseling, individual career planning, organizational human resources planning, career information systems, management/supervisory development, programs for special groups, and training. Within each category, career activities are discussed. The authors examine how career programs develop, issues and problems in career programs, and new directions in career development. The article outlines a sample one-day career planning workshop.

707. Palmer, W.J. "An Integrated Program for Career Development." *Personnel Journal*, 51, No. 6 (1972), 398-406; 451.

Systems which are designed to facilitate career development must be dynamic, financially sound, and an integrated part of the enterprise. Career development programs are most effective in a nurturing environment where qualified people can "grow" within their own interests and abilities. This can be accomplished by use of assessment programs, management replacement training, individual development plans, on-the-job training, job rotation, task force assignments, management development programs, and continuing education.

708. "Personnel Opinions: Elements of an Employee Development Program." *Public Personnel Review*, 31, No. 2 (1970), 134-137.

Three personnel practitioners respond to the question, "What are the elements of an employee development program?" The first stresses steps in the training process: specifying objectives, determining priorities, determining content, selecting techniques, administering training, and evaluating results. The second identifies elements of an employee development program: a full-time, enthusiastic training director; participation and commitment of middle and top-level executives; and a personnel system which dispenses rewards based on competence. The third discusses the change factors of risk vs. commitment as applied to the establishment of a new division of training.

709. Pilla, Barbara. "Women in Business." *Training and Development Journal*, 31, No. 11 (1977), 22-27.

    Describes Prudential Insurance Company's program in one satellite office--the Governmental Health Programs Office--to help women develop their talents and advance into managerial positions.

710. Portis, Bernard. "Career Development Requires Senior Executive Involvement/Management Initiative." *The Business Quarterly*, 43, No. 3 (1978), 9-12.

    Reports results of a survey of Canadian senior- and middle-managers concerning staffing, career planning, and management training. Career planning and management training were activities which respondents thought deserved greater attention in the future.

711. Rabinowitz, Samuel, and Douglas T. Hall. "Changing Correlates of Job Involvement in Three Career Stages." *Journal of Vocational Behavior*, 18, No. 2 (1981), 138-144.

    Examines the correlates of job involvement in the early, middle, and late career stages. Using perceptual data from 332 workers the authors found support for the hypothesis that "career stage moderated the relationship of job involvement and various situational, individual difference, and outcome measures." (p. 138)

712. Reardon, Robert C., Dorothy Domkowski, and Erwin Jackson. "Career Center Evaluation Methods: A Case Study." *Vocational Guidance Quarterly*, 29, No. 2 (1980), 150-158.

Describes and assesses the impact of the career center program and services offered within the Division of Student Affairs at Florida State University. The data-gathering methods used in the evaluation included user contacts, sign-in sheets, participant observation, client surveys, faculty awareness and utilization surveys, random interviewing, and case studies.

713. Rosenberg, De Anne. "Clearing the Way for the Growth of Women Subordinates." *Supervisory Management*, 21, No. 1 (1976), 9-12.

    Discusses five basic areas which management should consider to make sure that women subordinates have an equal chance for advancement. These include adopting results-oriented job descriptions, publicizing promotions and added responsibilities, developing career plans for each managerial training position, demanding good performance, and reevaluating managerial role models.

714. Ryan, T. Antoinette. "A Conceptual Model of Career Development." *Educational Technology*, 13, No. 6 (1973), 28-38.

    Presents a process model of career development which can be used to simulate real-life situations and generate delivery system models for specific settings and situations. The model helps organize and relate formal education (e.g., instruction, guidance, and administration) together with business, labor, industry, and community activities. The model gives a blueprint for planning, operating, and evaluating programs which affect career development.

715. Salvagno, Ralph G. "The Myths of Career Development." *Training and Development Journal*, 23, No. 3 (1969), 46-50.

    Career development myths are rooted in the disproportionate attention given to career program structure. Career development programs are the means for assisting individuals in the direction and progression of their occupational development. The stress of career development should be on stimulating gradual changes in on-the-job behavior and equipping the employee with the required knowledge about himself and reality.

716. Schoner, Bertram, and Thomas W. Harrel. "The Questionable Dual Ladder." *Personnel*, 42, No. 1 (1965), 53-59.

The dual ladder in theory seeks to make the technical and managerial routes to advancement equally rewarding. The authors examine differences in morale between managerial and technical personnel and assess the success of the dual ladder in giving equal recognition to both groups. Survey data were obtained from managers and engineers in one division of an electronics company. Results show high morale in both groups, but the dual ladder failed in its goal of granting equal pay and equal prestige for managers and technical personnel.

717. Weerts, Michael V. *Development of an Instrument to Assess Employer Sponsored Career Development Programs for Sub-Professional Employees.* Diss., Univ. of Northern Colorado, 1977.

    Identifies the practices/attitudes of major Colorado public/private employers toward career development of sub-professional employees; and presents a self-assessment questionnaire whereby employers can compare their practices to those of employers of comparable size and type of business.

718. Wellbank, Harry L., Douglas T. Hall, Marilyn A. Morgan, and W. Clay Hammer. "Planning Job Progression for Effective Career Development and Human Resource Management." *Personnel*, 55, No. 2 (1978), 54-65.

    Describes the Sears Roebuck method of job-based career development which seeks to link individual career planning with corporate human resource planning. By means of a job-progression development program Sears executives seek to identify: "paths" and "fast tracks" to target jobs; lateral and downward moves; sequencing of job assignments; training needs; and "people pools" for vacant positions. Job posting is one way to provide information about job progression.

719. Wintersheid, Beverly. "A Career Development System Coordinates Training Efforts." *Personnel Administrator*, 25, No. 8 (1980), 29-33.

    A career development system can help coordinate training efforts so that training is tied to individual career progression in the organization, individual career development is related to human resource needs of the organization, and the training budget is justified in light of the performance of the organization. The elements of a career development system are described and the relationship of the career development systems to existing programs is explained.

720. Wnuk, Joseph J. "Career Paths." *Training and Development Journal*, 24, No. 5 (1970), 38-40.

One possibility for dealing with the "people problem" in organizations is a career path program. The author defines career paths, specifies advantages of career paths, discusses implementation steps in establishing a career path program, and distinguishes career pathing with manpower planning.

ORGANIZATIONAL ENTRY

721. Becker, Howard S. "Personal Change in Adult Life." *Sociometry*, 27, No. 1 (1964), 40-53.

    Examines the processes of adult socialization in organizations by focusing on two processes: (1) "situational adjustment"--a process whereby adult roles are learned and the nature of the situation explains why people change as they do; and (2) "commitment"--a process whereby committed persons pursue "a consistent line of activity in a sequence of varied situations" and the "consistent activity persists over time." (p. 49) The relationship between these two processes is analyzed.

722. Becker, Howard S., and Anselm L. Strauss. "Career, Personality, and Adult Socialization." *American Journal of Sociology*, 57, No. 3 (1956), 253-263.

    Analyzes the thesis that "adult identity is largely a function of career movements within occupations and work organizations" (p. 253) by examining different facets of careers (e.g., recruitment, replacement) as they relate to institutions and to persons. The author emphasizes the importance of adult socialization when considering both the link between career advancement and informal learning and the connection between status passage and psychological stress.

723. Berlew, David E., and Douglas T. Hall. "The Socialization of Managers: Effects of Expectations on Performance." *Administrative Science Quarterly*, 11, No. 2 (1966), 207-223.

    Examines the effect of a company's initial expectations for young managers upon their eventual performance and success. The authors predicted and found first-year job challenge to be correlated strongly with subsequent performance and success. An organizational socialization model is presented.

724. Buchanan, Bruce 11. "Building Organizational Commitment: The Socialization of Managers in Work Organizations." *Administrative Science Quarterly*, 19, No. 4 (1974), 533-546.

   Identifies organizational experiences which have the greatest impact on managers' organizational commitment and discovers how the significance of such experiences vary with organizational tenure.

725. David, Harry. "Talent Scout for the Executive Suite." *Nation's Business*, 66, No. 9 (1978), 85-90.

   The President of H.D. Associates, a talent-search firm, discusses the basic principles used in filling key slots for companies, trade associations, and unions.

726. Evan, William M. "Peer Group Interaction and Organizational Socialization: A Study of Employee Turnover." *American Sociological Review*, 28, No. 3 (1963), 436-440.

   Tests the hypotheses that (1) the formation of peer group bonds is a necessary condition for successful organizational socialization, and (2) that the level of peer group interaction is negatively associated with the level of turnover. Results generally support the hypotheses.

727. "Executive Mobility." *Business Week*, No. 2432 (1976), 56-62.

   As the economy expands, professional recruiters are being employed by companies to fill top management vacancies. The pros and cons of using search firms vs. do-it-yourself recruiting are examined. The cross-fertilization associated with accelerated executive mobility benefits both the company and the executives.

728. Faulkner, Robert R. "Coming of Age in Organizations: A Comparative Study of Career Contingencies and Adult Socialization." *Sociology of Work and Occupations*, 1, No. 2 (1974), 131-139.

   Explains the importance of age-grading and age-related features in analyzing the contingencies impeding or facilitating interorganizational mobility, using data from interviews and official records. The personal and structural mechanisms for sustaining the motivation and commitment of second-level participants in two hierarchical work organizations are examined by focusing on career patterns in symphony orchestras and professional hockey. A feature of career socialization identified by the author is the management of mollification.

729. Feldman, Daniel C. "A Practical Program for Employee Socialization." *Organizational Dynamics*, 5, No. 2 (1976), 64-80.

 Surveys 118 community hospital employees to identify the indicators of positive socialization experiences, the impacts of socialization programs, the practices employers can follow at various stages of socialization, and the implications for the design of socialization programs. Among the recommended organizational practices are: informing recruits about the work group and reward structures, providing frequent feedback at the "break-in" stage, offering counseling at the "settling-in" stage, helping employees cope with home-work conflicts, using flexible scheduling, and matching individual needs with job demands.

730. Fukami, Cynthia G. *The Development of Organizational Identification in Professional Members of a Professional Organization: A Developmental Career Stage Approach*. Diss., Northwestern Univ., 1979.

 Investigates organization identification in a professional organization. A three-stage longitudinal model of career development (early, advancement, and maintenance) is presented. The study hypothesized that within each stage organizational identification would be positively related to the extent to which the needs of that stage have been satisfied. Results of the investigation were mixed.

731. Guion, Robert M., and Richard F. Gottier. "Validity of Personality Measures in Personnel Selection." *Personnel Psychology*, 18, No. 2 (1965), 135-164.

 Summarizes a sampling of research studies on the validities of personality tests for industrial use. The author's conclude that there is "no generalizable evidence that personality measures can be recommended as good or practical tools for employee selection." (p. 159)

732. Hall, Douglas T. "A Theoretical Model of Career Subidentity Development in Organizational Settings." *Organizational Behavior and Human Performance*, 6, No. 1 (1971), 50-76.

Describes a model which focuses on career identity changes occuring after a person has entered an occupation. This psychological success model sees growth in career commitment as a series of cycles of challenging goal setting, independent effort, success, subidentity growth, and increased career self-esteem and motivation, leading to additional goal setting.

733. Hall, Douglas T., and Benjamin Schneider. "Correlates of Organizational Identification as a Function of Career Pattern and Organizational Type." *Administrative Science Quarterly*, 17, No. 3 (1972), 340-350.

    Two types of organizations--the Roman Catholic Church and research and development laboratories--provide the settings to examine personal and organizational correlates of organizational identification. Comparing the results with those obtained in an earlier study of the U.S. Forest Service, the authors report that priests and foresters typically spend their entire career in a single organization (the single organization career pattern), while research professionals are more mobile (the multi-organization career pattern). The correlates of these career patterns are reported.

734. Hall, Douglas T., Benjamin Schneider, and Harold T. Nygren. "Personal Factors in Organizational Identification." *Administrative Science Quarterly*, 15, No. 2 (1970), 176-190.

    Examines the personal factors associated with organizational identification in the U.S. Forest Service. It is hypothesized and found that identification increased as a function of time and commitment to public service and that identification is related to the member's higher-order needs. The authors discuss the relationships of service orientation, organizational identification, and need satisfaction.

735. Hedland, Delva. "A Review of the MMPI in Industry." *Psychological Reports*, 17, No. 3 (1965), 875-889.

    Presents evidence critical of the industrial uses of the MMPI emphasizing the scarcity of validity studies on this test.

736. Ilgen, Daniel R., and William Seely. "Realistic Expectations as an Aid in Reducing Voluntary Resignations." *Journal of Applied Psychology*, 59, No. 4 (1974), 452-455.

Summarizes the results of a study in which new organizational members were given realistic information about a situation they were about to enter. This information was given after they decided to join the organization but prior to their arrival on the scene. Compared to a control group which was denied such information, the experimental group showed significantly less turnover.

737. Jolson, Marvin A., and Martin J. Gannon. "Wives--A Critical Element in Career Decisions." *Business Horizons*, 15, No. 1 (1972), 83-85.

Career choices of businessmen are significantly influenced by their wives. Corporations should minimize conflict between a man's career and the needs of his family by recruiting carefully, previewing jobs realistically, preparing special manuals for wives, and/or conducting interviews or group sessions with wives.

738. Keats, Stephen M. "How to Hire Americans." *Management Today*, June (1978), 19-29.

The search for U.S. executives to run non-American firms has become crucial. The author explains how to hire top managers for foreign-based companies opening subsidiaries in the United States.

739. Kinslinger, Howard J. "Application of Projective Techniques in Personnel Psychology Since 1940." *Psychological Bulletin*, 66, No. 2 (1966), 134-149.

Discusses the utility of projective instruments in personnel studies on selection, identification of successful workers, assessment of promotion potential, and prediction of job satisfaction and job adjustment. The author concludes that projective techniques will have practical utility in personnel psychology only after thorough job specifications in terms of personality traits have been prepared and after extensive cross-validity studies have been conducted.

740. Kotter, John Paul. "The Psychological Contract: Managing the Joining Up Process." *California Management Review*, 15, No. 3 (1973), 91-99.

The "joining-up" process refers to the assimilation of new employees into an organization. This research explores problems in the joining-up process to determine how it can be better managed. The concept of the psychological contract was useful. This is the contract between an individual and the employing organization, which outlines what each expect to give and receive from each other in their relationship. Effective management of the joining-up process affects the cost of getting new people on board and keeping them, as well as the level of productivity and commitment of employees once hired.

741. Lauer, Peter H. "How to Pick the Right Middle Manager." *The Personnel Administrator*, 23, No. 8 (1978), 64-66.

    Discusses five ways to locate middle managers: (1) recommendations of senior executives; (2) use of newspaper or trade advertising; (3) search by personnel departments; (4) recommendations by employment agencies; and (5) use of executive search firms.

742. Lee, Sang M. "An Empirical Analysis of Organizational Identification." *Academy of Management Journal*, 14, No. 2 (1971), 213-226.

    Analyzes the determinants and correlates of organizational identification among scientists. Results show differences between scientists with high organizational identification and those with low organizational identification on certain job variables, job attitudes, and motivation.

743. Levinson, Harry. "Criteria for Choosing Chief Executives." *Harvard Business Review*, 58, No. 4 (1980), 113-120.

    Offers a list of 20 dimensions of personality useful in selecting chief executives. The dimensions are organized into three groups--thinking, feelings and interrelationships, and outward behavior characteristics--according to psychological themes. The author mentions three caveats associated with use of the list.

744. Nash, Allan N. "Development of an SVIB Key for Selecting Managers." *Journal of Applied Psychology*, 50, No. 3 (1966), 250-264.

    Investigates whether measured interests of 461 managers from 13 varied Minnesota-based companies are related to a criterion of managerial effectiveness. The author seeks to develop an interest key applicable in varied situations. He discusses distinctions between interest patterns of "less" and "more effective" managers.

Organizational Entry

745. Schein, Edgar H. "How to Break in the College Graduate." *Harvard Business Review*, 42, No. 6 (1964), 68-76.

   Newly recruited college graduates who join organizations desire opportunities to test themselves, to maintain their individuality and integrity, to grow on the job, to be considered worthwhile, and to work for organizations that conform to their ideal of a rational enterprise. Many newly recruited graduates are disillusioned when these expectations are not met. Organizations should provide challenging initial assignments, train supervisors to properly handle graduates, and design meaningful work for them.

746. Schneider, Benjamin. "Organizational Climate: Individual Preferences and Organizational Realities." *Journal of Applied Psychology*, 56, No. 3 (1972), 211-217.

   Examines whether there is a congruence between perceptions of organizational climate by prospective employees and perceptions of those already employed by the organization. Results show low significant correlations between new employee expectations and the climate of the particular organization they join and no significant relationship between new employee preferences and organizational climate.

747. Stahlman, Pershing P. "Working Abroad: Some Problems and Pitfalls." *The Personnel Administrator*, 24, No. 8 (1979), 27-30.

   Much of the dissatisfaction experienced by Americans living and working abroad can be traced to unrealistic expectations. Recruiters must use the selection process to encourage prospective overseas workers to carefully consider their choices by projecting his family and himself into a worst case scenario. By giving examples of the problems and frustrations that may be encountered potential recruits will have more realistic expectations about working abroad.

748. "They Like Peace Corps Graduates." *Business Week*, No. 2724 (1976), 160-162.

   Multinational corporations and banks are recruiting Peace Corps trained volunteers because their experience with different cultures makes them adaptable to overseas assignments. The transition is easy for those who switch from volunteer jobs to corporate life.

749. Wanous, John P. "Effects of a Realistic Job Preview on Job Acceptance, Job Attitudes, and Job Survival." *Journal of Applied Psychology*, 58, No. 3 (1973), 327-332.

Reports on a field experiment by the telephone company contrasting the effects of an unrealistic (i.e., traditional) job preview and a realistic preview. While there was no difference in the rates of job acceptance between the two groups, those exposed to the realistic job preview had more realistic expectations, higher job survival rates and fewer thoughts of quitting. Implications for the organizational induction process and suggestions for future research are discussed.

750. Wanous, John P. "Tell It Like It Is at Realistic Job Previews." *Personnel*, 52, No. 4 (1975), 50-60.

Realistic job previews (RJPS) seek to present to prospective employees a balanced picture of both the satisfying and dissatisfying features of jobs. Based on data from 80 newly hired Bell Telephone operators, the author concludes that RJPs resulted in reduced turnover, increased job satisfaction, and fewer thoughts of quitting when compared to traditional methods of recruitment. Related research conducted in different settings has reached similar conclusions.

751. Zaharia, E.S., and A.A. Baumeister. "Job Preview Effects During the Critical Initial Employment Period." *Journal of Applied Psychology*, 66, No. 1 (1981), 19-22.

Examines the effects of two interventions using realistic job previews with prospective employees on the voluntary turnover rates of technicians in a residential facility for the retarded. Results indicate that "both interventions produced a small but statistically nonsignificant improvement in turnover rates." (p. 19)

COUNSELING/ COACHING/ MENTORING

752. Atkinson, Charles, et al. "Management Development Roles: Coach, Sponsor, and Mentor." *Personnel Journal*, 59, No. 11 (1980), 918-921.

    Presents the case for three management training techniques: (1) the coach (who instructs trainees in job-related tasks); (2) the sponsor (who counsels his protege from the voice of experience); and (3) the mentor (who guides his protege up the career ladder).

753. Bensahel, Jane G. "Let Your Protege Make His Own Way." *International Management*, 32, No. 5 (1977), 44-46.

    Executives should not be over-protective but should allow their proteges freedom to form their own alliances, to develop their own talents, and to make mistakes. Mentors should focus on developing new talent in their proteges, not on fashioning carbon copies of themselves.

754. Benton, A. Randolph. "Managerial Career Coaching." *Training and Development Journal*, 35, No. 7 (1981), 54-55.

    A progress report on a training program for supervisors designed to encourage career development through coaching. An important obstacle to program success is the tendency toward mental compartmentalization of career issues versus business issues.

755. Cook, Mary F. "Is the Mentor Relationship Primarily a Male Experience." *Personnel Administrator*, 24, No. 11 (1979), 82-86.

    Companies are increasingly aware of the need for mentoring programs which prepare employees to move up in the organization. The author cites reasons why women haven't had the mentoring experiences they have needed. Examples are given of organizations that have implemented formal sponsorship programs to help women and minorities advance into top management.

756. Gambill, Ted R. "Career Counseling: Too Little, Too Late?" *Training and Development Journal*, 33, No. 2 (1979), 24-27.

    Describes and assesses the career counseling program at Meridian Insurance. The objectives, key concepts, and major aspects of the career counseling program are reviewed. The author stresses the value of career counseling as an employee-development tool for the organization which will bring many benefits to both employees and the organization.

757. Gould, M.J. "Counseling for Self-Development." *Personnel Journal*, 49, No. 3 (1970), 226-234.

    Through one-on-one counseling and performance appraisal, organizational superiors can help employees gain the necessary insight to see what changes are necessary if subordinates are to accomplish their goals. Self-development consultations can help employees to organize data, establish realistic goals, and develop plans of action.

758. Halatin, T.J. "Why be a Mentor." *Supervisory Management*, 26, No. 2 (1981), 36-39.

    A mentor can be crucial to an individual's career development program. The author describes mentor relationship benefits to the mentor, the subordinate, and the organization as well as the dangers in such relationships. Seven guidelines are mentioned for supervisors wanting to establish and maintain effective mentor relationships.

759. Hastings, Robert E. "No Fault Career Counseling Can Boost Middle- and Upper-Management Productivity." *Personnel Administrator*, 27, No. 1 (1982), 22-27.

    An interview with an official of AmeriTrust, a major bank, headquartered in Cleveland, Ohio, concerning a counseling program incorporating career pathing and outplacement for persons in middle- and upper-management positions who are caught in changing job roles.

760. Henry, James D. "Are You Good at Career Counseling?" *Supervisory Management*, 19, No. 3 (1974), 22-27.

    Examines three stages in the career development process and considers appropriate managerial career counseling strategies in each stage.

761. Isaacson, Lee E. "Counseling Male Midlife Career Changers." *Vocational Guidance Quarterly*, 29, No. 4 (1981), 324-331.

Identifies factors leading to voluntary and involuntary midlife career changes by men and discusses counseling strategies for dealing with clients facing these transitions.

762. Jones, Pamela, Beverly Kaye, and Hugh R. Taylor. "You Want Me to Do What?" *Training and Development Journal*, 35, No. 7 (1981), 56-62.

Career development is an important part of an organizations human resource development program. To be effective career developers, managers must be skilled in the coaching, counseling, and helping functions. Managers must be prepared to deal with these new responsibilities.

763. Jones, William H. "Grief and Involuntary Career Change: Its Implications for Counseling." *Vocational Guidance Quarterly*, 27, No. 3 (1979), 196-201.

Involuntary career loss can be a devastating experience causing grief in an individual. A prerequisite to effective counseling of these individuals is an understanding of grief and its relationship to loss in general. Individual cases of grief caused by job loss are examined and suggestions for effective management of grief are offered.

764. Kaye, Beverly L. "Up is Not the Only Way." *Supervisory Management*, 25, No. 2 (1980), 2-9.

In the "developer" role, a manager's role is to coach subordinates making them aware of career options. Six career options are discussed: moving up, moving across, moving down, exploring, staying put, and moving out.

765. Klaus, Rudi. "Formalized Mentor Relationships for Management and Executive Development Programs in the Federal Government." *Public Administration Review*, 41, No. 4 (1981), 489-496.

Mentor relationships in the public sector are examined drawing primarily on three case studies of formal mentor systems. The cases include the Internal Revenue Service, the Science and Education Administration in the Department of Agriculture, and the Fourth Federal Executive Development Program administered by the Office of Personnel Management. Five concrete lessons, themes, and implications are reported.

766. Kravetz, Dennis J., and Stephanie E. Derderian. "Developing Career Guidance Programs Through the Job Family Concept." *Personnel Administration*, 25, No. 5 (1980), 39-44.

   Presents details on a comprehensive career guidance program including background, methods, position classification into job families, and career assessment devices useful for guidance purposes. Establishment of job families, use of career assessment devices, and development of career paths can be valuable components of a career counseling program. It is important to help employees probe the psychological characteristics of jobs and match them to employee expectations.

767. Leonard, Edwin D. "Counseling and Employee Development." *Personnel Administration*, 28, No. 5 (1965), 32-35.

   Effective employee development depends upon a creative relationship between employees and supervisors. Supervisory counseling can be a useful approach to employee development. The effectiveness of this approach to employee development depends upon the supervisor's attitude and counseling ability.

768. McLane, Helen J. "Jumping Ahead by Having a Mentor." *Data Management*, 19, No. 3 (1981), 38-39; 56.

   Questions and answers on why it benefits an information executive to have a mentor.

769. Meckel, Nelson T. "The Manager as Career Counselor." *Training and Development Journal*, 35, No. 7 (1981), 65-69.

   Managers must improve their counseling skills and increase their willingness to do career counseling if they are to enhance the career development of their subordinates. Eight specific suggestions are given for managers wishing to improve their career counseling skills.

770. Miller, Donald B. "Training Managers to Stimulate Employee Development." *Training and Development Journal*, 35, No. 2 (1981), 47-63.

   Describes a three-day course for managers designed to improve their career coaching and counseling skills. Westinghouse has found this course to be useful in introducing managers to new career management concepts and techniques.

771. Miller, Norman R. "Career Guidance--A Means of Tapping Hidden Potential." *Personnel*, 41, No. 4 (1964), 36-42.

Many people possess potential far above what they actually achieve in life. Such untapped potential can be brought out and constructively channeled. The author describes in-company counseling programs which help the employee define career goals and action plans. In analyzing the employees' potential, useful information can be obtained from appraisals, personnel and training records, questionnaires, biographical interviews, and tests. This data provides the framework on which the employee and the guidance counselor can build.

772. Missirian, Agnes K. *The Process of Mentoring in the Career Development of Female Managers.* Diss., Univ. of Massachusetts, 1980.

Surveys 100 top businesswomen to examine the effect of mentor/protege relationships on the career patterns of successful female managers. Results confirm the importance of mentoring in career development for females. The mentoring process is described in its three phases: initiation, development, and termination. A set of mentor behaviors is specified along with perceptions and feelings experienced by proteges during each phase of the mentoring process.

773. Phillips, Linda L. *Mentors and Proteges: A Study of the Career Development of Women Managers and Executives in Business and Industry.* Diss., Univ. of California, 1977.

Describes the career development of a sample of women managers/executives (N=331) in American business and industry. Specific attention is given to their success, career obstacles, and the influence of "significant others" on their careers. Most of the women stated that they had had one or more career mentors during their lifetimes. The role of these mentors in career development is explored. Suggestions on "institutionalizing" mentoring programs are presented.

774. Schaeffer, Dorothy. "Counseling--No Easy Task." *Supervision*, 43, No. 2 (1981), 7-8.

Effective employee counseling of problem employees requires identifying the problem and determining to what extent supervisory counseling is needed.

775. Shapiro, Eileen C., Florence P. Hazeltine, and Mary P. Rowe. "Moving Up: Role Models, Mentors, and the 'Patron System'." *Sloan Management Review*, 19, No. 3 (1978), 51-58.

    Examines the need for female "role models" and "mentors" as prerequisites for woman's success in the workplace. The authors suggest that role models are of limited effectiveness in helping women to gain positions of leadership and authority, but that mentors can facilitate access to such positions for their proteges. Careful consideration of a continuum of "patron relationships" developed by the authors can lead to more effective efforts at bringing women into positions of leadership, authority, and power.

776. Wolf, James F., and Frank P. Sherwood. "Coaching: Supporting Public Executives on the Job." *Public Administration Review*, 41, No. 1 (1981), 73-76.

    An executive coach can provide support for executive development on the job. The author discusses four kinds of coaching support (executive skill building, problem solving, and career counseling) and three methods of providing coaching assistance (individual assessment meetings, director observation and feedback, and survey feedback with work group).

777. "Women Finally Get Mentors of Their Own." *Business Week*, No. 2557 (1978), 74-80.

    More female mentors are guiding young women managers up the career ladder.

MANAGEMENT ASSESSMENT/ TRAINING/ DEVELOPMENT

778. "A Shortfall in Transit Managers." *Business Week*, No. 2598 (1979), 62-64.

    As top positions in transit authorities become vacant, agencies are having difficulty finding qualified recruits. With this scarcity of talent, managers who are qualified often move from job to job causing a high turnover rate in this field. Transit managers' salaries are only a fraction of what similar jobs in the private sector command. Correctives to this problem are found in management internship and training programs as well as new educational programs in transit at colleges and university.

779. Alderfer, Clayton P. "Effect of Individual, Group, and Intergroup Relations on Attitudes Toward a Management Development Program." *Journal of Applied Psychology*, 55, No. 4 (1971), 302-311.

    Examines the reactions of organization members to a management development program in a medium-sized bank. Findings indicate that one's attitude toward the program were related to his seniority, organizational rank, perceived career opportunities, and pay satisfaction. Other factors affecting attitudes were the person's status as an employee, officer, or trainee, and his sex.

780. Bell, Chip R. "Career Planning and Development: A Resource System." *Training and Development Journal*, 29, No. 8 (1975), 32-35.

    How do managers get subordinates from where they are to where they want to be? An advisory system is described which aims at providing managers multiple leadership/ training/ education options for meeting specific developmental needs of subordinates. The advisory system could be encompassed in a notebook located in each department office or plant. The notebook covers: (1) major function areas, (2) subfunctional areas, (3) education/ training alternatives, (4) workshop syllabus, (5) career planning workshop, and (6) feedback to the advisory system.

781. Bray, Douglas W. "Management Development Without Frills." *The Conference Board Record*, 12, No. 9 (1975), 47-50.

    Examines the contribution of the assessment center approach to full utilization of management personnel based on results of the Bell System's Management Progress Study.

782. Bray, Douglas W., and Donald L. Grant. "The Assessment Center in the Measurement of Potential for Business Management." *Psychological Monographs*, 80, No. 17 (1966), 1-27.

    Describes the assessment process in the Bell System's Management Progress Study. This report covers assessment procedures, analysis of assessment staff evaluations, contributions of selected techniques to the assessment process, and relationships of assessment results to subsequent managerial progress.

783. Brush, Donald H., and Lyle F. Schoenfeldt. "Identifying Managerial Potential: An Alternative to Assessment Centers." *Personnel*, 57, No. 3 (1980), 68-76.

    Assessment centers are useful for managerial selection purposes and also for developing individual managers. The author explains how centers can identify managerial strengths and weaknesses in terms of on-the-job needs and how to design corrective training internally, externally, and on the job.

784. Burack, Elmer H. "Self-Assessment: A Strategy of Growing Importance." *Training and Development Journal*, 33, No. 4 (1979), 48-52.

    A wide variety of organizations are using self-assessment approaches as these institutions take on more formalized career-related activities. The focus and content of self-assessment approaches are examined including behavioral-type instruments (inventories, scales), management-related instruments (inventories, scales), orientation materials, and organizational and logistical factors. Five ground-rules for successful use of self-assessment approaches in career-related programs are presented.

785. Byham, William C., and Carl Wettengel. "Assessment Centers for Supervisors and Managers: An Introduction and Overview." *Public Personnel Management*, 3, No. 5 (1974), 352-364.

786. Calero, Thomas M. *Technology and the Changing Circumstances of Managerial Careers.* Diss., Northwestern Univ., 1972.

   Seeks to better understand the impact technological change has upon the job responsibilities and actual job activities of managers and technical support personnel in several midwestern corporations. Results show a marked trend toward reevaluation of on-the-job experience vis-a-vis formal education with respect to moving up in management. A technological rationale is often used to justify the greater emphasis upon education.

787. Campbell, Richard J., and Douglas W. Bray. "Assessment Centers: An Aid in Management Selection." *Personnel Administration*, 30, No. 1 (1967), 7-13.

   Discusses the Bell System's assessment center procedures emphasizing the impact of the assessment center program. The assessment center is considered to be a valuable technique for the identification of management potential.

788. Clay, Hubert H., and Leif O. Olsen. "Some Dogmas of Development: Facts or Fallacies." *Personnel Administration*, 21, No. 1 (1967), 41-44.

   Management development is retarded by adherence to three questionable dogmas: (1) the appraisal process is aided by forms, (2) managers know how to develop subordinates, and (3) the performance interview is inviolate.

789. Ferguson, Wilburn C. "Motorola Supervisory Development Program." *Training and Development Journal*, 25, No. 6 (1971), 16-17.

   To eliminate the "formal training gap" that existed when employees were promoted to supervisors, the Motorola Government Electronics Division in Scottsdale, Arizona, initiated a supervisory development program. Once supervisors have been nominated by department heads and have chosen to participate, a program is designed to meet their specific needs. The four steps in the program are described and examples of forms used in implementing the program are provided.

790. Fitz-enz, Jac, Kathryn E. Hards, and G.E. Savage. "Total Development: Selection, Assessment, Growth." *Personnel Administrator*, 25, No. 2 (1980), 58-62.

   Assessment must be linked with other growth activities to create an efficient and effective development program. Within the framework of a career development system, this article presents a case history of how assessment is interdependent with selection and training.

791. Gannon, Martin J. "Attitudes of Government Executives Toward Management Training." *Public Personnel Management*, 4, No. 1 (1975), 63-68.

Measures the attitudes of federal government executives toward management training. Findings show that background characteristics were not related to the perceived importance of management training; interpersonal relations and managerial scientific techniques were ranked high as proper training objectives; trainees preferred training that was appropriate for long-term career growth, informal, and taught in a seminar-type university setting. Managers generally have positive sentiments concerning the efficacy of management training.

792. Ginsburg, Lee R., and Arnold Silverman. "The Leaders of Tomorrow: Their Identification and Development." *Personnel Journal*, 51, No. 9 (1972), 662-666.

The first hospital personnel identification and development center was established for first and second-level managers. The center operated within five parameters: (1) management potential must be validly measured, (2) the organization and the assessees must accept the assessment approach, (3) administration of the center is an integral part of the organization's management development program, (4) the approach is flexible, comprehensive, and (5) the procedure has a high payoff. The authors report that the center is predictive of managerial ability.

793. Grant, Donald L., Walter Katovsky, and Douglas W. Bray. "Contributions of Projective Techniques to Assessment of Management Potential." *Journal of Applied Psychology*, 51, No. 3 (1967), 226-232.

Examines the utility of projective tests in assessment centers and the relationships of projective data to managerial progress. Analysis of data from three projective instruments shows that these reports were especially influential on assessment-center staff evaluations in rating work motivation, dependency, and passivity. Projective variables also reliably related to managerial progression.

794. Harley, Joan, and Lois A. Koff. "Prepare Women Now for Tomorrow's Managerial Challenges." *Personnel Administrator*, 25, No. 4 (1980), 41-42.

Companies must help women employees to prepare for top administrative positions in the 1980s by offering "proactive" training to increase their proficiency, productivity, and promotability.

795. Hart, Gary L., and Paul H. Thompson. "Assessment Centers: For Selection or Development." *Organizational Dynamics*, 7, No. 4 (1979), 63-77.

Argues in favor of development-oriented assessment centers rather than selection-oriented centers. The authors describe one company's experience in using an assessment center for employee development. Results suggest that assessment center technology can be used effectively for career development and career planning.

796. Heneman, Herbert G., Jr. "As You Were Saying--Downward Management Development." *Personnel Journal*, 50, No. 9 (1971), 720-721.

Management development programs should be geared downward as well as upward and laterally. The "three-way" concept is necessary since managerial stamina and desire often diminishes over time. Differential development patterns and multiple career paths are helpful in dealing with executive deadwood.

797. "How RPI Helps Locate Talent." *Business Week*, No. 2552 (1978), 129-130.

The Rensselaer Polytechnic Institute's School of Management has developed a system to categorize management functions, identify characteristics of successful managers in specific jobs, and diagnose training needs for new executives. The designers of the system are monitoring accuracy in forecasting managerial ability by following the progress of recent graduates.

798. Hubben, Herbert. "Executive Development Practices and Problems--the Industrial Experience." *Public Personnel Review*, 25, No. 2 (1964), 103-106.

Summarizes recent industrial experience in executive development. The author sees industry favoring individually-tailored executive development approaches. Industrial managers will support these development programs if it is clear that key executives are committed to them. If there is frequent movement at top levels, and if there are financial rewards associated with achievement of individual executive development efforts. The trend is to identify a good employee and send that person to the best possible course where the training is tailored to his needs.

799. Jennings, Eugene E. "How to Develop Your Management Talent Internally." *Personnel Administrator*, 26, No. 7 (1981), 20-23.

Describes the methods used by companies that have successfully implemented management development programs. Developmental companies will pursue dual goals of ensuring long term fiscal viability and of developing highly talented people. Traditional companies spend too much time producing profits and not enough on human asset development.

800. Jorz, Joanne J., and Louise M. Richards. "A Curriculum Plan to Develop Training Professionals." *Training and Development Journal*, 31, No. 10 (1977), 22-24.

The five roles of the trainer are training administrator, consultant, career counselor, learning specialist, and program manager. A curriculum plan is presented whereby trainers can gain experience in each of these roles as part of a professional development program for federal government trainers.

801. Knowlton, William A., Jr., and Terrance R. Mitchell. "Effects of Causal Attributions on a Supervisor's Evaluation of Subordinates Performance." *Journal of Applied Psychology*, 65, No. 4 (1980), 459-466.

Investigates the impact of "a supervisor's attributions about the causes of a subordinate's poor performance on an evaluation of that subordinate." (p. 459) Results of analysis using data from 40 undergraduate students strongly support the hypothesis that "effort" attributions lead to more extreme evaluations than "ability" attributions.

802. Kraut, Allen I. "New Frontiers for Assessment Centers." *Personnel*, 53, No. 4 (1976), 36-39.

Assessment centers are useful not only to identify employees with management potential, but also to aid in recruitment, replacement, promotion, development, and coaching of job performance. The defining characteristics of assessment centers are summarized along with a brief discussion of potential uses, validity, cost/benefit issues, assessor training requirements, system-wide impacts, and potential pitfalls.

803. Leibowitz, Zandy B., and Nancy K. Schlossberg. "Training Managers for Their Role in a Career Development System." *Training and Development Journal*, 35, No. 7 (1981), 72-79.

Identifies nine career planning roles that supervisors might play: communicator, counselor, appraiser, coach, mentor, advisor, broker, referral agent, and advocate. A model training program is discussed which seeks to raise the consciousness of managers about the career planning needs of employees, helps managers assess their career planning skills, and introduces managers to career planning concepts.

804. Levinson, Harry. "Executive Development: What You Need to Know?" *Training and Development Journal*, 35, No. 9 (1981), 84-95.

    Presents eight suggestions for formal training programs directed at teaching tomorrow's successful managers and executives what they need to know.

805. Mahler, Walter R., and Hugh A. McLean. "Developmental Dialogues." *Training and Development Journal*, 26, No. 11 (1972), 50-54.

    A program emphasizing supervisor-manager dialogues was designed by the American Bankers Association to meet the training needs of first-level bank supervisors. The elements of the program and its results are described along with the advantages accruing to both the individuals and the organization.

806. Meahea, Laird W., and John F. Duffy. "An Integrated Model for Training and Development: How to Build on What You Already Have." *Public Personnel Management*, 9, No. 4 (1980), 336-343.

    The training and development literature is void of any integrative T/D model which would assist those responsible for implementing an effective program. The authors outline a model which integrates (a) job analyses, (b) needs assessment, (c) motivational theory, (d) performance appraisal, (e) assessment center technology, (f) feedback, (g) effective training evaluation, and (h) career path/development. The advantages of this model for organizations are enumerated.

807. Murphy, Joseph P. "Determining Needs With Supervisory Conferences." *Training and Development Journal*, 26, No. 6 (1972), 2-6.

    A series of structured supervisory meetings were conducted at the Omaha Public Power District to assess organization and personnel weaknesses. Through these conferences a new approach to supervisory training has been established where managers from all levels meet and discuss both problems and solutions.

808. Nash, Allan N. "Vocational Interests of Effective Managers: A Review of the Literature." *Personnel Psychology*, 18, No. 1 (1965), 21-37.

Reviews empirical literature which seeks to identify managerial potential through the use of vocational interest measures.

809. Norton, Steven D., Joe L. Balloun, and Branislav Kenstaninovich. "The Soundness of Supervisory Ratings as Predictors of Managerial Success." *Personnel Psychology*, 33, No. 1 (1980), 377-388.

Using a model of career development, three types of validity (criterion-related, content, and construct) are considered for supervisor's rating of non-managers as a predictor of managerial success. The authors argue that all three types of validity are inapplicable to this prediction situation. Suggestions are offered for developing a sound rating system.

810. Pankowski, Mary L. "Training and Development Needs of State Agency Employees." *Training and Development Journal*, 27, No. 7 (1973), 22-24.

Structured interviews and surveys were used to ascertain the needs for training and development among Florida's State agencies. Based on this kind of needs assessment, training and development organizations (both public and private) can design programs to meet recognized needs.

811. Perham, John C. "The Companies That Build Executive Talent." *Dun's Review*, 101, No. 5 (1973), 51-55.

Identifies companies that are doing the best job of training and developing executives and describes their activities. ITT, IBM, GE and others are heavy exporters of talented, all-purpose general executives. Other companies like Dow Chemical, Eastman Kodak, and GM are almost raid proof, since they groom their own executives and then keep them. Companies that 10 or 20 years ago had the best reputations for building up an executive talent bank are generally not the ones doing the best job today.

812. "Public Sector People Development." *Training and Development Journal*, 28, No. 7 (1974), 10-13.

Reports an interview with Frederick Fisher, Vice President, National Training and Development Service (NTDS) emphasizing state and local government training needs, NTDS philosophy and programs, public sector productivity, and the role of training and career development.

813. Quick, James C., et al. "Developing Administrative Personnel Through the Assessment Center Technique." *Personnel Administrator*, 25, No. 2 (1980), 44-46; 62.

The use of assessment centers for developmental purposes will increase in importance as increased effectiveness is required of individuals in diverse organizational settings. In this article four years of assessment center experience in American Airlines are applied to the development of management personnel in Texas State Government. A two-day, six exercise format for a typical center is described in detail.

814. Radar, Martha H. "Evaluating a Management Development Program for Women." *Public Personnel Management*, 8, No. 3 (1979), 138-145.

Examines the impact of a management development program for women on trainees' assertiveness and attitudes toward women. Training for upward career mobility was given to women administrators, supervisors, and professionals. While assertiveness and attitudes toward women significantly improved for administrators and professionals. The author concludes that promotion into a nontraditionally female job might be viewed by women with more traditional attitudes as a threat rather than as an opportunity.

815. Ross, Joyce D. "A Current Review of Public Sector Assessment Centers: Cause for Concern." *Public Personnel Management*, 8, No. 1 (1979), 41-46.

The use of assessment centers has become increasingly evident in public organizations. While many governmental jurisdictions have enthusiastically jumped on the bandwagon, there has been insufficient attention given to the legal and organizational standards necessary in conducting a valid and reliable assessment center. The author examines assessment center standards, pointing out possible legal challenges and encouraging public decision makers to critically evaluate the conduct of their assessment centers.

816. Schachter, Hindy L. "Simulations for Training and Assessment: The Problem of Relevance to the Real World." *Public Personnel Management*, 9, No. 3 (1980), 225-227.

In recent years, there has been increased use of simulations in training and assessing public managers. The author examines some of the difficulties facing developers as they attempt to replicate the complex environment of public agencies in solo and group simulations. Two strategies--self-evaluation and outside evaluation--are identified for making simulations more relevant to the "real" public agency world.

817. Sharinger, Dale H. "Avoidance of Pitfalls in Supervisory Development." *Training and Development Journal*, 35, No. 10 (1981), 92-96.

Presents an approach to teaching basic management to newly selected first-line supervisors. Upper level management needs to accept the role of trainer and model of a good manager if effective supervisory development is to occur. Some reasons why top managers have failed to accept this role are reviewed and some ways to facilitate managerial involvement are described.

818. Shusta, George. "Don't Make It Fancy--Just Good." *Training and Development Journal*, 28, No. 1 (1974), 10-14.

Three important requirements for an effective training and development program are: (1) emphasizing the basic, fundamental, grass roots approach to skill development, (2) selling the program to top management and gaining their strong support, and (3) coordinating the efforts of internal personnel with those of outside consultants.

819. Siegel, Gilbert B. "Management Development and the Instability of Skills: A Strategy." *Public Personnel Review*, 30, No. 1 (1969), 15-20.

Management development is defined as increasing the capacity in organizations for predictable behavior. The author examines the organizational-technological revolution that has led to an instability of skills. He summarizes various human motivation models (rational-economic man, social man, self-actualizing man) and concludes that the contemporary worker is most approximated by the self-actualizing man. He then posits the O-E-C syndrome (organizing, evaluating, coaching) as a managerial strategy which will allow us most to develop this type of employee.

820. Singleton, John. "How to Identify Your Negative Behavior Characteristics." *Supervisory Management*, 25, No. 7 (1980), 17-24.

Discusses the supervisor's responsibility to help subordinates identify negative behavior characteristics identify negative behavior characteristics and to counsel them about overcoming shortcomings. The author provides a list of characteristics that could have a positive and negative impact on employees' careers. Self assessment attitude surveys are described and the characteristics of effective feedback are listed.

821. Snyder, John T. "Training Actualization Through Accountability." *Training and Development Journal*, 29, No. 6 (1975), 34-37.

The trainer is part of the "loyal opposition" who supports the organization but continually looks for ways to change it to improve effectiveness. As change agents, trainers must be concerned with the growth and development of individuals. Trainers should assist managers to establish a climate in which individual needs can be met.

822. Stewart, Rosemary. "Patterns of Work and the Dictates of Time." *Personnel Management*, 8, No. 6 (1976), 25-28.

A knowledge of how work patterns and their time cycles affect managerial behavior can lead to more effective selection and career development programs. The author identifies four types of work patterns and the job titles belonging to each. These work patterns need to be considered when identifying training and development needs.

823. Strausbaugh, David, and Barry L. Wogman. "An Assessment Center Examination to Select Administrative Interns." *Public Personnel Management*, 6, No. 4 (1977), 263-269.

Summarizes the experience of the City of Philadelphia in developing and administering an assessment center to examine candidates for administrative internships. Based on this initial study, the authors suggest that the assessment center procedure is content-valid and gives no evidence of adverse impact on protected groups.

824. Taylor, Susan M., and Randall B. Dunham. "A Program for Planned Student and Personnel Practitioner Interactions." *Personnel Administrator*, 25, No. 10 (1980), 71-73.

825. Thorne, Edward H., and Jean L. Marshall. "Management Skill Development: An Experience in Program Design." *Personnel Journal*, 55, No. 1 (1976), 15-17; 38.

   Adapts the adult-education model to the industrial setting by describing the key elements involved in implementing a managerial skills development program.

826. Truskie, Stanley D. "Guidelines for Conducting In-House Management Development." *Personnel Administrator*, 26, No. 7 (1981), 25-27.

   Elaborates the guidelines for establishing a viable and effective in-house management development program. Results of such programs have shown behavioral improvement of managers in such areas as problem solving, decision making, planning, organizing, developing subordinates, and dealing with labor relations and affirmative action.

827. Warren, Alfred S. "Personnel Development and Education-Work Relations of General Motors." *Training and Development Journal*, 31, No. 1 (1977), 9-11.

   Describes General Motors' program for development of people through training and education.

MANAGING MOBILITY

828. Andrews, John D.W. "The Achievement Motive and Advancement in Two Types of Organizations." *Journal of Personality and Social Psychology*, 6, No. 2 (1967), 163-168.

    Investigates how executives with various motive patterns advance in different types of firms. In firms emphasizing achievement values, employee advancement is related to the strength of an executive's need for achievement. However, in firms emphasizing power striving values, this relationship is reversed.

829. Barker, Tony. "Omens for Over-Promotion." *Management Today*, March (1981), 83-87.

    Warns that damage to the business and to the executive can result from promoting managers without careful evaluation of their competence and potential. Corporate actions to develop employees so they can perform a more significant role should precede rather than follow promotions.

830. Beyer, Janice M., John M. Stevens, and Harrison M. Trice. "Predicting How Federal Managers Perceive Criteria Used for Their Promotion." *Public Administration Review*, 40, No. 1 (1980), 55-60.

    Surveys 634 federal government managers regarding their expectations of factors contributing to career advancement. Six criteria were assessed: (1) performance of unit supervised; (2) quality of supervisor's performance; (3) interpersonal skills; (4) administrative skills in applying formal policies; (5) seniority; and (6) technical skills. The performance criteria (1-4) were considered more important for promotions than factors 5 and 6.

831. Cardwell, James W. "The Other Side of Relocation--Relocating the Spouse." *Personnel Administrator*, 25, No. 9 (1980), 53-56.

Corporate relocation programs cannot disregard the special needs of the dual career couple since more than 50 percent of married women work. Four strategies for involving the couple in relocation decisions are described and four alternatives for penalizing the relocation to the special needs of the transferees and the spouse are provided.

832. Collie, H. Cris, and Peter J. DiDomenico. "Relocation Trends--Moving into the 80s." *Personnel Administrator*, 25, No. 9 (1980), 31-35; 66-68.

   Contrasts relocation trends in the 70s with those expected in the 80s. Statistical data are cited including highlights of Employee Relocation Council surveys on relocation trends and policies. The authors predict that in the future relocation will no longer be viewed as a benefit program. Instead, it will be seen as a corporate strategy for efficiently deploying human resources to meet productivity goals.

833. Corey, James H. "The Fear of Failure--the Supervisor's Greatest Enemy." *Supervisory Management*, 24, No. 12 (1979), 2-7.

   Describes the fear and insecurity experienced by newly promoted supervisors. Reasons for supervisory failure, the outward signs of fear, and strategies for eliminating fear are discussed. Management should accept responsibility for helping supervisors to grow emotionally and psychologically on the job.

834. Cummings, Paul W. "Supervisory Expectations Versus Organizational Reality." *Training and Development Journal*, 30, No. 9 (1976), 37-41.

   Analyzes survey data from first line production workers to examine supervisory vertical mobility. Results suggest that too little attention is given to analyzing organizational hierarchies to improve supervisory vertical mobility. Selective and inequitable supervisory vertical mobility can be changed by improved performance appraisals, career counseling, promotion criteria, and career development programs.

835. Diggin, Thomas E. "Upward Mobility--TECOM Puts It All Together." *Public Personnel Management*, 3, No. 3 (1974), 230-232.

   Describes the U.S. Army Test and Evaluation Command (TECOM) program for upward mobility of its lower level employees. The program seeks to use the abilities of

TECOM employees and to encourage them to become more qualified for job opportunities. TECOM includes the following six elements: career systems, career development plans, counseling and guidance, education and training, work force analysis, and EEO and women's programs.

836. Durrill, David C. "Job Posting--a Chance to Advance." *The Personnel Administrator*, 18, No. 1 (1973), 41-42.

   Describes the job posting procedures and rules followed by the Bank of Virginia Company. The decision to post jobs is based on the assumption that individuals are responsible for their own advancement. The company sensed an increase in morale and communication as a result of job posting.

837. Egan, Michael. "Exploring the Expatriate's World." *Personnel Management*, 8, No. 7 (1976), 25-29.

   Discusses the personnel implications of employees working outside their home countries. As increasing numbers of managerial and professional people are leaving the United Kingdom to work abroad, there is a high demand for U.K. expatriates at more senior levels. The author examines the reasons for this trend, the salaries, the culture shock, and the effects of overseas assignments on career development.

838. Estler, Suzanne E. "Evolving Jobs as a Form of Career Mobility: Some Policy Implications." *Public Personnel Management*, 10, No. 4 (1981), 355-364.

   Examines "evolving jobs" as an alternative process to hierarchical mobility, assesses the pros and cons resulting from this process, and considers the policy implications suggested by evolving jobs. The study focuses on intra-organizational mobility among nonteaching personnel in universities. The author expected to find employee frustration because of limited career opportunities. However, results showed that in many instances jobs were not unchanging; instead, they evolve around the individual holding them. Evolved jobs become instruments of career mobility.

839. Farnsworth, Terry. "What It Takes to Become a Company Hero." *International Management*, 36, No. 6 (1981), 45-46.

   Do the heroes who find a place in the "corporate hall of fame" deserve our praise? Five types of heroes are discussed: (1) the turnaround man; (2) the social lion;

(3) the miser; (4) the joker; and (5) the straight shooter. Companies which encourage and promote such employees will be sorry in the long run.

840. Foegen, J.H. "If It Means Moving, Forget It." *Personnel Journal*, 56, No. 8 (1977), 414-416.

   Winning the corporate promotion used to be contingent upon an employee's willingness to relocate. However, younger managers are increasingly refusing transfers and managers must learn to recognize and adapt constructively to this trend. Suggestions are offered on ways to deal with this problem.

841. Fulmer, Robert M., and William E. Fulmer. "Providing Equal Opportunities for Promotion." *Personnel Journal*, 53, No. 7 (1974), 491-497.

   Compares the advantages and disadvantages of job posting and employee request systems as selection methods for promotions for production employees. The absence of job posting may be considered illegal and the burden of proof is on management to justify its procedure. An employee request system contains most of the advantages of job posting but it poses fewer potential problems to management.

842. Gardiner, Charles V., and Kenneth L. Rich. "Relocation Policies: Boom and Bust." *Personnel Administrator*, 25, No. 9 (1980), 37-42; 64; 104-105.

   Stresses the importance of relocating employees only when necessary and offers practical hints on keeping down relocation costs. The authors identify five major issues a company must consider when formulating or assessing relocation policies.

843. Gittleman, H.M. "Occupational Mobility Within the Firm." *Industrial and Labor Relations Review*, 20, No. 1 (1966), 50-65.

   Analysis of the movement of workers among jobs at Waltham Watch Company in order to identify the determinants of mobility and to assess their relative influence. Concludes that intrafirm mobility is a function of technology, labor market conditions, and changes in the composition of output.

844. Glueck, William F. "Executive Mobility in Public Service and Business." *Public Personnel Review*, 31, No. 2 (1970), 95-101.

Examines the career development practices of private
corporations, the federal civil service, and the Air
Force. The author seeks to determine to what extent
career models have been developed in these sectors and
to what extent geographical mobility is essential to the
career plans of these organizations. Results indicate
that in terms of career development, the Air Force is
the most developed, followed by industry, and then
civilian government.

845. Glueck, William F. "Managers, Mobility, and Morale."
Business Horizons, 17, No. 6 (1974), 65-70.

Do American businessmen view relocation as beneficial
to them, their families, and their employer? The article
reports results of a survey of 463 midwestern business
executives who were asked about geographic mobility.
The author recommends that managers examine their transfer practices to assure that they are necessary, that
they are in both the manager's and company's best interest,
and that they contribute to employee morale and company
effectiveness.

846. Helmich, Donald L. "Organizational Growth and Succession
Patterns." *Academy of Management Journal*, 17, No. 1
(1974), 771-775.

Examines four patterns of succession to the position
of corporate executive: insider to insider, insider to
outsider, outsider to insider, and outsider to outsider.
Results show that companies experiencing succession
patterns of two insiders in a row are less apt to
experience increases in organizational growth. This
suggests that organizations seeking to grow in a dynamic
environment might favor outside promoted executives.

847. Helmich, Donald L. "Succession: A Longitudinal Look."
Journal of Business Research, 3, No. 1 (1975), 355-364.

Examines the succession of leaders and types of succession
related to organizational age in the petrochemical industry. Findings reveal that the older the organization
the greater the frequency of internal successions to
the presidency; the younger the organization the higher
the rates of succession and the longer the tenure in
office of internal successors.

848. "How to Ease Reentry After Overseas Duty." *Business Week*,
No. 2589 (1979), 82-84.

Executives accepting overseas assignments are finding themselves on "hardship duty" in the Middle East and underdeveloped countries. Some will not accept foreign assignments without "repatriation agreements" or written guarantees that their overseas assignment will not exceed two to five years and that they will be given a mutually acceptable position when they are returned home. Corporations are using such agreements to reduce employee anxiety about overseas duty.

849. Jennings, Eugene E. "The Supermobile." *Human Resource Management*, 11, No. 1 (1972), 4-17.

Supermobiles have career expectations which increase faster than corporations can fulfill them. Some corporations breed supermobiles by inflating expectations without producing the requisite achievement opportunities. Supermobiles with high expectations who perceive blocks in their career paths will likely move. Companies can reduce turnover among this group by not promising unrealistic promotional opportunities.

850. Kimball, Richard T. "Planned Professional Manpower Mobility." *The Conference Board Record*, 9, No. 9 (1972), 54-58.

Predicts increased job transience for professional employees for the next decade. Both individuals and managers will profit from a concept of planned mobility. The implications of professional manpower mobility are discussed.

851. Kunish, Robert D. "Relocating in an Unsettled Economy." *Personnel Administrator*, 25, No. 9 (1980), 25-28.

Summarizes real estate trends in the past decade which have had a significant impact on corporate relocation programs. The chain of events leading to current problems are reviewed and strategies are discussed for reducing relocation pains and providing assistance to the transferee.

852. Kushell, Robert E. "Identifying the Good, the Bad, and the Indifferent." *Supervisory Management*, 24, No. 4 (1979), 2-7.

Describes one management tool, the Promotable People Chart, which is useful in isolating personnel problem areas and evaluating the strength of a work team. Development of the chart requires the identification of four categories of employees: those with excellent promotion potential, moderate growth potential, questionable employees, and poor producers. The author discusses ways to use this tool to identify human resource potential, isolate performance problems, and increase productivity.

853. Levenson, Myra K., and Robert W. Hollman. "Personal Support Services in Corporate Relocation Programs." *Personnel Administrator*, 25, No. 9 (1980), 45-51.

    Considers the impact of corporate decisions on the family life of employees. The authors recommend the implementation of programs which address the emotional needs of employees and their families. Among the recommended personal supports are increased information, early communication with spouses, spouse job assistance, on-site relocation assistants, workshops for transferees, and case management systems.

854. Lupton, Daniel E. "Are Today's Managers Really All That Mobile?" *Personnel*, 49, No. 2 (1972), 60-64.

    Is increasing executive mobility a reality or a fallacy? A review of several surveys and analysis by the author suggests that managers, omitting top executives, are not job hopping from company to company. The article considers the implications of this reduced interorganizational mobility for managerial and organizational development.

855. Mack, James G. "How Companies Can Handle the Complexities of Relocation." *Personnel Administrator*, 25, No. 9 (1980), 59-61.

    Provides estimates of company costs involved in directly handling a home disposition versus costs involved in using a relocation company (third party program). Corporations can realize net savings in both dollars and in personal relocation services by using a third party program.

856. "Managers Move More But Enjoy It Less." *Business Week*, No. 2446 (1976), 19-20.

    Reluctance to relocate has led to conflict between companies and managers. The cost of transfers is up but the benefits to ease the pain are slackening off. Working wives and housing costs are major factors influencing executives' unwillingness to move.

857. McConkey, Dale D. "Why the Best Managers Don't Get Promoted." *The Business Quarterly*, 44, No. 2 (1979), 39-42.

   Examines the reasons why managerial selection is often made from a narrow rather than a broad pool of potentially eligible candidates. Five types of "insularity" may prevent selection of the "best" managers: line and staff, departmental/functional, sex, promotion from within, subjective, and quality of life. These types of insularity tend to narrow the total group from which promotees are selected.

858. McGregor, Eugene B. *Education and Career Mobility Among Federal Administrators: Toward the Development of a Comparative Model.* Diss., Syracuse Univ., 1969.

   Studies the relationship between education and career mobility of two groups of American federal administrators: high ranking civil servants and high ranking officials in three foreign affairs organizations. A comparative model of mobility is developed permitting empirical comparisons of different samples of officials for different periods of time. The structure of mobility and the correlates of mobility for the two samples are examined.

859. McGregor, Eugene B. "Politics and Career Mobility of Bureaucrats." *The American Political Science Review*, 68, No. 1 (1974), 18-26.

   Discusses the conceptualization, measurement, and political importance of career mobility among federal bureaucrats. A comparative typology of career mobility is developed. A comparison of the career mobility of higher civil servants and foreign affairs officials shows varying background characteristics makes a small mobility difference for the former but a much greater difference for the latter.

860. Ostrowski, Paul S. "Management Succession: Chance or Choice." *Management Review*, 57, No. 10 (1968), 65-69.

   Succession planning helps to maintain the continuity of managerial leadership in an enterprise. The process, prerequisites, implementation, and weaknesses of succession planning are described.

861. Pashigian, B. Peter. "Occupational Licensing and the Interstate Mobility of Professionals." *The Journal of Law and Economics*, 22, No. 1 (1979), 1-26.

    The interstate mobility of lawyers is significantly reduced by occupational licensing and limitations on the use of reciprocity.

862. Pitts, Robert A. "Unshackle Your Comers." *Harvard Business Review;* 55, No. 3 (1977), 127-136.

    Makes the case for transfering talented middle managers across corporate divisions. The author argues that "the inevitable result of shackling such persons (comers) to positions they have out-grown is the inevitable loss of these employees." (p. 128) Corporate managers should take steps to properly identify "comers" and to persuade division heads to release managers and to accept transfers. Administrative techniques are suggested which will aid in overcoming barriers to inter-divisional transfers.

863. Rosenbaum, James E. "Tournament Mobility: Career Patterns in a Corporation." *Administrative Science Quarterly*, 24, No. 2 (1979), 220-240.

    Analyzes the career mobility of employees in a large corporation over a 13-year time span. Two conflicting models of mobility are presented: a historical (tournament) model and an ahistorical (path independence) model. Results of empirical analysis support the tournament model showing that mobility early in one's career has a significant relationship with important aspects of one's subsequent career: career floors and ceilings and the likelihood of promotions and demotions in each successive period.

864. Schaeffer, Dorothy. "Counseling the Unpromotable." *Supervision*, 42, No. 8 (1980), 6-7.

    Whenever promotions are announced, supervisors may have to counsel with unhappy employees who were passed over. The author discusses how supervisors can explain their actions and still preserve employee's self-respect and enthusiasm for their job. A four-point plan is outlined.

865. Schwarzwald, Joseph, and Judith Goldenberg. "Compliance and Assistance to an Authority Figure in Perceived Equitable or Nonequitable Situations." *Human Relations*, 32, No. 10 (1979), 877-888.

Examines the issue of whether intra-departmental promotion is more effective than promotion from the outside. Findings are related to the theory of inequity.

866. Shetty, Y.K., and Newman S. Peery. "Are Top Executives Transferable Across Companies?" *Business Horizons* 19, No. 2 (1976), 23-28.

Are top managers interchangeable across firms and industries, or are such managers unlikely to be successful unless they have a thorough understanding of an industry and its environment? This study points out some of the serious constraints limiting the transferability of executives across companies and/or industries. Among the companies surveyed, those recruiting chief executives from within performed much better than those selected from outside.

867. Steinberg, Ronnie. "Typical and Alternative Routes to Promotion of Women and Minorities." *Journal of Public and International Affairs*, 3, No. 1 (1982), 13-26.

Analyzes the promotion process for positions in grades 23 to 38 in New York State government with special attention given to institutional barriers impeding advancement of women and minorities. The primary barriers were "eligibility requirements" and the "rule of three". Alternative methods of defining eligibility and different procedures for selection are considered.

868. Swinyard, Alfred W., and Floyd A. Bond. "Who Gets Promoted?" *Harvard Business Review*, 58, No. 5 (1980), 6-18.

Why are some executives promoted while others are not? Using survey data from 11,000 executives collected over ten years, the authors develop a profile of the promoted executive. They are better educated, hold an advanced degree in business administration, move up from being a group vice-president, and have been mobile. The most obvious changes in the past decade are the increases in both education and mobility.

869. Thomas, William C., Jr. "Generalist vs. Specialist: Careers in a Municipal Bureaucracy." *Public Administration Review*, 21, No. 1 (1961), 8-16.

Analyzes the career lines of bureau chiefs of New York City government. A proliferation of career pyramids or promotional channels was found. As a result of these channels, there is often higher interdepartmental than intradepartmental movement; in the latter instance, specialist skills are the paramount factors affecting individual advancement to higher levels. The study findings lead the author to question the relevance in big organizations of earlier discussions of the roles of the specialist and generalist.

870. Tomeski, Edward, and Konrad E. Sadel. "Job Satisfaction and the Systems Professional." *Journal of Systems Management*, 31, No. 6 (1980), 6-10.

The manager and the technical professional are pursuing two distinctly different career paths. Too often a technically competent person is promoted to a management position for which he is ill-suited. Organizations should recognize and reward competent technical professionals who may not want to be promoted to a management post.

871. Veiga, John F. "Do Managers on the Move Get Anywhere." *Harvard Business Review*, 59, No. 2 (1981), 20-38.

Discusses four questions: (1) How mobile are managers? (2) What is a typical career? (3) Are mobile managers a breed apart? (4) What are the payoffs? While some mobile managers get the top jobs, the rest find mobility frequently fails to pay off. Management should be circumspect about encouraging lateral moves, and it should seek to create realistic promotions and mobility patterns.

872. Vroom, Victor H., and Kenneth R. MacCrimnion. "Toward a Stochastic Model of Managerial Careers." *Administrative Science Quarterly*, 13, No. 1 (1968), 26-46.

A Markov chain model is used to describe career movements of managers and professionals within organizations. This allows a formal description of the results of present career policies to be made and allows predictions to be made of the effects of extending present policies into the future. A more rational basis for career management is thereby provided. Data are presented, a simple model is developed, and inferences are made from a sample of career movements of professionals and managers in an industrial organization.

MANAGING MID-LIFE TRANSITIONS

873. Balog, James. "Pyramids, Mesas, and Mid-Career Crises." *Financial Analysts Journal*, 35, No. 5 (1979), 25-29.

    Examines investment analysts' mid-career crises and compares industry's approach to organizing creative people with Wall Street's approach. The advantages and disadvantages of industry's pyramid structure vs. Wall Street's mesa structure are discussed and prescriptions for rejuvenating career satisfaction are offered.

874. Berkwitt, George J. "Deadwood in the Executive Suite." *Dun's Review*, 95, No. 3 (1970), 35-37.

    Following years of widespread expansion and easy profits many companies find themselves with too many executives doing too little work. Management must take steps to stop "rigor mortis" in the executive suite by measuring performance, firing executive deadwood, instituting executive outplacement programs, or encouraging executive creativity.

875. Brown, Duane. "Emerging Models of Career Development Groups for Persons at Midlife." *Vocational Guidance Quarterly*, 29, No. 4 (1981), 332-340.

    Presents and critiques four models of counseling/guidance now being used to deliver services to workers at midlife: the self-help model, the information model, the developmental model, and the structured group model. The critique is based on four criteria and the author finds no one model which meets all four criteria. The developmental model is viewed as offering the most promise.

876. Chernis, Cary. *Staff Burnout: Job Stress in the Human Services*. Beverly Hills, Cal.: Sage, 1980.

    Examines the roles, dynamics, and effects of staff burnout in social service organizations. The symptoms and significance of burnout for human services are explored, along with the sources of burnout, the impacts of job stress, prevention strategies, and future directions. Among the preventive measures suggested are staff development and counseling programs, redesign of staff roles, sensitivity in developing program goals and philosophies, and management development programs for administrators.

877. Cherniss, Cary, Edward S. Egnatios, and Sally Wacker. "Job Stress and Career Development in New Public Professionals." *Professional Psychology*, 7, No. 4 (1976), 428-436.

Examines three issues regarding new public professionals: (1) the aspects of career experience which contribute to psychological stress; (2) the effects of high job stress on performance and career development; and (3) the influence of the work setting on the coping process.

878. Connor, Samuel R., and John S. Fielden. "R_x for Managerial 'Shelf Sitters'." *Harvard Business Review*, 51, No. 6 (1973), 113-120.

"Shelf-sitters" are managers who have been passed over for promotions but are kept on the payroll. The authors present a two-fold plan: (1) companies should encourage and pay for second-career training of younger managers, and (2) companies should force early retirement (or demotion) on passed-over or "surplus" managers.

879. Cooper, Cary, and Derek Torrington. "Strategies for Relieving Stress at Work." *Personnel Management*, 11, No. 6 (1979), 28-31.

Explores the short- and long-term strategies which personnel managers might use to manage work stress. Short-term strategies dealing with performance appraisal, stress counseling, stress awareness, training, and clarity of promotion criteria are considered. Long-term strategies involving worker participation, selection and promotion criteria, grievance procedures, career development, and job mobility are discussed.

880. Finston, Howard V. "Career Frustration--American Style." *The Personnel Administrator*, 15, No. 6 (1970), 23-29.

Even though organizational climates are now less autocratic and more democratic, career frustration persists for many employees. The potential for participative management is not likely to be achieved unless it is supplemented by efforts to facilitate the personal growth of employees in the organization. Personal growth training efforts might include individual counseling, inter-group therapy, and sensitivity training. Instead of relying exclusively on participation and group involvement, attention should be given to the psychological health of the individual and the organization.

881. Fiore, Michael V., and Paul S. Strauss. *Promotable Now: A Guide for Achieving Personal and Corporate Success*. New York: John Wiley and Sons, 1972.

    Brings together aspects of need fulfillment psychology with cognitive dissonance theory and outlines an approach to restructuring management style. The model seeks to help the "dead end" manager to become more promotable. The authors describe a dynamic management set which they contend is an effective strategy for bringing about change. The career lattice model for identifying and developing managers is explained and extended to the employing organization as a need fulfilling unit.

882. Gershenfeld, Walter J. "What is the Problem Concerning Obsolescence of Managerial Personnel." *Personnel Administration*, 29, No. 5 (1966), 17.

    Managerial obsolescence resulting from technological change needs to be appraised at the societal, organizational, and individual levels. Organizations must engage in innovative planning and enact policy measures to deal with this increasing problem.

883. Goffman, Erving. "On Cooling the Mark Out: Some Aspects of Adaptation." *Psychiatry*, 15, No. 4 (1952), 451-463.

    Discusses the sense of disappointment which employees experience when they realize their career expectations are unrealistic. Just as the "mark" is a "sucker" taken in by a crook, so to is the disappointed employee sometimes taken in by the employing organization when deception concerning expectations occurs. Organizations should take steps to avoid the adverse consequences from disillusioned employees and to minimize the loss of self esteem experienced by employees.

884. Golembiewski, Robert T. "Mid-Life Transition and Mid-Career Crisis: A Special Case for Individual Development." *Public Administration Review*, 38, No. 3 (1978), 216-222.

Focuses on the "mid-life transition" as one developmental stage which employees experience during the course of employment. The author describes this transition and associates it with the experience of "mid-life crisis". During mid-career crisis, the employee seriously questions his/her personal identity and values. This often results in significant career shifts by those who have already achieved success in their work. The author considers challenges to organizations posed by mid-life transition and strategies that might be developed to deal with them.

885. Golightly, Henry O. "When an Executive Quits on the Job." *Business Horizons*, 21, No. 2 (1978), 14-17.

Discusses the on-the-job retiree who occupies an office, draws full pay, and goes through the motions of work; but, in effect, quits. The author identifies the signs of a manager who has quit, considers the effects of on-the-job retirement, and suggests some remedies for dealing with the problem. Recommendations include shaking up the routine, appealing to the individual's pride, and providing new challenges. If these strategies fail, job transfer, termination, or early retirement are suggested.

886. Hodgson, Richard C. "Recycling the Middle-Aged Executive." *The Business Quarterly*, 37, No. 1 (1972), 22-27.

Discusses the problems causing premature managerial obsolescence and remedial actions to help managers keep growing. The remedies include personal planning, formation of situational groups, and use of the Forty Plus organization.

887. Hood, John M. "The Company Man in Crisis." *Personnel Journal*, 54, No. 2 (1975), 93-96.

The psychological crisis facing aging middle managers is discussed. Increased availability of career change counseling is one potentially effective response organizations could make to deal with this problem.

888. Horgan, Neil J., and Robert P. Floyd, Jr. "MBO Approach to Prevent Technical Obsolescence." *Personnel Journal*, 50, No. 9 (1971), 687-693.

Presents a practical approach to the prevention of technical obsolescence in the organization. The role and responsibilities of the individual, management, and the training and development of staff are discussed.

The authors argue that "canned" courses for large groups of technical personnel are inappropriate and recommends a program designed to meet individual needs.

889. Hughes, Ellen C. "'Shelf Sitters' Reexamined." *Harvard Business Review*, 52, No. 3 (1974), 38-40, 44, 46, 160, 163, 164.

    Summarizes reader responses to a previous article (878) which recommended a formula for helping obsolescent executives to prepare for a second career. In general readers felt it was inhumane to insist that "shelf-sitters" be required to leave; instead, the employing organization should help find a place for them via transfers, retentions, and/or demotions. Among the different ideas proposed were: up-or-out policies after five years, accommodate employees in return for their many years of service, discard the belief that promotions are synonomous with success, and eliminate excess staff via attrition.

890. Lachter, Lewis E. "Are You Considering a Second Career?" *Administrative Management*, 32, No. 4 (1971), 28, 32.

    Administrative managers are increasingly switching to a new set of responsibilities at mid-career. Second career executives can be a valuable addition to the firm. Programs are needed which provide executives opportunities to enter new areas within the corporate structure. Five examples of second careers are given.

891. Laurence, Barbara S. "The Myth of the Midlife Crisis." *Sloan Management Review*, 21, No. 4 (1980), 35-49.

    There is widespread acceptance of the notion that everyone passes through a "midlife crisis." However, we should avoid uncritical acceptance of this concept, which the author contends is a myth. Her data from a small sample of individuals who recently made midlife career changes illustrates that such changes do not always result from crisis and that midlife crisis is not a universal life experience. She suggests the need for an alternative approach, which is more interactive and longitudinal, stressing both psychological and environmental factors.

892. Leider, Richard J. "Why a Second Career?" *The Personnel Administrator*, 19, No. 2 (1974), 40-45.

    The priorities of executives often change as they go through the "mid career crisis" and seek new purposes in work. The author summarizes societal trends leading to the emergence of second careers and points to the need for revitalization of career systems to deal with these developments.

893. Levinson, Harry. "On Being a Middle-Aged Manager." *Harvard Business Review*, 47, No. 4 (1969), 51-60.

   Discusses middle-aged managers by looking at various symptoms of the aging process: health, psychological factors, changes in point of view, family relationships, work style, and personal goals. The personal and organizational implications of the changes in the middle-aged manager are examined and steps toward constructive action are recommended.

894. Levinson, Harry. "When Executives Burn Out." *Harvard Business Review*, 59, No. 3 (1981), 73-81.

   Discusses the nature of managerial burnout, why modern organizations give rise to this type of exhaustion, and some managerial strategies to combat it.

895. Mahler, Walter R. "Educating the Executive in the Future." *Training and Development Journal*, 32, No. 7 (1978), 50-53.

   Presents nine predictions concerning the future of executive education. Such education in the future will gain in popularity, be more influenced by "customers," adapt to the needs of homogeneous students, be related to the stages of an executive's career, use innovative teaching techniques, involve executives teaching each other, involve cross-cultural learning, and be more individualized.

896. Mahler, Walter R. "Every Company's Problem: Managerial Obsolescence." *Personnel*, 42, No. 4 (1965), 8-16.

   Identifies six different types of obsolescence: abrupt, creeping, pseudo, ability, attitudinal, and industrial. Ten suggestions are offered for individuals wishing to cope with obsolescence and nine preventive measures are listed for the company in dealing with this threat.

897. Manuso, James S. "Executive Stress Management." *The Personnel Administrator*, 24, No. 11 (1979), 23-28.

   Argues that organizational efforts to deal with employee stress could cut corporate costs. The author identifies stressors, recommends treatments, and discusses ways to manage stress.

898. Marshall, Judi, and Cary L. Cooper. "Managers Under Stress." *Management Today*, December (1976), 19-22.

The United Kingdom has experienced increased managerial stress as new managers are underutilized, managerial authority is undermined by worker participation, and job challenge is lacking due to pressures from below and power restrictions from above. Government interference in private enterprise is another source of dissatisfaction.

899. Miller, Neil. "Career Choice, Job Satisfaction, and the Truth Behind the Peter Principle." *Personnel*, 53, No. 4 (1976), 58-66.

Concludes that there may be more myth than fact in the Peter Principle. Hazy thinking and haphazard decision-making characterize the ways individuals make career choices and the employment/promotion practices of many companies. To reverse the downturn in job satisfaction at midcareer, the author suggests the need for meaningful career paths for managers, specific definitions of job requirements, and carefully planned training programs. The initiative for career development is not likely to come from employees themselves; instead, some external force from the organization is needed.

900. Morano, Richard. "Continuing Education in Industry." *Personnel Journal*, 52, No. 2 (1973), 106-112.

Continuing education programs are needed to combat technological obsolescence. The author discusses the need for life long learning and outlines four assumptions about adult learners. If companies can motivate employees to undertake the task of learning adult education programs can significantly contribute to both employee and company goals.

901. Murphy, Patrick P., and Harman, D. Burk. "Career Development of Men at Work." *Journal of Vocational Behavior*, 9, No. 3 (1976), 337-343.

Makes the case for revising previous career development theory to include an additional developmental stage occuring at midlife. The authors offer a definition of a developmental stage and examine findings from recent studies of male middlescence for indications of the presence of such a stage. The implications for career development theory and counseling practice resulting from the acceptance of this stage are discussed. Suggestions are offered for practitioners on ways they may assist those entering their middle years to deal with the mid-life stage and avoid the crisis it may induce.

902. Norman, Beverly. "Career Burnout." *Black Enterprise*, 11, No. 12 (1981), 45-48.

   Career burnout is a serious occupational hazard with symptoms of rage, frustration, and fatigue. The causes and consequences of career burnout are considered, especially for young black professionals. Individual and corporate strategies to prevent or relieve burnout are discussed.

903. Orth, Charles D., III. "How to Survive the Mid-Career Crisis." *Business Horizons*, 17, No. 5 (1974), 11-18.

   Discusses the factors leading to mid-career change, the directions and extent of change, and the problems such change poses for individuals and organizations. Organizations should consider new kinds of managerial training, new guidance and counseling procedures, and more sophisticated career development and early retirement programs. Profiles of four people in second careers are provided.

904. Peterson, William D., and Susan E. Spooner. "Career Crises for Helping Professionals: Who Counsels the Counselor in Crisis." *Journal of College Student Personnel*, 16, No. 1 (1975), 80-84.

   Examines the potential causes of career crises, reviews reactions to career crises, and explores techniques for handling the crisis. Concrete examples are provided. Sources of help for professionals in crisis are mentioned.

905. Potter, Beverly A. *Beating Job Burnout*. San Francisco: Harbor, 1980.

   Reviews the symptoms and causes of burnout and ways to diagnose and prevent it. Special attention is devoted to motivation, tailoring the job to fit the individual, changing jobs, and thought control. Three useful appendices spell out what companies can do as well as individual relaxation exercises and self-programming strategies.

906. Schultz, Duane. "Managing the Middle-Aged Manager." *Personnel*, 51, No. 6 (1974), 8-18.

   Managers and others going through the mid-life crisis often suffer health problems, depression, fear, hostility, and alienation. Those who manage middle-aged managers need to be aware of the nature of this crisis and take positive steps to help resolve it. To help their employees through these difficult "transition" years, many employers are establishing mid-career clinics. Such clinics should help employees recognize the nature of the problem and provide both personal and vocational counseling.

907. Sheppard, Harold L. "The Emerging Pattern of Second Careers." *Vocational Guidance Journal*, 20, No. 2 (1971), 89-95.

    Discusses the need to radically alter our traditional work patterns as a result of changing technology and increased longevity. The author suggests a means for identifying candidates for flexible or second careers and indicates some of the social-psychological dimensions in which they differ from the noncandidates for second careers.

908. Thompson, Paul H., and Gene W. Dalton. "Are R & D Organizations Obsolete?" *Harvard Business Review*, 54, No. 6 (1976), 105-116.

    Surveys of over 200 professionals in five large R & D organizations reveal that there are four different stages in the technical employee's career. Recommendations based on the author's career-stage model are directed at managerial improvements designed to prevent organizational obsolescence.

909. Twigger, Tony. "The Managerial Career." *Management Today*, December (1978), 55-57; 114.

    Examines the attitudes of a sample of British managers in electrical companies toward their careers. Results show that many managers do not believe their careers follow predictable paths, and that few organizations intervene to help employees cope with the stress and strain of job changes within a managerial career. Large organizations should provide career counseling to advise employees.

910. Ullmann, Charles A. "Second Careers for Military Retirees." *Vocational Guidance Journal*, 20, No. 2 (1971), 89-95.

    Describes the Department of Defense's Referral Program that assists servicemen to obtain second careers. It provides both counseling services and a computerized man-job matching system to facilitate the occupational relocation of military servicemen at mid-career.

MANAGING THE OLDER WORKER

911. Bartlett, Douglas M. "Retirement Counseling: Making Sure Employees Aren't Dropouts." *Personnel*, 51, No. 6 (1974), 26-35.

    Discusses the correlates of successful retirement and the employer's responsibilities for providing pre- and post-retirement counseling. The what, when, where, who, and how of retirement counseling is addressed.

912. Broussard, William J., and Robert J. Delargey. "The Dynamics of the Group Outplacement Workshop." *Personnel Journal*, 58, No. 12 (1979), 855-857.

    When job cut-backs necessitate termination of an employee or group of employees, outplacement counseling procedures can be usefully employed. This form of career guidance and assistance can be provided in outplacement workshops which help instill confidence and introduce techniques so employees can constructively search for jobs. The ingredients for a successful workshop are presented.

913. "Climbing Down the Ladder." *Management Review*, 67, No. 6 (1978), 6-7.

    An alternative to early retirement is offered by companies in Denmark which give top executives less stressful jobs with less money and prestige.

914. Cuddihy, Robert. "How to Give Phased-Out Managers A New Start." *Harvard Business Review*, 52, No. 4 (1974), 61-69.

    Describes the experience of the Aluminum Company of Canada, Ltd. (Alcan) with massive managerial cutbacks and their efforts to make the separation procedure more socially responsible. Redundant executives were identified three to six months before termination so that internal alternative job possibilities could be considered and external job searching was facilitated by coaching and counseling. The author recommends steps other companies could take to deal with dismissals.

915. Driessnack, Carl H. "Outplacement: A Benefit for Both Employee and Company." *The Personnel Administrator*, 23, No. 1 (1978), 24-26, 29.

While companies are not accustomed to providing benefits out of charity, there are sound financial reasons for implementing outplacement programs. Among the advantages cited by the author are reduced severance pay and improved employee and public relations. The role of the company and the viewpoint of the displaced individual are discussed in relation to re-employment assistance.

916. Driessnack, Carl H. "Outplacement--the New Personnel Practice." *Personnel Administrator*, 25, No. 10 (1980), 84-93.

Outplacement involves removal of marginal employees with minimal disruption and cost to the organization and with maximal benefit to the employees involved. This article describes how outplacement works and how it can benefit displaced individuals and organizations with a surplus of personnel. Among the topics discussed are use of outside consultants, economic and humanitarian considerations, and finding suitable outside employment.

917. Giovannini, Peter C., and Vito V. Soranno. "Retirement Planning: Choice or Chance." *Training and Development Journal*, 28, No. 9 (1974), 40-42.

Describes the retirement planning program of the Port Authority of New York and New Jersey. The following eight points are covered in a five-session program: (1) the need to plan for retirement; (2) physical and psychological aspects; (3) Social Security/Medicare benefits; (4) pension benefits; (5) company health and insurance benefits; (6) finances/investments; (7) estate planning; and (8) use of time during retirement.

918. Goldner, Fred H. "Demotion in Industrial Management." *American Sociological Review*, 30, No. 5 (1965), 714-724.

Examines the management of one large business firm which provides examples of the individual and organizational mechanisms that can be used to make demotions socially acceptable. In this case the manager's acceptance of the possibility of demotions provided the organization with the flexibility to move them around to suit its productive needs without jeopardizing individual commitment to the firm.

919. Hedaa, Laurids. "...Or De-escalation?" *Across the Board*, 16, No. 4 (1979), 23-25.

   A survey was conducted which explores manager's reactions to demotions. Results show managers prefer demotion to early retirement. The author recommends greater flexibility in career patterns and legitimation of downward mobility in career paths and pension plans.

920. Holly, William J., Jr., and Hubert S. Field, Jr. "The Design of a Retirement Preparation Program: A Case History." *Personnel Journal*, 53, No. 7 (1974), 527-530.

   Presents a case history of the activities of a privately-owned utility firm in designing its retirement program. Ingredients of a successful program include: top management support, voluntary attendance of retirees and spouses, cooperation, and program coordination by the personnel department.

921. Holt, Lawrence J. "Retirement: A Time to Enjoy or Endure?" *The Personnel Administrator*, 24, No. 11 (1978), 69-73.

   Since retirement is a significant period in a person's life, it takes advance preparation. Organization executives are recognizing an obligation to assist potential retirees in planning for this retirement period. The causes of the trend toward early retirement are summarized, along with the difficulties facing the retiree. To assist employees in coping with the problems, the author enumerates the possible objectives of retirement preparation programs and outlines the core session of a typical retirement preparation workshop.

922. Kets de Vries, Manfred F.R. "The Midcareer Conundrum." *Organizational Dynamics*, 7, No. 2 (1978), 45-62.

   Examines the changes and stress symptoms associated with midlife/midcareer transitions and develops a conceptual framework outlining alternative reactions of managers to this transition phase. Suggestions are provided on how the individual, the organization, and society can limit the adverse effects of the midlife/midcareer phase. The role of counseling in prevention of obsolescence is considered.

923. Koyl, Leon F. *Employing the Older Worker: Matching the Employee to the Job*. Washington, D.C.: National Council on Aging, 1974.

Describes a method of examining older workers to determine their fitness for work. Since the results obtained can be related to job requirements, the data in this manual are useful in matching the person to the job and vice versa. A seven-category scale is used to organize and rate data from a physical exam and to rate and profile the requirements of a specific job. The outcome provides a basis for matching the two.

924. Kravetz, Dennis J. "Counseling Strategies for Involuntary Terminations." *The Personnel Administrator*, 23, No. 10 (1978), 49-54.

To effectively assist the terminating employee, an employee relations counselor must recognize and respond to the emotional stages the employee is going through. Among the psychological reactions are shock and disbelief; rage, anger; defense mechanisms; distress, despair, or depression; reflective grief; and positive behavior. Specific counseling activities are discussed which might lessen the psychological impact of involuntary terminations.

925. Lundren, Earl F. "Needed--Retirement Counseling Programs in Business." *Personnel Journal*, 44, No. 8 (1965), 432-436.

Employees who are approaching retirement need to be prepared to emotionally accept it. If employees are to achieve the financial condition, activity level, and health status necessary for successful retirement, companies will need to aid them through a program of preretirement counseling. Retirees from companies having such preparatory programs are found to be more satisfied with retirement.

926. Manion, A. Vincent. "Retiring Early?" *The Personnel Administrator*, 17, No. 5 (1972), 18-21.

A recent research survey of 201 diverse industries investigated early retirees to determine the social, health, and financial characteristics of the sample; the reasons for their retirement decisions; their attitudes toward work and leisurely pursuits; and their attitudes regarding retirement planning and counseling. The author discusses implications of the survey results for personnel administration.

927. McIntosh, Stephen S. "Outplacement--the New Responsibility in Termination." *The Personnel Administrator*, 18, No. 2 (1973), 10-13.

Describes the efforts of the Barberton, Ohio, Works of PPG Indsutries, to deal with the effects of a major cutback by developing an outplacement or unemployment training program for terminating employees. The outplacement training program included: (1) self-confidence building and focus on the meaning of work; (2) the actual job search (e.g., locating openings using employment agencies); (3) financial relief available (e.g., transitional employment, unemployment compensation); (4) resume development; and (5) the cover letter.

928. Meyer, Evelyn, and Carol Ann Kradlak. "Adding Pizzazz to Your Retirement Education Program." *The Personnel Administrator*, 24, No. 11 (1979), 63-67.

    Identifies two key factors affecting the success of retirement education programs: the preparation of the retirement education program planner and the effectiveness of the program and follow-up mechanism. The authors identify the objectives, topical coverage, training and cost considerations, format, and supplementary materials required for a successful retirement education program. Such programs can be pepped up by insuring a suitable environment, proper pacing, adequate preparation of outside speakers, appropriate handouts, relevant group activities, relaxed learning climate, good audio-visual aids, and consistent follow-up.

929. Mirsberger, Gerald E. "Counseling the Older Employee." *Personnel Administration*, 17, No. 5 (1972), 22-23.

    Five objectives of a retirement planning program which combines the goals of the participant and the company are to: (1) aid employees in insuring an acceptable lifestyle in retirement, (2) encourage prospective retirees to think positively about retirement, (4) encourage planning for retirement, and (5) provide management with information on plans of prospective retirees to insure proper manpower planning for replacement.

930. Mithers, Joan. "Turn Your Employee Career Guidance Program into an Effective Pre-Retirement Vehicle." *Personnel Administrator*, 25, No. 10 (1980), 49-52.

    Career development programs can be adapted to focus on older workers. Pre-retirement planning can keep valued employees active longer and bring benefits to the organization. A career development workshop for older workers is outlined which helps employees find fulfillment either in a post-retirement career or in retirement. The author summarizes the advantages to the employer in sponsoring this kind of program, discusses program costs, and delineates the content of such a program.

931. Pellicano, Don. "Retirement Counseling." *Personnel Journal*, 52, No. 7 (1973), 614-618.

    Recommends the hiring of an outside consultant to establish and oversee retirement counseling programs. Use of consultants removes the need for a permanent staff of retirement counselors. It also protects the organization from legal recourse for advice that older employees judge to be unsatisfactory subsequent to retirement.

932. Pogalies, Joan. "Widespread Concerns for the Aged." *The Personnel Administrator*, 17, No. 5 (1972), 16-17.

    A brief discussion of pre- and post-retirement programs is followed by a listing of agencies which might be helpful in developing such programs.

933. Pyron, H.C. "Preparing Employees for Retirement." *Personnel Journal*, 48, No. 9 (1969), 722-727.

    A survey of 100 companies describes an "intensive-comprehensive" pre-retirement counseling program. Only 12 percent of respondents implemented counseling programs conforming to the criteria of this model. The author believes such a model can increase the effectiveness of older workers and improve morale.

934. Quinn, Joseph F. "Job Characteristics and Early Retirement." *Industrial Relations*, 17, No. 3 (1978), 315-323.

    Explores the influence of the work environment on the potential retiree's decision by focusing on the actual working conditions and the nature of the job. Results support the hypothesis that individuals are more likely to retire from jobs with undesirable job characteristics. The nature of the job and conditions of employment do influence early retirement decisions, particularly for employees with health limitations.

935. Rosen, Benson, and Thomas H. Jerdee. "The Influence of Age Stereotypes on Managerial Decisions." *Journal of Applied Psychology*, 61, No. 4 (1976), 428-432.

Investigates the influence of age stereotypes on simulated managerial decisions of business students using an in-basket exercise. Results confirm the hypothesis that stereotypes regarding older employee's physical, emotional, and cognitive traits lead to discrimination against older employees. The implications of results for career satisfaction and worker motivation are discussed.

936. Scherba, John. "Outplacement: An Established Personnel Function." *The Personnel Administrator*, 23, No. 7 (1978), 47-50.

    Argues that outplacement programs should be offered by every personnel department, regardless of size. Recognizing that such programs may vary according to characteristics of the department (size, expertise, workload), the author discusses how an effective outplacement program can be developed and implemented in-house. Among the services companies might provide are: interview training, job search training, resume preparation, resume typing and reproduction, job leads, counseling, advertising, letters to employers, and facilities.

937. Staley, Mark J. "Pre-retirement Planning: A Primer." *The Personnel Administrator*, 20, No. 5 (1975), 44-46.

    An effective pre-retirement planning program (PREPP) must carefully consider not only what is to be done but also how and when it is to be accomplished. The criteria to consider before starting a PREPP are listed, along with possible objectives to accomplish and topics to be covered in a pre-retirement planning program. The author provides hints on how to get started with a PREPP and teaching tips of do's and don't's.

938. Tatzmann, Manfred. "How to Prevent Retirement Shock." *The Personnel Administrator*, 17, No. 5 (1972), 45-48.

    Surveys and interviews on group pre-retirement programs reveal five primary areas of concern for older employees: (1) money, (2) attitudes, (3) health, (4) housing, and (5) unspoken concerns. The author discusses each of these and stresses the rewards for the employer resulting from an effective assistance program.

939. Thompson, Velma M. "Unemployed Aerospace Professionals--Lessons for Programs for Mid-Life Career Redirection." *Policy Analysis*, 3, No. 3 (1977), 375-385.

Examines the problems of middle aged professionals facing involuntary career changes and assesses programs designed to help unemployed aerospace personnel. The author reviews the literature on mid-life career redirection programs summarizing the reasons for failure of unsuccessful programs and the ingredients present in successful ones. Effective programs supplement technical retraining with provision of job information and counseling services.

940. Van Der Meulen, Peter D. "Retirement Planning at Ampex." *The Personnel Administrator*, 17, No. 5 (1972), 49.

The Ampex Corporation's pre-retirement counseling program, for employees between 15 and 65 is briefly described. The program consisted of eight weekly two-hour sessions on retirement problems and solutions as well as supplemental programs to suit special populations.

941. Walker, James W. "Will Early Retirement Retire Early?" *Personnel*, 53, No. 1 (1976), 33-39.

The popularity of early-retirement is diminishing as a result of changing financial conditions, age discrimination laws, and individual attitudes. After outlining the factors which led organizations to develop early retirement arrangements and the factors which influence individuals to retire early, the author traces countervailing forces which are gaining strength. Management should be aware of the pros and cons of early retirement and adopt policies based on a realistic appraisal of the issues and current trends.

942. Wood, Stephen. "Management Reactions to Job Redundancy Through Early Retirements." *The Sociological Review*, 28, No. 4 (1980), 783-807.

Presents a case study of a division of a multi-national company in which an early retirement scheme was used to deal with managerial job redundancies. The article's focus is primarily on the reactions of personnel who had not been asked to leave the firm at the time of the study. The research illustrates the way in which job redundancies can be managed and the divisions that can arise between redundants and non-redundants.

PUBLIC SECTOR

943. Barad, Cary B. "Developing and Using an In-House Interest Inventory." *Personnel*, 54, No. 6 (1977), 57-61.

    The Social Security Administration has developed and used an in-house interest-inventory system. Responses from employees on a number of statements concerning organizational job activities are matched with groupings of occupations based on the similarity of their responses and those of satisfied employees in each of the occupational clusters. Interest profiles are designed to help employees plan their own career and they are not to be used in agency personnel actions or in determining the ability/potential of an employee to succeed in different types of work.

944. Birkenstock, John, Ronald Kurtz, and Steven Phillips. "Career Executive Assignments--Report on a California Innovation." *Public Personnel Management*, 4, No. 3 (1975), 151-155.

    In 1963, the State of California pioneered an innovative program entitled "Career Executive Assignments" to help meet the needs of top level civil service administrators. This program created an autonomous civil service personnel system, which has become a prototype of separate career executive merit systems. The article traces the evolution of the program from its inception, through infancy and adolescence, into an evolving maturity.

945. Campbell, Alan K., and Lynn D. Strakosch. "The Presidential Management Intern Program: A New Approach to Selecting and Developing America's Future Public Managers." *Public Administration Review*, 39, No. 3 (1979), 232-236.

    Examines six aspects of the Presidential Management Intern Program (PMI): purpose, selection process/criteria, intergovernmental cooperation, affirmative action, career development, and evaluation strategy. A profile of the first PMI class is presented.

946. Cole, Richard L., and David A. Caputo. "Presidential Control of the Senior Civil Service: Assessing the Strategy of the Nixon Years." *The American Political Science Review*, 73, No. 2 (1979), 399-413.

Assesses President Nixon's success in obtaining managerial control over the federal bureaucracy by manipulating the civil service personnel system. Findings show that Republicans were more successful in attaining top career positions during the Nixon years. Independent career executives were more likely during the Nixon years than previously to share the sentiments of Republican executives by supporting Nixon policies and goals.

947. Cotton, Chester C., and Richard F. Fraser. "On-the-Job Career Planning: One Organization's Approach." *Training and Development Journal*, 32, No. 2 (1978), 20-24.

Describes career development within the Agricultural Research Service (ARS) of the U.S. Department of Agriculture. The individual development plan is the "blueprint" for the ARS development process; the supervisor-employee relationship gives direction for the effort; and the training and development unit manages, supports, monitors, and evaluates the program.

948. Fay, Lew. "Management Development Through Mobility and Versatility." *Public Personnel Review*, 25, No. 4 (1964), 240-244.

The City of San Diego undertook efforts to develop generalists with varied qualifications to fill management ranks instead of relying on professional and technical specialists. The author was Personnel Director in San Diego during this time, and he cites several case histories of career men as evidence substantiating the success of their program. The author relates the jurisdiction's examination procedures, competitive promotions, and job rotation practices to management development.

949. Fisher, John F., and Robert J. Erickson. "California's Executive Assignment: Meeting the Challenge for Better Management." *Public Personnel Review*, 25, No. 2 (1964), 82-86.

Two men who helped develop California's new personnel system, geared especially for high-level civil service officers, trace the emergence of the idea, the enabling legislation, problems in implementation, and the long-range outlook of the program. The key to realizing the potential of this system, in the author's view, is its being integrated into the overall management development program of the state civil service.

950. Fisher, John F., and Neely D. Gardner. "A Development Program for Personnel Technicians." *Public Personnel Review*, 21, No. 2 (1960), 110-113.

Examines the employee development process followed by the California State Personnel Board. The process assumes that development should be based on the unique needs of each individual. Employee development is a three-way responsibility shared by (1) the individual who is responsible for his own development; (2) the manager/supervisor who is responsible for encouraging development of subordinates; and (3) the organization which is responsible for holding managers/supervisors accountable for creating a "climate" conducive to development.

951. Garson, G. David. "The Institute Model for Public-Sector Management Development." *Public Personnel Management*, 8, No. 3 (1979), 242-255.

Drawing on experience in the North Carolina Government Executives Institute (GEI), the author examines the institute model of management development for high-level government executives. After presenting five principles of interactive education, the author presents the GEI curriculum and an approach to evaluating training programs. An evaluation of the first two GEI graduating classes reveal that on three evaluative criteria, the GEI Model is discovered to be effective in back-home agency effect.

952. Gilbert, G. Ronald, and John V. Sauter. "The Federal Executive Institute's Executive Development Programs." *Public Personnel Management*, 8, No. 6 (1979), 382-390.

Reviews some of the practices of executive development in the Federal Government, with particular emphasis on OPM's Federal Executive Institute (FEI). The authors report mixed findings: some behaviors support the theory that executive development is functioning well; other behaviors identify questions about the theory and practice of executive development. The paper considers the implications of the Civil Service Reform Act's Senior Executive Service provisions for the practice of executive development.

953. Golembiewski, Robert T. "Organization Development in Public Agencies: Perspectives on Theory and Practice." *Public Administration Review*, 29, No. 4 (1969), 367-377.

Summarizes OD experiences in public agencies at different levels, and presents a variety of perspectives on the characteristics of OD programs. The author discusses seldom recognized problems facing government agencies in their applications of OD programs. He foresees increasing applications of OD programs in public agencies, recognizes the need for these programs to be tailored more closely to the constraints of the public agency environment, and outlines roles for students of public administration who have developed appropriate competencies.

954. Grandpre, Donn R. "One Thing Wrong With the Federal Service: What Would I Do About It?" *Personnel Administration*, 23, No. 4 (1960), 4-5.

The author calls for career service personnel to fill top positions in government (including secretaries of the departments) due to their extensive experience, availability, and natural competence.

955. Hebel, John J. "Generalist Versus Specialist in the Bureau of Indian Affairs." *Public Administration Review*, 21, No. 1 (1961), 16-23.

Previous organizational arrangements in the Bureau of Indian Affairs (BIA) of the Department of the Interior were distributed with the introduction of a generalist, in the form of an area director, into the organizational structure. Prior to the change, the BIA was characterized by specialist dominance and independence, resulting from the broad functional responsibilities and centralized organization of the Bureau. The change in structure has led to a power equilibrium between specialists and generalists where neither dominates.

956. Henry, Nicholas. "A Mini-Symposium on Internships in Public Administration." *Public Administration Review*, 39, No. 3 (1979), 231-259.

Focuses on internships at each level of government and reports some empirical findings about internships. The initial article reviews the first year of experience with the federal Presidential Management Intern Program; the third evaluates the Phoenix Management Intern Program; and the final two articles assess perceptions of satisfaction-dissatisfaction with internships and the worth of public administration internships.

Public Sector   261

957. Lang, Kurt. "Military Career Structures: Emerging Trends
      and Alternatives." *Administrative Science Quarterly*,
      17, No. 4 (1972), 487-498.

      Within the occupational structure of the U.S. military,
      tactical operations, account for only a minority of all
      officer assignments. An inflation of assignments to
      tertiary sector activities has occured in the technical
      management area. These developments in combination
      with shortages in many engineering/scientific fields,
      undermine the validity of several premises on which
      military careers have heretofore been based. Alternative
      models supplementing military officer recruitment include
      the paraprofessional force, contracting of services from
      civilian organizations, and lateral recruitment.

958. Leibowitz, Zandy B., and Nancy K. Schlossberg. "Critical
      Career Transitions: A Model for Designing Career
      Services." *Training and Development Journal*, 36, No.
      2 (1982), 12-19.

      Identifies four categories of "critical career
      transitions" (moving into new roles, lateral moves, job
      loss, non-movement) and outlines three components of
      organizational career transition programs (structuring
      suport systems, providing cognitive information, planning).
      Examples of career transition workshops for technical
      specialists moving to management, for those reaching
      plateaus in their careers, and for those making pre- and
      post-retirement plans are provided.

959. Lomas, W. Richard. "The Federal Personnel System and the
      Challenge of the Space Age." *Western Political Quarterly*,
      28, No. 2 (1965), 263-274.

      Examines the federal civil service system and assesses
      its ability to meet technological, social, and economic
      changes. Career patterns, training, and career planning
      are briefly discussed.

960. Mailick, Sidney, and Solomon Hoberman. "Executive Develop-
      ment and Organizational Development." *Public Personnel
      Review*, 24, No. 3 (1963), 173-178.

      Describes and evaluates the executive development
      program for New York City including sponsorship, financing,
      objectives, and training. The program was designed for
      high-level officials, operated continuously, and was con-
      cerned with both organizational and individual change.
      In accomplishing program objectives, the City established
      a close working relationship with New York University,
      and organized the program around present and future needs of
      city departments.

961. Musolf, Lloyd D. "California's Career Executive Assignment: A Perilous but Necessary Voyage." *Public Personnel Review*, 25, No. 2 (1964), 87-89.

    Presents the pros and cons of California's new personnel system for top-level executives and likens it to Ulysses' voyage. Having weighed the "allures and risks", the author concludes that the plan deserves sympathetic consideration.

962. Musolf, Lloyd D. "Separate Career Executive Systems: Egalitarianism and Neutrality." *Public Administration Review*, 31, No. 4 (1971), 409-419.

    The adoption of separate personnel systems for the higher civil service must consider the values underlying American personnel systems. Two such values are especially relevant: egalitarianism and political neutrality. This article sets forth the way in which two separatist systems--California's Career Executive Assignment and the proposed Federal Executive Service--address these values and how each system relates to the ill-fated Senior Civil Service initiative of the 1950s.

963. Ourairatana, Arthitya. *A Study of Selected Career Executive Development Programs in the United States Federal Service: 1962-1966.* Diss., Univ. of Colorado, 1968.

    Examines three selected executive development programs organized for mid and upper-level federal careerists during the years 1961 to 1966. The three programs are: National Institute of Public Affairs' Career Education Awards, U.S. Civil Service Commission's Executive Seminar Centers, and Brookings Institution Conferences for Federal Managers and Program Executives. The author concludes that the three executive development programs have contributed significantly to the federal service.

964. Patton, Thomas H., and Lester E. Dorey. "Long Range Results of a Team Building OD Effort." *Public Personnel Management*, 6, No. 4 (1977), 31-50.

    Drawing on data from 28 federal and military executives participating in seven seminars/workshops on organizational development through team building, the authors found participants reporting changes in ability to resolve interpersonal conflict, set goals using MBO, manage time, build trust, motivate and communicate with subordinates, confront unacceptable performers, and reward employees. The authors suggest that this OD design may be broadly applicable in government employment.

965. Perham, John C. "Unique Job Swap for Executives." *Dun's Review*, 109, No. 5 (1977), 89-91.

Describes the President's Executive Interchange Program which gives selected middle level managers in the private and public sectors an opportunity to work for a year in the other sector. Special attention is given to choosing the participants, bridging the gap between sectors, and dealing with reentry problems.

966. Pomerleau, Raymond. "The State of Management Development in the Federal Service." *Public Personnel Management*, 3, No. 1 (1974), 23-28.

Examines three theoretical perspectives which illustrate present practices in management development: (1) cognitive skills, refers to implanting of technical abilities through traditional training; (2) Affective modes, refers to attempts to raise one's consciousness about the culture of the organization and one's ability to work well in that culture; and (3) Broadening of perspectives, refers to educational practices which alter the conventional thinking of managers. The first two are amenable to quantitative evaluation; the third has been widely adopted despite lack of empirical evidence that it improves managerial performance.

967. Raksasataya, Amara. *Executive Development in the United States: With Special Emphasis on Top Federal Career Executives*. Diss., Indiana Univ., 1960.

Provides a theoretical and academic exploration of the various issues of executive development and studies the Brookings Institution Executive Conference Program. The analysis yields both a theoretical and practical framework for executive development in public administration.

968. Rehfuss, John A. "Executive Development: Executive Seminar Center Style." *Public Administration Review*, 30, No. 5 (1970), 553-561.

Outlines the operation of the U.S. Civil Service Commission Executive Seminar Centers and assesses the lecture method of instruction. Concern about the overuse of lectures and the need to diversify the program curriculum leads the author to propose four alternatives: modified lecture, solid core, export of training technology, and management exchange and feedback. The article alludes to unresolved issues over the broadening of specialists into generalists. The Commission will have to decide whether to provide almost all middle managers with one or a few courses or whether to devoted most middle management training resources to a small, select group.

969. Segal, David R., and Daniel H. Willick. "The Reinforcement of Traditional Career Patterns in Agencies Under Stress." *Public Administration Review*, 28, No. 1 (1968), 30-39.

Personnel decisions are often being dictated by external pressures rather than by internally-generated organizational pressures. External pressures toward more universalistic recruitment criteria have led such agencies as the United States Army, Navy, and Foreign Service to react by emphasizing recruitment from traditional sources as criteria for advancing to top levels within these organizations. By contrast, in both the Air Force and Marine Corps, this is not the case, since traditional criteria do not exist in the former, and the latter has been under less environmental stress.

970. Thie, Harry J., and Robert C. Lorbeer. "Better Personnel Management Through Applied Management Science." *Interfaces*, 6, No. 3 (1976), 68-73.

Successful accomplishment of the Army's mission requires effective management of Army personnel resources. The Department of the Army's policy is to use personnel in slots consistent with their military qualifications and personal characteristics. The authors discuss computer models which enable personnel managers to restructure job classifications within career development fields.

971. Benedict, Truman G. "What Kind of Federal Career Service?" *Personnel Administration*, 23, No. 4 (1960), 25-28, 49.

The author discusses concepts of career, merit, and promotion in the Federal government pointing up problems and making recommendations for change.

972. Warner, W. Lloyd, et al. "A New Look at the Career Civil Service Executive." *Public Administration Review*, 22, No. 4 (1962), 188-195.

Research on the background of federal career civil civil servant executives (over 7,640 managers at the GS 14 level or higher) are compared with other kinds of federal executives and with top business leaders. The author examines such questions as level of entry, representative bureaucracy and career lines in the federal government. The groups of executives are compared on the basis of education levels, institutions of higher education from which four-year degrees were received, interorganizational mobility, and socioeconomic origins.

973. Wynia, Bob L. "Executive Development in the Federal Government." *Public Administration Review*, 32, No. 4 (1972), 311-317.

Calls attention to some of the weaknesses in the existing system of executive development and foresees the creation of a new and better "education and training" system. Present government practice indicates that once employees are hired, they are, by and large, on their own to upgrade skills, gain new knowledge, and learn new methods. With the passage of the Intergovernmental Personnel Act, the implementing agencies have the opportunity to initiate some long overdue research and to put in place a comprehensive education and training system.

AUTHOR INDEX

References are to item numbers

Ackerman, Leonard 684
Albee, Lou 261
Alderfer, Clayton P. 779
Allan, Peter 479
Allen, Lynn 277
Allen, Pinney 126
Allen, Robert E. 169
Allison, Elisabeth 126
Allpander, Guvenc G. 531
Almquist, Elizabeth M. 127, 530
Andberg, Wendy L. 128
Anderson, Richard J. 170
Anderson, Stephen D. 1
Andrews, John D.W. 828
Angrist, Shirley S. 530, 532
Anthony, Ted F. 216
Aplin, John C. 604
Arffa, Marvin S. 129
Armstrong, Janet C. 459
Asser, Mary Helen 533
Astin, Helen S. 350, 351
Atanasoff, George E. 80
Atkinson, Charles 752
Austin, David L. 610

Bachhuber, Thomas D. 2
Bailey, John A. 314
Baker, H. Kent 210
Balloun, Joe L. 809
Balog, James 873
Bank, Ira M. 81
Barad, Cary B. 943
Barker, Tony 829
Barkhaus, Robert S. 3
Barnes, Alma S. 534

Barnes, Lousi B. 438
Baron, Alma S. 534,535
Barrow,Cynthia A. 165
Bartlett, Douglas M. 911
Bartlett, Willis E. 82, 83
Bartling, Herbert C. 52
Bartol, Kathryn M. 315, 536
Bartol, Robert A. 536
Baruch, Rhoda 302
Bates, George E. 262
Baumeister, A.A. 751
Baxter, James C. 171, 200
Bayer, Ann 460
Beachley, Catherine 53
Becker, Howard S. 721, 722
Becker-Haven, Jane F. 25
Begosh, Donald G. 4
Bell, Chip R. 780
Bell, Robert R. 211
Bellas, Carl J. 685
Benedict, Truman G. 971
Bensahel, Jane G. 753
Benson, Carl A. 212
Benton, A. Randolph 754
Berardo, Don 213
Berger, Lance A. 611
Berger, Mike 214
Berkwitt, George J. 874
Berlew, David E. 723
Berliner, Don 172
Bernstein, Peter 316
Best, Fred 5
Betz, Ellen L. 317, 376
Betz, Nancy E. 537, 555, 560
Beyer, Janice M. 830
Bird, Caroline 538

267

Birkenstock, John 944
Black, Gordon S. 503
Blank, Jeff R. 54
Blau, Peter M. 55, 130
Blood, Milton R. 411
Bohn, Martin J. 46
Bolles, Richard N. 6, 84, 85, 177
Bolyard, Charles W. 3
Bond, Floyd T. 867
Bonnell, Roy O., Jr. 158
Boocock, Sarane S. 86
Borchard, David C. 131
Borgen, Fred H. 56
Borrow, Henry 87
Bowen, Donald D. 663
Bowin, Robert B. 377
Boynton, Robert E. 352
Bradley, Richard W. 88
Brady, William F. 173
Bray, Douglas W. 353, 387 781, 782, 787, 793
Brennan, Lawrence D. 174
Brennan, William L. 263
Brenner, Marshall H. 7
Britten, Robert H. 686
Broadwall, Martin M. 215
Brodsky, Archie 442
Bronzaft, Arline L. 548
Broussard, William J. 912
Brown, Duane 875
Brumfield, Peggy D. 539
Brush, Donald H. 783
Buchanan, Bruce, II 724
Burack, Elmer H. 784
Burck, Harman D. 120, 901
Bureau of Labor Statistics 57
Burnett, Kent F. 25
Burnstein, Eugene 378
Buskirk, Richard H. 318
Butkus, Alvin A. 245
Byham, William C. 785
Bylinsky, Gene 481

Calero, Thomas M. 786
Campbell, Alan K. 945
Campbell, N. Jo 356
Campbell, Richard J. 353, 787

Campbell, Robert E. 89
Caputo, David A. 946
Cardwell, James W. 831
Career Information Center 58
Carey, E. Niel 90
Carnegie Commission on Higher Education 59
Carol, Arthur 246
Carr, James W. 504
Carroll, Archie B. 216
Cateora, Phillip R. 599
Chalofsky, Neal 514
Chamberlain, Anne 264
Champoux, Joseph E. 402
Chance, Barbara J. 601
Cheloha, Randall S. 399
Chenery, Mary F. 111
Chenoweth, Lillian C. 540
Cherniss, Cary 876, 877
Cherrington, David 400
Christensen, Edwin R. 18
Claiborn, Charles D. 94
Clarke, John R. 265
Clay, Hubert H. 788
Cleckley, Betty Jane 482
Clement, Ronald W. 505
Cleveland, Harlan 8
Coates, Charles H. 354
Cohen, Leonard 175
Cohen, Michael 483
Cohen, William A. 176
Cole, Andre 639
Cole, Mary E. 541
Cole, Richard L. 946
Colla, Coleman 466
Collie, H. Cris 832
Collins, Shelia K. 355
Conen, Loretta K. 445
Connor, Robert J. 208
Connor, Samuel R. 878
Connors, John F. 687
Constandse, William J. 401
Cook, David R. 688
Cook, Mary F. 755
Cooney, Rosemary S. 542
Cooper, Cary 879, 898
Cooper, Jacqueline F. 60
Cooper, Lloyd G. 689

Author Index

Cooperman, Irene G. 543
Corey, James H. 833
Cosgrave, Gerald P. 9
Costello, John 484
Cotton, Chester C. 947
Couch, Peter D. 217
Cowle, Jerry 266
Crites, John O. 91, 92, 267, 319, 553
Cross, William C. 93
Crotty, Philip T. 247, 248
Crumrine, Janice 390
Crystal, John C. 177
Cuddihy, Robert 914
Cummings, Paul W. 834
Cunningham, David 447

Dalton, Gene W. 320, 438, 908
Danker-Brown, Pamela 203
Darian, Jean C. 544
Dauw, Dean C. 268
David, Harry 725
Davidson, Jeff 612
Davis, Anthony J. 186
Dayton, Charles W. 178
Deci, Edward L. 432
Deitch, Cynthia H. 545
Delargey, Robert J. 912
Denues, Celia 132
Derderian, Stephanie E. 766
De Salvia, Donald 488
Deutsch, Arnold R. 179
Dever, Scott 269
Diamond, Esther E. 61
Di Domenico, Peter J. 832
Diggin, Thomas E. 835
Dill, William R. 440
Dillard, John M. 356
Dilley, Joseph S. 110
Di Marco, Nicholas J. 379
Dittrich, John E. 690
Dixon, David N. 94
Djeddah, Eli 10
Domkowsky, Dorothy 712
Donaho, Melvin W. 196
Dornan, J.M. 321
Douglas, Priscilla D. 546
Driessnack, Carl H. 915, 916

Drossel, Margaret 664
Du Bato, George S. 95
Dubin, Samuel S. 441
Dubing, Robert 402
Duffy, John F. 806
Duncan, Otis D. 55
Dunham, Randall B. 824
Dupree, Flint O. 180
Durrett, Mary E. 66
Durrill, David C. 836
Dye, Thomas R. 485
Dyer, Lee D. 270, 271

Earwood, Larry 691
Edelwich, Jerry 442
Egan, Michael 837
Egnatios, Edward S. 877
Egner, Jean R. 96
Ekehammar, Bo 133
Elias, Susan F. 203
Ellis, Priscilla 134
Eng, Jo Ellen 613
Entrekin, L.V. 272
Epperson, Douglas L. 62
Epstein, Gilda F. 547, 548
Epstein, Jack 614
Erickson, Erik H. 273
Erickson, Robert J. 949
Estler, Suzanne E. 838
Evan, William M. 726
Evans, Martin G. 615
Everett, J.E. 272

Farmer, H.S. 550
Farmer, James A., Jr. 274
Farnsworth, Terry 839
Farr, James L. 399
Faulkner, Robert R. 728
Faux, Victor A. 23
Fay, Lew 948
Fazel, Mohammed 692
Feingold, S. Norman 98
Feldman, Daniel C. 729
Feldman, Howard S. 665
Ferguson, Lawrence L. 616
Ferguson, Wilburn C. 789
Ferrari, Erma P. 11
Ferrari, Sergio 551

Field, Hubert S. 920
Fielden, John S. 878
Finkelhor, Marian K. 552
Finston, Howard V. 880
Fiore, Michael V. 881
Fishel, Jeff 506
Fisher, Dalmar 705
Fisher, John E. 357
Fisher, John F. 949, 950
Fitz-enz, Jac 790
Fitzgerald, Louise F. 99, 553
Fletcher, Frank M. 12
Floyd, Robert P., Jr. 888
Foegen, J.H. 840
Follett, Charlene V. 128
Ford, George A. 13
Ford, John 487
Ford, Robert N. 275
Form, William H. 638
Forrest, David J. 115
Forrester, Gertrude 63
Foster, Lawrence W. 554
Foster, Mary Sue 617
Foulkes, Fred K. 618
Fox, Frederick V. 403
Fox, Marcia R. 181
Frantzich, Stephen E. 507
Fraser, Richard F. 947
Frédian, Alan J. 268
French, Wendell L. 223
Friant, R.J., Jr. 218
Friedland, Nehemia 28
Fukami, Cynthia G. 730
Fulmer, Robert M. 841
Fulmer, William E. 841

Gale, Barry 64
Gale, Linda 64
Gambill, Ted R. 756
Gannon, Martin J. 619, 633, 737, 791
Garbin, Albeno P. 322
Gardiner, Charles V. 842
Gardner, Neely D. 629, 950
Garfinkle, Joan P. 404
Garson, G. David 951
Geeting, Baxter 323
Geeting, Corrinne 323

Gelatt, H.B. 100
Gemmill, Gary 488, 489
Gershenfeld, Walter J. 882
Gibson, James L. 405
Gifford, J. Nebraska 324
Gilbert, G. Ronald 952
Ginsberg, Lee R. 792
Ginsburg, Sigmund G. 443
Ginzberg, Eli 65, 101
Giovannini, Peter C. 917
Gittleman, H.M. 843
Gleason, Richard D. 219
Glueck, William F. 135, 844, 845
Goffman, Erving 883
Goldenberg, Judith 865
Goldman, Daniel R. 380
Goldner, Fred H. 490, 918
Golembiewski, Robert T. 884, 953
Golightly, Henry O. 885
Goodale, James G. 136
Goodson, William D. 693
Gordon, Francine E. 556
Gordon, George G. 491
Gottfredson, Cary D. 137
Gottier, Richard F. 731
Gottsdanier, Josephine S. 613
Gould, M.J. 757
Gould, Roger L. 276
Gould, Sam 381
Grandpre, Donn R. 954
Granick, David 620
Granovetter, Mark S. 182
Grant, Donald C. 353, 782, 793
Grass, Donald 694
Greenhaus, Jeffrey H. 138
Greenwood, James W., III 444
Greenwood, Jaems W., Jr. 444
Grey, Ronald J. 491
Grosky, Oscar 406
Grotevant, Harold T. 66
Gruber, Edward C. 174
Grubel, Herbert G. 508
Grupp, Fred W., Jr. 407
Guerrier, Yvonne 695
Guest, David 358

Author Index

Gugielmino, Paul J.   325
Guion, Robert M.   731
Guttmann, Jean E.   531
Guzzo, Richard O.   359

Hacker, Andrew   509
Hackett, Gail   537, 555
Hackman, J. Richard   382
Hageseth, Jon A.   113
Haire, Mason   696
Hakel, Milton D.   14
Halatin, T.J.   758
Haldane, Bernard   220
Hall, Douglas T.   136, 326, 341, 383, 384, 408, 423, 556, 557, 558, 621, 622, 663, 706, 711, 718, 723, 732, 733, 734
Hall, Francine S.   557, 558, 622, 623
Hall, Mary S.   15
Hall, Richard H.   67
Haller, Archibald   327
Hamilton, Jack A.   102
Hammer, W. Clay   718
Hammond, D. Corydon   62
Hansen, L. Sunny   559
Hanson, Marlys   277, 697
Hardesty, Sarah A.   560
Hards, Kathryn E.   790
Harel, Gedaliahu   445
Harley, Joan   794
Harmon, Leonore W.   16, 139, 409
Harrell, Thomas W.   716
Harren, Vincent A.   17, 140
Harrington, Thomas F.   68
Harris, Barbara   587
Harrison, Evelyn   561
Hart, Darrell H.   18
Hart, Gary L.   795
Hartley, Shirley F.   598
Harwood, Richard K.   2
Haskell, M.A.   624
Hastings, Robert E.   278, 698, 759
Hawkins, James E.   183
Hawley, Peggy   141
Hay, Christine   562

Hayano, David M.   510
Hazeltine, Florence P.   775
Healy, Charles C.   123
Hebal, John J.   955
Hedaa, Laurids   919
Hedland, Delva   735
Heidrick, Garner   511
Heilman, Madeline E.   359
Heisler, W.J.   489, 492
Helfrich, Linda M.   155
Helliwell, Tanis   446
Helm, Carl   103
Helmich, Donald L.   846, 847
Hendel, Darwin D.   128
Heneman, Herbert G., Jr.   796
Henry, James D.   760
Henry, Nicholas   956
Herbert, Theodore T.   563
Herr, Edwin L.   104, 105
Herrick, Neil Q.   428
Higginson, Margaret V.   30
Hill, Alfred W.   699
Hilton, Thomas L.   106
Hjelm, Victor S.   512
Hoberman, Solomon   960
Hodgson, Richard C.   886
Hofstede, Geert   360, 410
Holbert, Neil B.   463
Holland, Joan E.   146
Holland, John L.   107, 137, 142, 143, 144, 145, 146, 329, 662
Hollandsworth, James G.   184
Hollman, Robert W.   853
Hollman, Thomas D.   14
Holly, William J., Jr.   920
Holmberg, Steven H.   210
Holt, Lawrence J.   921
Hood, John M.   887
Hopke, William E.   69
Hopkins, R.M.   224
Hoppock, Robert   70
Horgan, Neil J.   888
Horner, Matina   385, 386
Horton, Joseph A.   147
Howard, Ann   387
Howard, John   447
Howes, Nancy J.   361

Hoyt, Daniel R. 19
Hubbard, Howard G. 513
Hubben, Herbert 798
Huber, George P. 207
Huddleston, Michael R. 158
Hughes, Ellen 889
Hulin, Charles L. 411
Hummel, Dean L. 20
Hutcheson, Peggy 514

Idema, Thomas H. 493
Ilgen, Daniel R. 736
Illfelder, Joyce K. 388
Isaacson, Lee E. 761
Ivey, Allen E. 108

Jackson, Dorothy J. 96
Jackson, Douglas N. 199
Jackson, Erwin 712
Jackson, John H. 465
Jacobs, Frederick 577
Jacques, Elliott 281
Jacques, Philip F. 565
Jameson, Robert J. 185
Janis, Irving 148
Jarman, Betty Jane 566
Jennings, Eugene E. 494, 799, 849
Jepson, David A. 109, 110, 368
Jerdee, Thomas H. 303, 588, 935
Jindal, Gopi R. 282
Johns, Ted 221
Johnson, Donald M. 249
Jolson, Marvin A. 463, 737
Jones, G. Brian 29, 102
Jones, Lawrence K. 111
Jones, Pamela 762
Jones, Rochelle 464
Jones, William H. 763
Jones, William S. 666
Jongeward, Dorothy 625
Jorz, Joanne J. 800

Kahne, Hilda 567
Kahnweiler, William 121
Kaplan, Rosalyn 605

Karpicle, Susan 21
Katkovshy, Walter 793
Katz, Arthur J. 250
Katz, Martin 112
Katz, Ralph 431
Kaufman, H.G. 251, 448
Kay, Janice 626
Kay, M. Jane 627
Kaye, Beverly L. 667, 762. 764
Keats, Stephen M. 738
Keavney, Timothy 169, 465
Kejner, Mathilde 414
Kellog, Marion S. 628
Kelly, John J. 131
Kennedy, John J. 283
Kennedy, Marilyn M. 284
Kenstaninovich, Branislav 809
Kesselman, Gerald A. 672
Kets de Vries, Manfred F.R. 662, 922
Keys, J. Bernard 211
Kimball, Richard T. 850
Kinslinger, Howard J. 739
Kinzel, Robert 285
Kirkhart, Larry 629
Kivlighan, Dennis M. 113
Klaus, Rudi 765
Klegon, Douglas 22
Klein, Stuart M. 405
Kleinger, Brian H. 222
Klimoski, Richard J. 515
Klingner, Donald E. 186, 668
Knowlton, William A. 801
Knudson, Harry R. 223
Koehn, Hank E. 630
Koff, Lois A. 794
Kolinko, Tom 554
Kopelman, Richard E. 516
Korman, Abraham K. 149, 362, 412, 413
Korwood, Robert 358
Kotter, John P. 23, 740
Koyl, Leon F. 923
Kradlak, Ann 928
Kraut, Allen I. 802
Kravetz, Dennis J. 766, 924
Kremple, Robert J. 466

Author Index

Krizian, Adolph 252
Kroll, Arthur M. 24
Krumboltz, John D. 25, 29, 114
Kryger, Barbara R. 187
Kuehl, Charles R. 379
Kunisch, Robert D. 851
Kurtz, Ronald 944
Kushell, Robert E. 852

Lachter, Lewis E. 890
Landau, Samuel B. 631
Lang, Dorothy 413
Lang, Kurt 957
Lansbury, Russell 517
Laserson, Nina 467
Latham, Gary P. 188
Lathrop, Richard 189
Lauenstein, Milton C. 253
Lauer, Peter H. 741
Laurence, Barbara S. 891
Lauterbach, Albert 495
Lave, Judith R. 532
Lawler, Edward E. 382, 389
Leach, John J. 700
Lederer, Murial 190
Lee, Nancy 568
Lee, Sang M. 742
Lee Dore, Russell 632
Leibowitz, Zandy B. 803, 958
Leider, Richard J. 286, 468, 669, 682, 892
Leonard, Edwin D. 767
Leonard, Frank S. 648
LeShan, Eda J. 287
Lesher, Richard L. 254
Levenson, Myra K. 853
Leventhal, Gerald S. 631
Levine, Adeline 390
Levinson, Daniel J. 288
Levinson, Harry 449, 743, 804, 893, 894
Levitt, Eleonor Sosnow 569
Lewis, J.D. 19
Life Insurance Agency Management Association 701

Lippett, Gordon 13, 26, 670, 671, 702
Lipsitt, Laurence 363
Livingston, J. Sterling 364
Lodahl, Thomas M. 414
Loeb, Stephen E. 633
Lomax, W. Richard 959
Lopata, Helena Z. 570
Lopez, Feliz E. 672
Lorbeer, Robert C. 970
Loring, Rosalin- 571
Loughary, John W. 289
Lovelady, Steven M. 290
Lukowski, Susan 191
Lundren, Earl F. 925
Lunneborg, Patricia W. 572
Lupton, Daniel E. 854
Lyden, Fremont J. 518

MacCrimmion, Kenneth R. 872
Mack, James G. 855
MacMillan, Keith 695
Mager, Robert F. 391
Magoon, Thomas M. 107, 154, Mahler, Walter R. 291, 805, 895, 896
Mahoney, Thomas A. 573
Mailick, Sidney 960
Mallett, Sheldon D. 71
Manion, A. Vincent 926
Manring, Susan L. 415
Mansfield, Rober 150, 384, 416
Manuso, James S. 897
March, James C. 519, 634
March, James G. 519, 634
Mardon, J. 224
Maret, Elizabeth 540
Margerison, Charles 292
Marguilies, Newton 635
Marinelli, Robert P. 665
Marsh, P.J. 703
Marshall, Jean L. 825
Marshall, Judi 898
Martier, Alison 706
Martin, Lee 293
McArthur, Charles 23, 151
McClelland, David 392

McClosky, Michael 225
McConkey, Dale D. 857
McCord, Bird 636
McCoy, Vivian R. 469
McDaniels, Carl 20
McDonagh, Edward C. 513
McEwan, Bruce 637
McGill, Michael E. 294
McGregor, Eugene B. 858, 859
McIntosh, Stephen S. 927
McKelvey, Bill 417
McLane, Helen J. 768
McLean, Hugh A. 805
Meahea, Laird W. 806
Medley, H. Anthony 192
Meier, Kenneth J. 497
Meir, Elchanan I. 27, 28
Meyer, Evelyn 928
Meyer, Herbert E. 226
Meyer, John L. 193
Meyer, Pearl 470
Meyers, Thomas K. 227
Mezey, Michael 520
Michelsen, Richard 532
Mickelson, Richard 530
Milkovich, George T. 304
Miller, Anna L. 584
Miller, Delbert C. 638
Miller, Donald B. 770
Miller, Ernest G. 518
Miller, James E. 450
Miller, Neil 899
Miller, Norman R. 771
Miner, John B. 365
Miners, Howard 331
Mines, Herbert T. 295, 366
Mirides, Ellyn 639
Mirsberger, Gerald E. 929
Missirian, Agnes K. 772
Mitchell, Anita M. 29
Mitchell, Howard M. 194
Mitchell, Terrance R. 801
Mithers, Joan 930
Moch, Michael K. 418
Moment, David 704, 705
Montana, Patrick J. 30, 673
Moore, Charles G. 31

Moore, Lynda L. 674
Morano, Richard 900
Moravec, Milan 675
Moreland, John R. 152
Morgan, Marilyn A. 367, 706, 718
Morrill, Weston A. 108, 115
Morris, James H. 419
Morrison, Ann M. 496
Morrison, David E. 451
Morrison, Donald G. 228
Morrison, Robert F. 420
Mortimer, Jeylan T. 33
Moses, Knolly 229
Munley, Patrick H. 153, 574
Murphy, Joseph P. 807
Murphy, Patrick P. 901
Murray, Norman J.M. 255
Murray, Thomas J. 230, 640
Musolf, Lloyd D. 961, 962
Myint, Thelma 351

Nalbandian, Carol 14
Nash, Allan N. 744, 808
Neapolitan, Jerome 471
Near, Janet P. 393
Nemec, Margaret M. 676
Newstrom, John W. 38
Nigro, Lloyd G. 497
Noeth, Richard J. 368
Norman, Beverly 902
Norton, Steven D. 809
Noughaim, Khalil E. 383
Nygren, Harold T. 734

Oates, David 256
O'Donovan, Thomas 369
O'Hara, Paula 575
O'Hara, Robert P. 344
Ohnesorge, James H. 14
Okosky, Charles E. 34
Oldham, Destry 83
O'Leary, Virginia E. 576
Oliver, Laurel W. 116
Olson, Leif O. 788
Olson, Richard P. 297

Author Index

Omvig, Chryton P. 117
O'Neill, George 35
O'Neill, James M. 154
O'Neill, Nena 35
O'Reilley, Charles A. 421
Orr, Warren G. 231
Orth, Charles D., III 577, 903
Ortiz, Flora I. 521
Ory, John C. 155
O'Shea, Arthur J. 68
Osgood, Donald W. 522
Osipow, Samuel H. 36, 332
Ostrowski, Paul S. 860
Otte, Fred L. 641
Ourairatana, Arthitya 963
Overstreet, Phoebe L. 124

Paine, Whiton S. 452
Palm, Harold J. 249
Palmer, W.J. 707
Pankowski, Mary L. 810
Papanek, Hanna 578
Parker, Robert A. 232
Parry, Kirk 394
Parry, Samuel 246
Pashigian, B. Peter 861
Patchner, Michael A. 156
Patton, Arch 642, 643
Patton, Thomas J. 964
Paul, Carol Ann B. 370
Peacock, Andrew C. 304
Peery, Newman S. 866
Pellegrin, Roland J. 354, 371
Pellicano, Don 931
Perham, John C. 72, 73, 74, 75, 76, 644, 811, 965
Perrone, Philip A. 333
Perrucci, Robert 455
Pesi, Michael 453
Peterson, Candida 579
Peterson, Elwood R. 118
Peterson, William D. 904
Phillips, Linda L. 773
Phillips, Steven 944
Phillips, Susan D. 298, 372
Picker, Ann M. 580
Pickering, John W. 485

Pietrofesa, John J. 334
Piggott, Lucille C.J. 373
Pilla, Barbara 709
Pinkstaff, Marlene 581
Pinto, Patrick 37, 505
Pipe, Peter 391
Pisciotte, Joseph P. 512
Piton, Margaret 191
Pitts, Robert A. 862
Plotsky, Frances A. 157
Pogalies, Joan 932
Pomerleau, Raymond 966
Poole, Brian A. 619
Popper, Hermaine I. 39
Porter, Albert 234
Porter, J. Richard 541
Porter, Lyman W. 402
Portes, Alejandro 327
Portis, Bernard 710
Potter, Albert L. 299
Potter, Beverly A. 905
Powell, Gary N. 582
Prangley, Robert E. 619
Prediger, Dale 119
Presthus, Robert 645
Price, Raymond L. 320
Purvis, June 523
Pyron, H.C. 933

Quadagno, Jill S. 300
Quay, John G. 301
Quick, James C. 813
Quinn, Joseph F. 934
Quinn, Robert P. 422

Rabinowitz, Samuel 423, 429, 711
Radar, Martha H. 814
Raksasataya, Amara 967
Rand, Lorraine M. 584
Rapoport, Rhona 585, 586
Rapoport, Robert 585, 586
Rapoza, Rita S. 559
Raynor, Keith 18
Reardon, Robert C. 120, 121, 158, 712
Rechnitzer, Peter 447
Reha, Rose 257

Rehfuss, John A. 968
Reid, Graham L. 196
Reid, J.N. 235
Reif, William E. 38
Reissman, Frank 39
Renwick, Patricia 424
Reynes, Tony 197
Rice, Beryl C. 425
Rich, Kenneth L. 842
Richards, Allan R. 407
Richards, Louis M. 800
Ripley, Theresa M. 289
Ritti, R.R. 490
Robbins, Paula 472
Rockmore, Wayne 672
Rodgers, Frank A. 363
Roe, Anna 159
Roe, Anne 302, 335
Roff, Harry 646
Roland, Alan 587
Rosen, Benson 303, 588, 935
Rosen, Hjalmar 374
Rosenbaum, James E. 863
Rosenberg, De Anne 713
Rosenberg, Howard R. 258
Rosenfeld, Rachel A. 375
Rosenthal, Beth 198
Ross, Joyce D. 815
Rothman, Robert A. 454, 455
Rothstein, Mitchell 199
Rothstein, William G. 40
Rowe, Mary P. 775
Rozelle, Richard M. 200
Rubinton, Natalie 122
Ruchelman, Leonard I. 524
Rush, James C. 304
Russell, Joyce E.A. 78
Ryan, Colleen 469
Ryan, T. Antoinette 714

Sadek, Konrad E. 498, 870
Saline, Lindon E. 236
Salmans, Sandra 525
Salmon, Richard D. 201
Saltoun, Jane 41
Salvagno, Ralph 715
Samler, Joseph 473
Sandberg, Carl H. 282

Sandifer, Beverly A. 184
Sarachek, Bernard 647
Sasser, W. Earl, Jr. 648
Sauter, John V. 952
Savage, G.E. 790
Schachter, Hindy L. 816
Schaeffer, Dorothy 774. 864
Schalders, William N. 677
Scheele, Adele 237
Schein, Edgar H. 336, 395,
  474, 649, 650, 651, 678,
  745
Schein, Virginia Ellen 587
Scherba, John 936
Schissel, Robert F. 590
Schlossberg, Nancy K. 803,
  958
Schmidt, Peggy J. 202
Schmittlein, David L. 228
Schneider, Benjamin 733, 734,
  746
Schoenfeldt, Lyle F. 783
Schoner, Bertram 716
Schoonmaker, Alan N. 305
Schrage, Harry 396
Schroeder, Wade W. 114
Schultz, Duane 906
Schwartz, Irving R. 306, 679
Schwarzwald, Joseph 865
Schwed, Peter 475
Scott, Dru 625
Scott, William A. 652
Seely, William 736
Seeman, Melvin 426, 427
Segal, David R. 969
Seidenfeld, J. Martin 238
Sekaran, Una 417
Seligman, Daniel 337
Seling, Mark J. 56
Seybolt, John W. 653
Shannon, Donald S. 690
Shapiro, Eileen C. 775
Shappell, D.L. 160
Sharinger, Dale H. 817
Shearer, Richard L. 456
Sheehy, Gail 307
Sheppard, Harold L. 428, 907
Sherwood, Frank P. 776

Author Index

Shestak, Melvin B. 324
Shetty, Y.K. 866
Shikiar, Richard 187
Shimberg, Benjamin 259
Shockley, Pamela S. 591
Shusta, George 818
Sidwell, P. Philip 42
Siegel, Gilbert B. 819
Sigelman, Carol K. 203
Silverman, Arnold 792
Simmons, Judy 592
Simpson, Janice C. 593
Singleton, John 820
Slaney, Robert B. 77, 78, 80, 161, 162
Smith, Abbott P. 526
Smith, Elsie J. 594
Smith, Michael H. 204
Smith, R. Douglas 88
Smith, Ralph E. 595
Sneath, Frank 654
Snodgrass, Gregory 123
Snyder, John T. 821
Sofer, Cyril 308
Soranno, Vito V. 917
Speas, Carol M. 205
Splaver, Sarah 527
Spokane, Arnold R. 71, 107
Spradley, James P. 458
Staats, Elmer 43
Stahl, O. Glenn 44
Stahlman, Pershing P. 747
Stake, Jayne E. 596
Staley, Constance M. 591
Staley, Mark J. 927
Staw, Barry M. 403
Steers, Richard M. 419
Steger, Joseph A. 456
Steinberg, Ronnie 868
Stephan, Cookie 601
Stephenson, Harriet 239
Stevens, John M. 830
Steward, Rosemary 822
Storey, Walter D. 45
Stover, Ronald G. 322
Strakosch, Lynn D. 945
Strand, Stanley 174
Strausbaugh, David 823

Strauss, Anselm L. 722
Strauss, Paul S. 881
Stringer-Moore, Donna M. 597
Stumpf, Stephen A. 338, 429
Super, Donald E. 46, 124, 309, 339, 340, 341
Sussman, John A. 240
Swanson, Barbara S. 541
Swenson, Allan A. 310
Swinyard, Alfred W. 867

Tarnowieski, Dale 342, 430
Tatzmann, Manfred 938
Taylor, Hugh R. 762
Taylor, Mary G. 598
Taylor, Susan M. 824
Tennyson, W. Wesley 343
Thal, Nancy L. 599
Theodore, Athena 600
Thie, Harry J. 970
Thomas, Edward G. 117
Thomas, Eugene L. 311, 476
Thomas, William C., Jr. 869
Thompson, Paul H. 320, 795, 908
Thompson, Velma M. 939
Thorne, Edward H. 825
Tiedeman, David V. 47, 344, Tomeski, Edward A. 498, 870
Tomlinson-Keasley, C. 397
Torrington, Derek 879
Tracey, Terence J. 154
Traxel, Robert G. 206
Tresemer, David 398
Trice, Harrison M. 830
Truskie, Stanley D. 826
Tsaklanganos, Angelos A. 655
Tuckman, Bruce W. 48
Tulloch, Rodney W. 117
Tully, Judy C. 601
Turecamo, Dorrine A. 602
Twigger, Tony 909

Ullman, Joseph C. 207
Ullmann, Charles A. 910
Ulrich, Heinz 208

Vaitenas, Rimantis 477

Vance, Carmen L.   604
Vance, Forrest L.   71
Van Der Meulen, Peter D.   940
Van Maanen, John   431, 656
Vash, Carolyn L.   457
Veiga, John F.   499, 500, 871
Veninga, Robert L.   458
Villanueva, A.B.   260
Vroom, Victor   163, 432, 872

Wacker, Sally   877
Walker, James W.   505, 658, 680, 681, 941
Wallace, B.S.   440
Walsh, W. Bruce   164, 165, 345
Walter, Verne   241
Walters, Roy H.   659
Walz, Garry R.   346
Wanous, John P.   166, 749, 750
Warnath, Charles F.   125
Warner, W. Lloyd   501, 972
Warren, Alfred S.   827
Watley, Donivan J.   605
Weaver, Charles N.   433
Weaver, Nancy P.K.   131
Weaver, Peter   312
Webber, Ross A.   434
Weerts, Michael V.   717
Weiss, W.H.   242
Welch, C. William   243
Welch, Susan   606
Wellbank, Henry L.   718
Wells, Theodore   571
Wertheim, Edward G.   167
Wettengel, Carl   785
Wheeler, Don   148
Whitney, Douglas   329
Widom, Cathy S.   167
Wiener, Yoash   477
Wilders, Malcolm   529
Wilensky, Harold L.   347
Williams, Constance M.   168
Williams, Cortez H.   660
Williams, Donald C.   502
Williams, Gregory   608
Willick, Daniel H.   969
Wintersheid, Beverly   719
Wittebort, Susan   435

Wnuk, Joseph J.   720
Wogman, Barry L.   823
Wolf, James F.   776
Wolff, Michael F.   661
Wood, S.   49
Wood, Stephen   942
Wortzel, Laurence H.   167
Wynia, Bob L.   973

Yankelovich, Daniel   50, 436
Yeager, Joseph C.   682
York, Reginald O.   657
Yost, Edward B.   563

Zaharia, E.S.   751
Zaleznik, Abraham   437, 438, 662
Zehring, John W.   209
Zenger, John H.   51, 683
Zytowski, Donald G.   349

TITLE INDEX

Absenteeism, Job Involvement, and Job Satisfaction in an Organizational Setting   399
Accelerating Pay Rates for Managers Who Switch Employees   502
Achievement Motivation Can Be Developed   392
The Achievement Motive and Advancement in Two Types of Organizations   828
Adding Pizzazz to Your Retirement Education Program   928
Affirmative Action for Women   625
Age, and Midcareer Crises: An Empirical Study of Academics   272
An Age-Graded Model for Career Development Education   48
Alienation at the Top   410
Almost Random Careers: The Wisconsin School Superintendency, 1940-1972   519
Ambition and the Political Vocation: Congressional Challengers in American Politics   506
Ambition Theory and the Office of Congressman   520
The American Occupational Structure   55
An Analysis of Demographic Characteristics and Career Patterns of Women Administrators in Higher Education   546
An Analysis of the Job Search Behavior Patterns and Re-Employment Experiences of Unemployed Middle-Aged Managers   270
Analyzing Performance Problems or You Really Oughta Wanna   391
Anatomy of Career Commitment in Women
Applicability of the Holland (1973) Model of Vocational Development with Spanish-Speaking Clients   68
Application of Projective Techniques in Personnel Psychology Since 1940   739
An Application of Roe's Vocational Choice Model   160
Are Job Banks Improving the Labor Market Information System?   207
Are R & D Organizations Obsolete?   908
Are Today's Managers Really All That Mobile?   854
Are Top Executives Transferable Across Companies?   866
Are You Considering a Second Career?   890
Are You Good at Career Counseling?   760
Are You a Potential Burnout?   446
Are You Promotable?   242

As You Were Saying--Downward Management Development   796
An Assessment Center Examination to Select Administrative Interns   823
The Assessment Center in the Measurement of Potential for Business Management   782
Assessment Centers: An Aid in Management Selection   787
Assessment Centers: For Selection or Development   795
Assessment Centers for Supervisors and Managers: An Introduction and Overview   785
The Association of Managerial Style and Worker Job Change Receptivity in Varying Situations   657
Attitude: Success Element for Women in Business   630
Attitudes of Government Executives Toward Management Training   791
Avoidance of Pitfalls in Supervisory Development   817

Background Characteristics and Career Development of Personnel Managers   504
Beating Job Burnout   905
Beginning Again in the Middle   460
A Behavioral Model of Middle-Manager Career Mobility: An Empirical Analysis   499
Behavioral Training for Increasing Effective Job-Interview Skills: Follow Up and Evaluation   184
Better Management of Managers' Careers   616
Better Personnel Management Through Applied Management Science   970
The Big Switch   464
A Biographical Data Analysis of Career Patterns in Engineering   515
Blue Collar Jobs for Women   190
The Boom in Executive Jobs   73
The Boom in Executive Self Interest   642
Breaking Out of the Lockstep   5
Breakthrough: Women into Management   571
Bright Prospects in the Executive Job Market   480
Britain's Management Squeeze   646
Building Organizational Commitment: The Socialization of Managers in Work Organizations   724
Burn-out: Stages of Disillusionment in the Helping Professions   442
Burn Out--When You Can't Do Your Job--and Don't Know Why   439
The Burnt-out Administrator   457
The Business Executive as a Career Type   513

California's Career Executive Assignment: A Perilous but Necessary Voyage   961
California's Executive Assignment: Meeting the Challenge for Better Managers   949

Career Adaptivity: The Effective Adaptation of Managers to
 Changing Role Demands 420
Career Adjustment Counseling of 'Young-Old' Women 83
Career Anchorage: Managerial Mobility Motivations--A Replication
 380
Career Burnout 902
Career Center Evaluation Methods: A Case Study 712
Career Characteristics of Top U.S. Bankers 511
Career Choice and Attitudes Towards Work Among Professionals-
 in-Training 134
Career Choice, Job Satisfaction, and the Truth Behind the Peter
 Principle 899
Career Choice Starts at Home 151
Career Choices of Married Women: Effects on Conflict, Role
 Behavior and Satisfaction 556
Career Concerns of Black Managers 647
Career Continuity and Retirement Plans of Men and Women
 Physicians: The Meaning of Disorderly Careers 300
Career Counseling: Too Little, Too Late? 756
Career Crises for Helping Professionals: Who Counsels the
 Counselor in Crisis 904
Career Decision-Making 106
Career Development 329, 343
Career Development: Choice and Adjustment 344
Career Development Concepts: Significance and Utility 314
Career Development and Counseling of Women 559
Career Development: Designing Our Career Machine 47
Career Development During the High School Years 350
Career Development: Exploration and Planning 341
Career Development in the First Year at Work 416
Career Development: A Future Oriented Historical Approach 704
Career Development: Growth and Crisis 24
Career Development: Maximizing Options 698
Career Development of Men at Work 901
Career Development by Objectives 38
Career Development: Preparing Round Pegs for Square Holes 684
Career Development Requires Senior Executive Involvement/ Manage-
 ment Initiative 710
Career Development Responsibilities of Managers 697
Career Development: Self Concept Theory 340
Career Development: Some Questions and Tentative Answers 700
Career Development: The State of the Art Among the Grassroots
 653
Career Development Strategies in Industry: Where Are We and
 Where Should We Be? 706
A Career Development System Coordinates Training Efforts 719
Career Development: Theory and Research 334
Career Development: Who Is Responsible? 699
Career Development and the Woman Manager--A Social Power Perspec-
 tive 582

Career Development of Women Administrators in Social Work, Nursing, and Education   355
Career Development for Women: An Affirmative Action First   626
The Career Development Workshop   703
Career Development of Young Women During the Post High School Years   351
Career Dynamics: Matching Individuals and Organizational Needs   651
Career Education: A Call for Action   254
Career Executive Assignments--Report on a California Innovation   944
Career Exploration in Adulthood   298
Career Frustration--American Style   880
The Career Game   31
Career Guidance: A Handbook of Methods   89
Career Guidance in the Life Insurance Industry   701
Career Guidance--A Means of Tapping Hidden Potential   771
A Career Guidance Program for Small Rural High Schools   93
Career Guidance: Who Needs It, Who Provides It, Who Can Improve It   101
Career Influences, Educational Experiences, and Professional Attitudes of Women and Men in Veterinary Medicine   128
The Career Information Center, a Working Model   58
Career Knockouts: How to Battle Back   284
Career Life Planning for Americans   30
Career-Life Planning and Development Management   668
Career and Life Planning Guide   289
Career Management   628
Career Management A Career?   652
Career Management Programs   614
Career or Marriage?: Aspirations and Achievements of Able Young Women   605
Career Mobility and Organizational Commitment   406
Career and Motherhood   587
Career Orientations and Perceptions of Rewarded Activity in a Research Organization   336
Career Paths   720
The Career Patterns of Mature American Women   540
Career Patterns of Technically-Trained Professionals: A Person-Environment Interaction Model   415
Career Patterns of Top Executives in New York City Government   479
Career Patterns of Women Administrators in Higher Education: Barriers and Constraints   533
Career Perceptions of Managerial and Professional Personnel   363
Career Personality, and Adult Socialization   722
Career Perspective: Your Choice of Work   132
Career Planning   301

Career Planning for Adults 277
Career Planning and Career Management: Perspectives of the Individual and the Organization: An Annotated Bibliography 37
Career Planning: Coming In From the Cold 683
Career Planning and Development: A Resource System 780
Career Planning and Development: Which Way Is Up? 43
Career Planning for Employee Development 663
Career Planning--Or How to Succeed in Business by Really Trying When the Other Way Doesn't Work 34
Career Planning: Not Leaving the Future to Chance 4
Career Planning: Personnel in the Third Party Role 682
Career Planning for Prison Inmates 665
Career Planning: Search for a Future 9
Career Planning for the Younger Manager 42
The Career Plateau: Causes and Effects 393
Career Problems of Young Managers 434
Career Process: A New Concept for Vocational Behavior 108
Career Prospects for Managers-to-Be: A Look at the 1980s 65
Career Roles, Psychological Success, and Job Attitudes 338
Career Satisfaction and Success: A Guide to Job Freedom 220
Career Stage as a Moderator of Performance Relationships with Facets of Job Satisfaction and Role Perceptions 429
Career Stages: A Partial Test of Levinson's Model of Life Career Stages 304
Career Success and Personal Failure: Alienation in Professionals and Managers 413
Career Women: The 'Revolting Minority' 627
Careers in Human Resource Development 514
Careers in Organizations 326
Careers in State and Local Government 209
Careers Via Closed Circuit Television 53
Careers, Work, and Leisure Among the New Professionals 517
Careers for You 11
Causes of Mid-Life Change from High-Status Careers 311
Central Life Interests and Organizational Commitment of Blue-Collar and Clerical Workers 402
Change of Life Priorities 475
Changing Correlates of Job Involvement in Three Career Stages 711
Changing Demands on the Training Professional 505
The Changing Success Ethic (An A.M.A. Survey Report) 342
Characteristics of Career Success: An Additional Input to Selecting Candidates for Professional Programs 361
Characteristics of the Successful Personnel Manager 358
The Childhood and Adolescent Career Plans of College Women 139
Children Explore Careerland Through Vocational Role Models 81
Choosing to be a Managerial Woman: An Examination of Individual Variables and Career Choice 554

Choosing a Second Career 461
Choosing to Work: An Action-Oriented Job Finding Book 175
Classroom to Boardroom: What You Learned May Not Help You 253
Clearing the Way for the Growth of Women Subordinates 713
Climbing Down the Ladder 913
Coaching: Supporting Public Executives on the Job 776
College Graduates and Jobs 59
The Colleges 632
Coming of Age in Organizations: A Comparative Study of Career Contingencies and Adult Socialization 728
The Coming Flood of New Executives 643
The Coming Glut in Executives 640
Coming: The Great Executive Exodus 644
Community Colleges and Public Service Careers 260
The Companies that Build Executive Talent 811
Companies and Careers 661
The Company Man in Crisis 887
Comparative Impact of the SC11 and the Vocational Card Sort on Career Salience and Career Exploration of Women 60
A Comparative Study of Work Opportunities of Women 542
Comparison of the Career Development of Women Executives in Institutions of Higher Education with Corporate Women Executives 604
Comparison of Pencil-and-Paper and Tactile-Board Forms of the Self-Directed Search 121
Competency-Based Learning Packages--A Case Study 255
The Complete Job Book 179
Compliance and Assistance to an Authority Figure in Perceived Equitable and Nonequitable Situations 865
A Comprehensive Model of Career Development in Early Adulthood 319
Computer Simulation Techniques for Research on Guidance Problems 103
Concepts, Curiosity, and Careers 12
A Conceptual Model of Career Development 714
Consistent and Inconsistent Career Preferences and Personality 165
Consistent Occupational Preferences and Personality 164
Contents and Techniques of Management Development Programs for Women 531
Continuing Education and the Experienced Manager 247
Continuing Education in Industry 900
Continuing Education and Job Performance 251
Contrasting Orientations and Career Patterns of Executives and Lower Managers 369
Contributions of Projective Techniques to Assessment of Management Potential 793
A Conversation with Peter F. Drucker 15

Title Index 285

Correlates of Organizational Identification as a Function of Career Pattern and Organizational Type 733
A Cost-Effective Career Planning Program Requires a Strategy 675
Counseling and Employee Development 767
Counseling Male Midlife Career Changers 761
Counseling--No Easy Task 774
Counseling the Older Employee 929
Counseling Psychology 25
Counseling Psychology: Career Interventions, Research and Theory 107
Counseling for Self-Development 757
Counseling Strategies for Involuntary Terminations 924
Counseling the Unpromotable 864
CREATE: A New Model for Career Change 469
Creating Successful Career Development Programs 641
Criteria for Choosing Chief Executives 743
Critical Career Transitions: A Model for Designing Career Services 958
Crystallizing Career Goals 667
A Current Review of Public Sector Assessment Centers: Cause for Concern 815
A Curriculum Plan to Develop Training Professionals 800

Deadwood in the Executive Suite 874
Death and the Mid-Life Crisis 281
Decision Behavior and Outcome of Midlife Career Changers 459
Decision-Making: A Conceptual Framework of Reference for Counseling 100
Decision Making in the Employment Interview: An Experimental Approach 199
Decision-Making and Vocational Development 105
Decline of the Generalist Myth 645
...Or De-escalation 919
The Definition and Measurement of Job Involvement 414
Demotion in Industrial Management 918
De-Recruitment: The Other Side of the Congressional Career Equation 507
The Design of a Retirement Preparation Program: A Case History 920
Determining Development Needs With Supervisory Conferences 807
Developing Administrative Personnel Through the Assessment Center Technique 813
Developing Career Guidance Programs Through the Job Family Concept 766
A Developing Concept of Careers 44
Developing an In-House Career Planning Workshop 677
Developing Life Plans 670, 671

Developing Managers in a Low Growth Organization 695
Developing Professional Skills and Expertise 702
Developing a Replicable Career Decision-Making Counseling Procedure 123
Developing the Top-Level Executive for the 1980s and Beyond 325
Developing and Using an In-House Interest Inventory 943
The Development of Career Choices: The Relationship Between Patterns of Commitment and Career Outcomes in Adulthood 372
Development of a Career-Orientation Scale for Women 590
The Development of an Integrated Career Planning Program at Gulf Power Company 672
Development of an Instrument to Assess Employer Sponsored Career Development Programs for Sub-Professional Employees 717
The Development of Organization Identification in Professional Members of a Professional Organization: A Developmental Career Stage Approach 730
A Development Program for Personnel Technicians 950
Development Programs for Mature Managers 248
Development of an SVIB for Selecting Managers 744
A Developmental Cross-Sectioning of Women's Careers and Marriage Attitudes and Life Plans 584
Developmental Dialogues 805
Developmental, Emotional, and Interest Factors in Voluntary Mid-Career Change 477
Dimensions of Counseling for Career Development 115
Directions: A Guide to Career Planning 2
Do Managers on the Move Get Anywhere 871
Does Career Planning Rock the Boat? 681
Don't Make It Fancy--Just Good 818
Dual Career Families 585
Dual Careers: How Do Companies and Couples Cope with the Problems 557
The Dual Track Career System Within the Internal Revenue Service 685
The Dynamics of the Group Outplacement Workshop 912

Early Determinants of Vocational Choice 159
The Economic Rationale of Occupational Choice 246
EDP Managers Put On a Business Suit 481
Educating the Executive in the Future 895
Education and Career Mobility Among Federal Administrators: Toward the Development of a Comparative Model 858
Education and Job Satisfaction, 1962-1977 422
Education and the Uncommon Wheel: An Analysis of the Views of Thirty American Corporate Leaders of the Role of Educational Experiences in the Development of Successful Managerial Careers 250

Title Index

Educational Factors, Professional Activity, and Job Tenure
  Among Public Accountants   633
An Educational Strategy for Proessional Career Change   274
The Effect of Career Education on Career Maturity   117
Effect of Individual, Group, and Intergroup Relations on
  Attitudes Toward a Management Development Program   779
The Effect of Job History on Managerial Success   367
The Effect of Parental Messages on the Career Patterns of
  Professional Women   566
Effectiveness of a Counseling Intervention Program for Teaching
  Career Decision-Making Skills   96
Effects of Causal Attributions on a Supervisor's Evaluation of
  Subordinates Performance   801
Effects of Matching Treatment Approaches and Personality Types
  in Group Vocational Counseling   113
Effects of Need and Commitment on Career Exploration Behaviors
  94
Effects of a Realistic Job Preview on Job Acceptance, Job
  Attitudes, and Job Survival   749
The Effects of Supervisory Behavior on the Path-Goal Relation-
  ship   615
Effects of Vocationally Relevant Information on the Expressed
  and Measured Interests of Freshman Males   71
The Efficient Executive   221
The Eight-Year Career Development Plan   224
The Elected and Appointed: Two American Elites   509
An 11-Year Follow-Up of Measured Interest and Vocational
  Choice   52
Eliminate Your Obsolescence   450
Emerging Models of Career Development Groups for Persons
  at Midlife   875
The Emerging Pattern of Second Careers   907
Emphasizing Career Planning in Human Resource Management   669
An Empirical Analysis of Organizational Identification   742
Employee Attitudes as a Function of Age and Length of Service:
  A Reconceptualization   405
Employee Reactions to Job Characteristics   382
Employee Satisfaction Through Career Development   691
Employing the Black Administrator   660
Employing the Older Worker: Matching the Employee to the Job
  923
Encouraging Women Through a Career Conference   157
The Encyclopedia of Careers and Vocational Guidance   69
Erik Erickson's Theory of Psychosocial Development and
  Vocational Theory   153
Evaluating a Management Development Program for Women   814
Every Company's Problem: Managerial Obsolescence   896
Everything a Woman Needs to Know to Get Paid What She's Worth
  538

Evolving Jobs as a Form of Career Mobility: Some Policy Implications 838
Executive Career Guidance 268
Executive Development: Executive Seminar Center Style 968
Executive Development in the Federal Government 973
Executive Development and Organizational Development 960
Executive Development Practices and Problems--The Industrial Experience 798
Executive Development in the United States: With Special Emphasis on Top Federal Career Executives 967
Executive Development: What You Need to Know? 804
An Executive Guide to Getting into Print 243
Executive Job Hunters Get a Guide 97
Executive Jobs: A Banner Year 72
Executive Jobs: Best Year Ever 76
Executive Mobility 727
Executive Mobility in the Federal Service: A Career Perspective 497
Executive Mobility in Public Service and Business 844
Executive Odyssey: Looking for a Job at Fifty-Five 264
Executive Stress Management 897
Executives and Supervisors: Contrasting Definitions of Career Success 371
Executives and Supervisors: Informal Factors in Differential Bureaucratic Promotions 354
Executive Training and Productivity: Managerial Views in Latin America 495
The Executive's Guide to Finding a Superior Job 176
Executives vs. the Career Woman 549
The Expanding Role of the Personnel Function 618
Expectancy Theory Applied to the Process of Professional Obsolescence 445
Expressed and Inventoried Vocational Interests: a Comparison of Instruments 77
Expressed Vocational Choice and Vocational Indecision 161
Exploding the Myth of Executive Job-Hopping 486
Explorations of a Theory of Vocational Choice and Achievement: 11. A Four Year Prediction Study 142
Exploring Careers 57
Exploring the Expatriate's World 837
Expressed and Inventoried Interests Revisited: Prespicacity in the Person 56

Facilitating Career Development: Strategies for Counselors 120
Facing the Mid-Life Crisis 294
A Factorial Investigation of Career Salience 138
Factors Determining Labor Force Participation of Married Women 573

Factors Influencing the Rising Labor Force Participation Rates of Married Women With Pre-School Children   544
Fail: Bright Women   385
The Fall and Rise of Harold Ottman   278
Fatalism as a Factor in Managerial Job Satisfaction, Job Strain, and Mobility   489
Fear of Failure, Achievement Motivation, and Aspiring to Prestigeful Occupations   378
Fear of Failure in Career Development   41
The Fear of Failure--the Supervisor's Greatest Enemy   833
Fear of Success: Popular, but Unproven   398
Fear of Success, Sex Role Attitudes, and Career Salience, and Anxiety Levels of College Women   388
The Federal Executive Insitute's Executive Development Programs   952
The Federal Personnel System and the Challenge of the Space Age   959
Female Modesty in Aspiration Level   548
Finding and Using Executive Talent   366
The First Job Dilemma   474
A Focus on Careers   249
The Football Club Manager--A Precarious Occupation   529
Formalized Mentor Relationships for Management and Executive Development Programs in the Federal Government   765
Formative Years in Business: A Long Term AT & T Study of Managerial Lives   353
Forty Plus: A Self-Help Group for Job-Less Executives   290
The Four Stages of Professional Careers--A New Look at Performance by Professionals   320
A Fresh Look at Retirement   262
From Barriers to Ladders   552
From Executive Suite to Halls of Ivy   462
From Manpower Planning to Human Resources Planning Through Career Development   674

Gaining EEO Compliance With A Stable Work Force   623
The Generalist and Organizational Mobility   483
Generalist versus Specialist in the Bureau of Indian Affairs   955
Generalist vs. Specialist: Careers in a Municipal Bureaucracy   869
Get the Right Person for the Job: Managing Interviews and Selecting Employees   193
Getting Ahead in the Company: How to Keep Track of Where You Are and Where You're Going   218
Getting Down to Basics About Landing That Job   173
Getting a Job: A Study of Contracts and Careers   182
Go Abroad, Young Man   227

Goals and Directions in Personal Planning 225
Governmental and Corporate Elites: Convergence and Differentiation 485
Grief and Involuntary Career Change: Its Implications for Counseling 763
Guidance of the College Bound: Problems, Practices and Perspectives 104
A Guide to R & D Career Pathing 694
Guidelines for Conducting In-House Management Development 826
Guidelines for Executive Job Changes 466

Headhunters 198
Helping Women to Resolve the Home Career Conflict 550
Here Come the Young Turks 328
Highway to Managerial Success 292
How 'Career Anchors' Hold Executives to Their Career Paths 395
How Companies Can Handle the Complexities of Relocation 855
How Long Should a Manager Stay in the Same Job 389
How Not to Become a Chief Executive 230
How Recruiters Influence Job Choices on Campus 135
How RPI Helps Locate Talent 797
How Retirement Opens Room at the Top 279
How Syntax Helps Its Professionals Plan their Careers
How to Break in the College Graduate 745
How to Climb the Communications Ladder to Success 232
How to Develop Managers for the Future--A Systems Approach 659
How to Develop Your Management Talent Internally 799
How to Ease Reentry After Overseas Duty 848
How to Give Phased-Out Managers a New Start 914
How to Help Your Child Plan a Career 20
How to Hire Americans 738
How to Identify Your Negative Behavior Characteristics 820
How to Listen Assertively 323
How to Pick the Right Middle Manager 741
How to Prevent Retirement Shock 938
How to Survive Getting Fired--and Win! 266
How to Survive the Mid-Career Crisis 903
How to Survive Your Company's Merger 280
How to Take Career Crossroads Without Skidding 291
How to Tell When a Good Employee is Job Hunting 612
How to Work for a Living and Like It: A Career Planning Book 51
How Working Mothers Manage: Socioeconomic Differences in Work, Child Care, and Household Tasks
HRD--A Professional Manifesto 689
Human Resource Planning: Managerial Concerns and Practices 658

Identifying and Developing Women for Management Positions 636
Identifying the Good, the Bad, and the Indifferent 852

Title Index

Identifying Managerial Potential: An Alternative to Assessment Centers 783
Identity: Youth and Crisis 273
If It Means Moving, Forget It 840
I'll Never Work for a Woman Supervisor Again 602
The Impact of Doctoral Social Work Education Upon Career Selection and Professional Activities 156
Impact of Dual Career Couples on Employers: Problems and Solutions 597
Implementing a Career Life Planning Program 673
Improving Employee Development Programs 688
Increasing Organizational Effectiveness Through Better Human Resource Planning and Development 678
Increasing Upward Mobility--The Stuff Achievement is Made Of 213
Individual Career Planning: Managerial Help for Subordinates 680
Individual Development Process 321
The Individual, the Organization, and a Career: A Conceptual Scheme 650
Individualism in Management 305
Individualizing Educational and Vocational Guidance Designing a Prototype Program 102
Individuals and Their Careers: Some Temporal Considerations for Work Satisfaction 431
Industrial Sociology 638
The Influence of Age Stereotypes on Managerial Decisions 935
The Influence of the Certified Administrative Manager Program on Career Development of Certified Administrative Managers 252
Influence of Role Pressures on the Perceiver: Judgement of Videotaped Interviews Varying Judge Accountability and Responsibility 200
Influence of Sex Role Attitudes and Cognitive Styles on Career Decision Making 140
The Influence of Volunteer Experience on Career Choice 129
Influences of Puerto Rican, Black, and Anglo Parents' Career Behavior on their Adolescent Children's Career Development 356
Inheriting a Career: the Influence of Sex, Values, and Parents 136
The Institute Model for the Public-Sector Management Development 951
Instruction in Career Decision Making and Decision-Making Styles 122
An Instrument for Measuring the 'Need to Work' 394
An Integrated Model for Training and Development: How to Build on What You Already Have 806

An Integrated Program for Career Development   707
Integrating Personal and Professional Development   26
Interests of Career and Homemaking Oriented Women   574
International Differences in Executive Reward Systems: Extent, Explanation, and Significance   620
Interview Behaviors of Mentally Retarded Adults as Predictors of Employability   203
An Investigation of Different Levels of Agreement Between Expressed and Inventoried Vocational Interests Among College Women   78
An Investigation of Two Measures of Career Indecision   162
Involuntary Job Rotation and Work Behavior   614
Is Career Planning a Useless Exercise?   8
Is the Mentor Relationship Primarily a Male Experience   755
Is Risk Management a Dead-End Job?   435
Is There Enough Room at the Top for Women Managers   564
Issues Concerning Collaborating Careers   579
Issues and Problems in Developing Managerial Careers and Potential   609
The Italian Woman Executive   551

Jobs-Career Key: A Test of Occupational Information   54
Job Characteristics and Early Retirement   934
Job Choice: The Impact of Intrinsic and Extrinsic Factors on Subsequent Satisfaction and Commitment   421
Job Enlargement, Individual Differences, and Worker Responses   411
Job-Hopping to the Top   496
The Job Hunter's Guide to Eight Great American Cities   201
Job Hunting After Forty   261
Job Posting--A Chance to Advance   836
Job Preview Effects During the Critical Initial Employment Period   751
Job Satisfaction Among State Executives in the U.S.   407
Job Satisfaction and the Systems Professional   870
Job Satisfaction in the United States in the 1970s   433
Job Search and the Effectiveness of Job-Finding Methods   196
Job Search Success of Middle-Aged Managers and Engineers   271
The Job Seekers Guide: A Workbook for Improving Your Career Situation   186
Job-Seeking Interview Skills Training: A Comparison of Four Instructional Techniques   205
Job Stress and Burnout: Research, Theory, and Intervention Perspectives   452
Job Stress and Career Development in New Public Professionals   877
Jumping Ahead by Having a Mentor

Keeping Up With Organizational Change   654

Landing the Right Executive Job   265
The Leaders of Tomorrow: Their Identification and Development   792
Learning to be a Middle Manager   217
Lessons of Leadership: The Man Who Runs General Motors   330
Let 1st-Level Supervisors Do Their Job   648
Let Your Protege Make His Own Way   753
Letters of Recommendation: A Question of Value   171
The Life Career Game   86
The Life and Career Plans of Young Adult College Women: A Follow-Up Study   16
The Life Cycle of the Social Role of Housewife   570
A Life-Span, Life Space Approach to Career Development   309
Long Range Results of a Team Building OD Effort   964
Luck and Careers   337

Making It On Your First Job: When You're Young, Inexperienced and Ambitious   202
Making It to the Top   240
Making Vocational Choices: A Theory of Careers   144
Male-Female Professionals: A Model of Career Choice   126
Man in a World of Work   87
MBO Approach to Prevent Technical Obsolescence   888
Management Development and the Instability of Skills: A Strategy   819
Management Development Roles: Coach, Sponsor and Mentor   752
Management Development Through Mobility and Versatility   948
Management Development Without Frills   781
Management of Disappointment   437
The Management Obsolescence Inventory   214
Management Reactions to Job Redundancy Through Early Retirements   942
Management Skill Development: An Experience in Program Design   825
Management Succession: Chance or Choice   860
The Manager as Career Counselor   769
The Managerial Career   909
Managerial Career Coaching   754
Managerial Career Development and the Generational Confrontation   705
The Managerial Growth Sector   235
The Managerial Job Market: Quality Counts   484
Managers Focus on Planning Their Lives   256
Manager's Guide to Successful Job Hunting   206
Managers, Mobility, and Morale   845
Managers Move More But Enjoy It Less   856

Managers' Personal Patterns of Management Theory and Policy as
    Factors in Managerial Career Attainment   352
A Manager's Personal Training and Development Need-Determination
    Questionnaire   239
Managers Predict Their Future   374
The Manager's Role in Developmental Planning   666
Managers Under Stress   898
Managing Down the Line   331
Managing Executive Stress   444
Managing Management Manpower   696
Managing the Middle-Aged Manager   906
Managing Your Career   222
Mandatory Continuing Education: Some Questions to Ask   259
Manpower Development   690
Manpower Obsolescence: A New Definition and Empirical Investiga-
    tion of Personal Variables   456
A Marketing Approach to the Professional Hiring Process   282
Memo to Job Seekers: Writing a Professional Resume   170
Men in Mid-Career: A Study of British Managers and Technical
    Specialists   308
Men, Women, and Work: Reflections on the Two-Person Career   578
Mentors and Proteges: A Study of the Career Development of Women
    Managers and Executives in Business and Industry   773
The Midcareer Conundrum   922
Mid-Career Renewal   286
Midcareer Socialization of Educational Administrators   521
Middle Managers Mobility Patterns   377
Middle Managers' New Values   430
Midlife: A Time to Discover, A Time to Decide
Mid-Life Transition and Mid-Career Crisis: A Special Case for
    Individual Development   884
Military Career Structures: Emerging Trends and Alternatives
    957
A Mini-Symposium or Internships in Public Administration   956
Mobicentric Man   494
The Mobile Manager at Mid-Career   500
Mobility and Career Development for Black Professionals   212
A Model for the Measurement of Vocational Maturity   91
A Model of Career Decision Making for College Students   17
Model of Careers in a Simple Hierarchy: Generalizing the
    Junior Professionals' Decision Rule   228
A Model of Coping with Role Conflict: the Role Behavior of
    Educated Women   408
A Model of Guidance for Career Decision Making   112
Motorola Supervisory Development Program   789
Moving Up   10
Moving Up: Role Models, Mentors, and the 'Patron System'   775
Moving Up to Supervision   215

Moving Women into 'Male' Jobs   617
Multiple Subtypes Among Vocationally Undecided College Students:
  A Model and Assessment Instrument   111
Multivariate Analysis of Male and Female Professional Career
  Choice Correlates   167
Must the Past be Prologue? Or, Why Can't We Do Things Differently?
  610
The Myth of Managerial Tenure   234
The Myth of the Midlife Crisis   891
The Myths of Career Development   715

The National Career Directory: An Occupational Information
  Handbook   64
The National Job-Finding Guide   208
Need for Achievement, Career Mobility, and the Mexican American
  College Graduate   381
Need Fulfillment in the Career Development of Women   376
Needed--Retirement Counseling Programs in Business   925
A Neglected Personnel Problem   401
Networking: Here's How at Equitable   676
Networking: Who You Know May Be As Important As What You Know
  229
The New Careers Concept: Potential for Public Employment of
  the Poor   624
New Data on Women Managers   534
New Frontiers for Assessment Centers   802
New Light on Lateral Entry   501
A New Look at the Career Civil Service Executive   972
The New Psychological Contracts at Work   436
No Fault Career Counseling Can Boost Middle- and Upper-Management Productivity   759
Nontraditional Occupations: Not for Women Only   99

Obsolescence or Life Long Education: A Choice for the Professional   441
Obsolescence and Professional Career Development   448
Occupational Change in Mid-Career: An Exploratory Investigation
  471
Occupational Changes in the Adult Years   302
Occupational Choice: A Conceptual Framework   130
Occupational Choice of Male Graduate Students as Related to
  Values and Personality: A Test of Holland's Theory   168
Occupational Information: Where to Get It and How to Use It in
  Counseling and Teaching   70
Occupational Knowledge and Career Development in Adolescence
  66
Occupational Licensing and the Interstate Mobility of Professionals   861

Occupational Literature 63
Occupational Mobility Within the Firm 843
Occupational Psychology 46
Occupational Value Socialization in Business and Professional Families 33
Occupations and the Social Structure 67
Old Bankers Are Not Written Off 296
Omens for Over-Promotion 829
On Being a Middle-Aged Manager 893
On Cooling the Mark Out: Some Aspects of Adaptation 883
On-the-Job Career Planning: One Organization's Approach 947
On the Meaning of Alienation 426
On the Personal Consequences of Alienation at Work 427
One Thing Wrong With the Federal Service: What Would I Do About It? 954
Opportunities for Women in International Business 599
Oderly Careers and Social Participation: The Impact of Work History on Social Integration in the Middle Mass 347
Organization Development in Public Agencies: Perspectives on Theory and Practice 953
Organizational Careers and Professional Expertise 455
Organizational Careers: Some New Perspectives 656
Organizational Choice: A Study of Pre- and Postdecision Processes 163
Organizational Climate: Individual Preferences and Organizational Realities 746
Organizational Development and Changes in Organizational Climate 635
Organizational Entry: Moving from Outside to Inside 166
Organizational Growth and Successive Patterns 846
Organizational Research on Job Involvement 423
Orientation and Conflict in Career 438
The Other Side of Relocation--Relocating the Spouse 831
Outcome Measurement in Career Counseling Research 116
Outplacement: A Benefit for Both Employee and Company 915
Outplacement: An Established Personnel Function 936
Outplacement--the New Personnel Practice 916
Outplacement--the New Responsibility in Termination 927
Out Where the Grass Looks Greener 293
An Overview of the Supervisors Job 216

Paraprofessions: Careers of the Future and the Present 527
The Part-Time MBA: Impacts on the Mid-Career Development of Managers 258
Passages 307
A Path Up for Women Bankers 313
Patterns of Work and the Dictates of Time 822
Peer Group Interaction and Organizational Socialization: A A Study of Employee Turnover 726

Title Index

The Perceived Cause of Work Success as a Mediator of Sex Discrimination in Organizations 359
Perceived and Real Sex Differences in College Students Career Planning 21
Performance Sampling in Social Matches 634
Personal Change in Adult Life 721
Personal, Educational, and Career Patterns of Men and Women Administrators in the Massachusetts Community Colleges 370
Personal Factors in Organizational Identification 734
Personal Support Services in Corporate Relocation Programs 853
The Personality Characteristics of Professional Career Women: A Study of the Concurrent Validity of John Holland's Theory of Vocational Choice 147
Personal Development and Education--Work Relations of General Motors 827
The Personnel Managers' Front-Life Role in the Marketing Field 522
Personnel: A New Route to the Top 525
Personnel Opinions: Elements of an Employee Development Program 708
Perspectives on Career Guidance: An Administrator's View 98
The Peter Principle and the Efficient Market Hypothesis 508
The Pink Slip: A Contingency Plan 299
Placement Firms: Can They Help? 195
Planned Professional Manpower Mobility 850
Planning for Career Growth 1
Planning for a Career in Human Resource Management 19
Planning Job Progression for Effective Career Development and Human Resource Management 718
Planning, Preparation, and Chance in Occupational Entry 18
Planning the Way to the Top 219
Planning Your Executive Career 223
Planning Your Future: A Workbook for Personal Goal Setting 13
Playing Favorites in Large Organizations 357
Plotting a Route to the Top 233
Politics and Career Mobility of Bureaucrats 859
Positive Changes From a Career Development Program 613
Potential for Career Growth 621
A Practical Problem for Employee Socialization 729
Predicting Field of Job Entry from Expressed Vocational Choice and Certainty Level 368
Predicting How Federal Managers Perceive Criteria Used for Their Promotion 830
Predicting Managers' Career Success In An International Setting 360
The Prediction of Managerial Performance: A Review 362
Prepare Women Now for Tomorrow's Managerial Challenges 794
Preparing Employees for Retirement 933

Preparing for a Move to Middle Management   211
Preparing Women for Management Roles   257
Pre-retirement Planning: A Primer   927
Presidential Control of the Senior Civil Service: Assessing the Strategy of the Nixon Years   946
The Presidential Management Intern Program: A New Approach to Selecting and Developing America's Future Public Managers   945
Prison Can be Bad for Your Career   316
The Problem of the Burned Out Executive   443
Problems of Knowledge and Obsolescence Among Professionals: A Case Study in Dentistry   454
The Process of Adult Life: A Study in Developmental Psychology   276
The Process of Mentoring in the Career Development of Female Managers   772
A Professional Framework for Self-Development   231
The Professional Job Changing System: World's Fastest Way to Get a Better Job   185
Professional-Paraprofessional Cooperation in Career Development   118
The Professional Poker Player: Career Identification and the Problem of Respectability   510
The Professional Woman   600
Professionalization as Career Immobility   490
Professionalizing the Workforce   637
A Profile of New York State Legislators   524
Profile of a Woman Officer   583
Profiles and Careers of Colorado State Legislators   512
Profiles of Five Second-Careerists   467
A Program for Planned Student and Personal Practitioner Interactions   824
Promotable Now: A Guide for Achieving Personal and Corporate Success   881
Promoting Career Planning Through Reinforcement   114
The Promotion Beliefs of Managers as a Factor in Career Progress: An Exploratory Study   488
Promotion: What Does It Take to Get Ahead   492
Propensity for Career Change Among Supervisors   465
The Pros and Cons of Changing Jobs   487
Providing Equal Opportunities for Promotion   841
The Psychological Contract: Managing the Joining Up Process   740
Psychological Stages of Careers in Engineering: An Expectancy Theory Taxonomy   516
The Psychology of Careers   339
The Psychology of Occupations   335
The Psychology of Vocational Choice   143

Title Index

Public Sector People Development 812
Put Your Degree to Work 181
Pyramids, Mesas, and Mid-Career Crises 873

The Quadrant Construct: A Conceptual Framework for Midlife Counseling 306
The Questionable Dual Ladder 716
The Quick Job-Hunting Map 84

The R & D Entrepreneur: Profile of Success 396
Racial Differences in Job Satisfaction: Testing Four Common Explanations 418
Realistic Expectations as an Aid in Reducing Voluntary Resignations 736
Recruitment of Women to Public Office: A Discriminant Analysis 606
Recycling the Middle-Aged Executive 886
Redesigning and Reassigning Your Way to a Better Job 275
The Reinforcement of Traditional Career Patterns in Agencies Under Stress 969
The Relationship Between Intrinsic-Extrinsic Needs and Occupational Preferences 28
The Relationship of Career-Related Self-Efficacy Expectations to Perceived Career Options in College Women and Men 537
The Relationship of Career Salience, Attitudes Toward Women, and Demographic and Family Characteristics to Marital Adjustment in Dual-Career Couples 560
Relationships of Age and Seniority with Career Variables of Engineers and Scientists 384
Relationships Between Sex Role Stereotypes and Requisite Management Characteristics Among Female Managers 589
The Relative Effectiveness of Alternative Job Sources 169
Relative Influence of Prestige as a Determiner of Intelligence Judgments for Occupations 14
Relocation--Executive Style 269
Relocation Policies: Boom and Bust 842
Relocation Trends--Moving into the 80s 832
Relocation in an Unsettled Economy 851
Remodeling the Executive for the Corporate Climb 226
Resolving Executives' Early Retirement Problems 285
Resumes for Better Jobs 174
The Resume Writer's Handbook 204
Retirement: A Time to Enjoy or Endure 921
Retirement Counseling 931
Retirement Counseling: Making Sure Employees Aren't Dropouts 911
Retirement Planning at Ampex 940
Retirement Planning: Choice or Chance 917

Retiring Early? 926
A Review of the MMPI in Industry 735
Risk Taking Managers: Who Gets the Top Jobs? 491
The Role of Managerial and Professional Motivation in the Career Success of Management Professors 365
Role Variables: Their Influence on Female Motivational Constructs 397
Rusting Out, Burning Out, Bowing Out: Stress and Survival on the Job 447
R_x for Managerial 'Shelf Sitters' 878

Sabbaticals for Executives 655
Schoolteaching as a Professional Career 523
The Season's of a Man's Life 288
The Second Career
Second Careers for Military Retirees 910
Second Careers: War Wives and Widows 543
A Second Look at Second Careers 473
Secrets of Success: A Plan Book for Making it in the 1980s 324
Selection, Development, and Socialization of Women Into Management 535
Self Assessment and Career Development 23
Self-Assessment and Career Planning: Matching Individual and Organizational Goals 679
Self-Assessment: A Strategy of Growing Importance 784
Self-Directed Career Exploration: A Comparison of CHOICES and the Self-Directed Search 158
The Self-Directed Search 145
A Self-Efficacy Approach to the Career Development of Women 555
Self-Esteem as a Moderator of the Relationship Between Self-Perceived Abilities and Vocational Choice 149
Self-Esteem, Self-Perceived Abilities, and Vocational Choice 150
Self Motivated Personal Career Planning: A Break-through in Human Resource Management 241
Separate Career Executive Systems: Egalitarianism and Neutrality 962
Sex and Career Decision-Making Styles 572
Sex Role Self-Concept and Career Decision Making 152
Sex Stereotyping in the Executive Suite 588
Sex Stereotyping in Occupational Choice: The Case for College Women 127
Sex-Typical and Sex-Atypical Interests of Kuder Occupational Interest Criterion Groups: Implications for Counseling 61
Sexual Discrimination in the Use of Letters of Recommendation 187

Shelf-Sitters Reexamined   889
Shifting Gears   35
A Shortfall in Transit Managers   778
Should Executives Go Back to School   245
The Significance of Occupations in Work Careers: An Empirical and Theoretical Review   40
A Simple Arithmetic Approach to Career Planning and Recruitment   49
A Simulation Study of Administrators' Behavior Toward Employees Who Receive Job Offers   631
Simulations for Training and Assessment: The Problem of Relevance to the Real World   816
The Situational Interview   188
Skills for Success: A Guide to the Top   237
The Social Characteristics and Career Patterns of Women Administrators in North Carolina Colleges and Universities   373
Social Learning and Career Decision Making   29
The Socialization of Managers: Effects of Expectations on Performance   723
The Sociology of Professions: An Emerging Perspective   22
The Sociology of Second Place: Social and Cultural Constraints on the Advancement of Women   545
Some Attitudinal Barriers to Occupational Aspirations in Women   576
Some Dogmas of Development: Facts or Fallacies   788
The Soundness of Supervisory Ratings as Predictors of Managerial Success   809
The Stability of Post-Decision Dissonance: A Follow-Up Study of the Job Attitudes of Business School Graduates   432
Staff Burnout: Job Stress in the Human Services   876
The Staffing Grid: An Integrated Approach to Organizational Development   611
Standard and Poor's Register of Corporations, Directors, and Executives   79
Starting Over: How to Recharge Your Life-Style and Career--With Firsthand Accounts of the New Pioneers Who've Done It   310
The State of Management Development in the Federal Service   966
The States and Sex-Typed Dimensions of Occupational Aspirations in Young Adolescents   601
Status Attainment Process   327
Status of Career Planning on College and University Campuses   693
Status of Holland's Investigative Personality Types and Their Consistency Levels Seven Years Later   154
Stepping Up to Supervision: Making the Transition   210
Strategy and Tactics for Getting A Government Job   191
Strategies for Relieving Stress at Work   879

Strategies for the Second Half of Life 312
Strategies for Self Education 440
Stress and the Public Administrator 451
Stress Management: Separating Myth from Reality 453
Stress Reactions in Organizations: Syndroms, Causes, and Consequences 662
Structural Influences on Organizational Commitment 419
The Structure of Occupations by Interests--A Smallest Space Analysis 27
Struggle for the Executive Suite: Blacks vs. White Women 592
Studies and Projects to Improve Vocational Guidance Services 88
A Study of Holland's Theory of Vocational Choice as It Applies to the Job Satisfaction Among Male and Female Supervisors 404
A Study of Individual Characteristics and Career Aspirations 155
A Study of New Careers and Upward Mobility of New Professionals in Neighborhood Health Centers 482
A Study of Professional Career Satisfaction of Women Social Workers in Relation to Career Patterns, Career Saliency, Professional Role Conception Congruence and Race 425
A Study of Selected Career Executive Development Programs in the United States Federal Service: 1962-1966 963
The Subtle Revolution: Women at Work 595
Successful Midlife Career Change 472
Succession: A Longitudinal Look 847
The Supermobile 849
Supervisory Expectations Versus Organizational Reality 834
Surprising Boom in Executive Jobs 75
Sweaty Palms: The Neglected Art of Being Interviewed 192
Symposium on Organizational Development 629
Systems Career Path Development 493

Take Charge of Your Own Career 32
Taking the Mystery Out of Career Development 692
Talent Scout for the Executive Suite 725
Targeting the Top 568
Task Success, Task Popularity, and Self Esteem as Influences on Task Liking 412
Technology and the Changing Circumstances of Managerial Careers 786
Tell It Like It Is at Realistic Job Previews 750
Test of a Psychological Cost-Benefit Model for Career Choice 133
Testing for Career Adjustment and Development 267
Tests and Developmental Career Guidance: The Untried Relationship 119

Title Index

A Theoretical Model of Career Subidentity Development in Organizational Settings 732
Theories of Career Development 36
A Theory of Political Ambition: Career Choices and the Role of Structural Incentives 503
They Like Peace Corps Graduates 748
Thinking Clearly About Career Choices 148
Threads: A Tapestry of Self and Career Exploration 3
Three Approaches to Counselor Free Career Exploration Among College Women 80
The Three Boxes of Life 6
3 Steps to Supervisory Maturity 238
Today's Young Managers: They Can Do It, But Will They? 387
Too Old or Not Too Old 303
Total Development: Selection, Assessment, Growth 790
Tournament Mobility: Career Patterns in a Corporation 863
Toward a Career-Based Theory of Job Involvement: A Study of Scientists and Engineers 417
Toward a Career Psychology of Women: What Do We Know? What Do We Need to Know? 553
Toward a Stochastic Model of Managerial Careers 872
Toward an Understanding of Achievement-Related Conflicts in Women 386
Training Actualization Through Accountability 821
Training and Development Needs of State Agency Employees 810
Training Managers to Stimulate Employee Development 770
Training Managers for Their Role in a Career Development System 803
The Trapped Administrator: Effects of Job Insecurity and Policy Resistance Upon Commitment to a Course of Action 403
Trends in Occupational Differentiation by Sex 608
The Troubled Transition: Why College and University Graduates Have Difficulty Developing Careers in Business 364
Turbulence in the Working World: Angry Workers, Happy Grads 50
Turn Your Employee Career Guidance Program into an Effective Pre-Retirement Vehicle 930
The Two Career Couple 558
The Two-Person Career
Typical and Alternative Routes to Promotion of Women and Minorities 868
A Typology of Mid-Life Career Changers 476

The Uncle Sam Connection: An Insiders Guide to Federal Employment 183
Understanding and Doing Something About Professional Development 236
Unemployed Aerospace Professionals--Lessons for Programs for Mid-Life Career Redirection 939

The Unemployed Senior Executive 295
Unique Job Swap for Executives 965
Unmasking the Career Development Bogeymen 686
Unshackle Your Comers 862
Up the Ladder 603
Up is Not the Only Way 764
Up from Poverty: New Career Leaders for Non-Professionals 39
Update on Executive Jobs 74
Upward Mobility--TECOM Puts It All Together 835
Use of High School Data to Predict Work Performance 7
Use of Interest Inventories with Native Americans: A Case for Local Norms 62
Utility Theory 498

Validity of Personality Measures in Personnel Selection 731
The Values of Younger Workers 400
Vocational Behavior and Career Development, 1975: A Review 332
Vocational Behavior and Career Development, 1976: A Review 317
Vocational Behavior and Career Development, 1977: A Review 349
Vocational Behavior and Career Development, 1978: A Review 345
Vocational Behavior and Career Development, 1979: A Review 322
Vocational Behavior and Career Development, 1980: A Review 315
Vocational Choices of Men and Women: A Comparison of Predictors from the Self-Directed Search 137
Vocational Decision-Making Models: A Review and Comparative Analysis 110
Vocational Decision-Making Strategy Types: An Exploratory Essay 109
Vocational Development 333
Vocational Development Process 346
Vocational Development of Professional Women: A Review 569
Vocational Guidance for All: Is Differentiated Staffing the Answer? 90
Vocational Indecision: More Evidence and Speculation 146
Vocational Interests of Effective Managers: A Review of the Literature 808
Vocational Maturity: Its Past, Present and Future Development 82
The Vocational Maturity of Ninth Grade Boys 124
Vocational Psychology: The Study of Vocational Behavior and Development 92
Vocational Theories: Direction to Nowhere 125
VOGUE: A Demonstration System of Occupational Information for Career Guidance 95

Walking Out on Success--For Many It's Paying Off 478
Want a Job? Get Some Experience. Want Experience? Get a Job 172
What Color is Your Parachute? 85

Title Index

What Do You Really Want From Your Job? 424
What Happens When There Are Two of You 263
What is the Problem Concerning Obsolescence of Managerial Personnel 882
What It Takes to Become a Company Hero 839
What Kind of Federal Career Service? 971
What Makes a Successful Executive: An Executive Personnel Consultant's Opinion 244
What Should You Ask the Company Interviewer? 194
What to Do So the Obsolescent Executive Won't Be You 449
What to Do When You Get Fired 283
What Women Think Men Think: Does It Affect Their Career Choice 141
What's New in Career Management 622
When an Executive Quits on the Job 885
When Executives Burn Out 894
When Executives Shift to Academic Careers 463
When Mothers Are Also Managers 607
Where are the Leaders? 687
Where Do I Go From Here With My Life? 177
Where Have All the Robots Gone? Worker Dissatisfaction in the 70s 428
Which Way: Manager-Directed or Person-Centered Career Pathing 45
Whither T and D--and You 526
Who Gets Promoted? 867
Who's Hiring Who 189
Why Be A Mentor 758
Why the Best Managers Don't Get Promoted 857
Why City Managers Leave the Profession: A Longitudinal Study in the Pacific Northwest 518
Why Executives Change Jobs 470
Why a Second Career? 892
Why Your Salesman Quit 528
Widespread Concerns for the Aged 932
Will Early Retirement Retire Early? 941
Winning Ways in Motivating Junior Staff 379
Wives--A Critical Element in Career Decisions 737
The Woman Boss 593
Woman's Place: Options and Limits in Professional Careers
Women in Business 709
Women in Business: Great Expectations 575
Women Educational Administrators: Career Patterns and Perceptions 580
Women as Effective Managers: A Strategic Model for Overcoming Barriers 563
Women and Fear of Success: A Problem in Replication 390
Women Finally Get Mentors of Their Own 777

Women in Management   541
Women in Management: The Obstacles and Opportunities They Face   562
Women in Management: Patterns for Change   577
Women in Management: Strategies for Removing the Barriers   639
Women in Management Training Programs: What They Think About Key Issues   591
Women in Managerial and Professional Positions: in the United States and the Soviet Union   536
Women in the Professions: Career Considerations and Job Placement Techniques   567
Women at Work: Overcoming the Obstacles   581
Women Working Within the System: Possibilities and Constraints   565
Women and the Workplace: A Corporate Perspective   539
Women's Career Aspirations and Achievements: College and Seven Years Later   530
Women's Occupational Careers: Individual and Structural Explanations   375
Women's Self Estimates of Competence and the Resolution of the Career/Home Conflict   596
The Wonderful Crisis of Middle Age   287
The Work/Stress Connection: How to Cope with Job Burnout   458
Working Abroad: Some Problems and Pitfalls   747
Working Couples   586
The Working Mother: A Critique of the Research   594
The Working Woman: Barriers in Employment   561

You Sell Products--Now Learn to Sell Yourself Likewise   197
You Want Me to Do What?   762
The Young Person's Job Search: Insights from a Study   178
Young Top Management: The New Goals, Rewards, Lifestyles   348
Your Career: Choices, Chances, Changes   131
Your Career in Federal Civil Service   180
Your Career: How to Plan It, Manage It, Change It   318

Ref
Z
7164
V6
W45
1983